Peat Marwick McLintock:

Guide to Acquisitions in the US

Peat Marwick McLintock:

Guide to Acquisitions in the US

Christopher G Sneath
Partner, Peat Marwick McLintock, London

Herbert S Adler
Co-Director, Mergers and Acquisitions Department KPMG Peat Marwick Main

London
Butterworths
1989

United Kingdom	Butterworth & Co (Publishers) Ltd, 88 Kingsway, LONDON WC2B 6AB and 4 Hill Street, EDINBURGH EH2 3JZ
Australia	Butterworths Pty Ltd, SYDNEY, MELBOURNE, BRISBANE, ADELAIDE, PERTH, CANBERRA and HOBART
Canada	Butterworths Canada Ltd, TORONTO and VANCOUVER
Ireland	Butterworth (Ireland) Ltd, DUBLIN
Malaysia	Malayan Law Journal Sdn Bhd, KUALA LUMPUR
New Zealand	Butterworths of New Zealand Ltd, WELLINGTON and AUCKLAND
Singapore	Butterworth & Co (Asia) Pte Ltd, SINGAPORE
USA	Butterworths Legal Publishers, ST PAUL, Minnesota, SEATTLE, Washington, BOSTON, Massachusetts, AUSTIN, Texas and D & S Publishers, CLEARWATER, Florida

A CIP Catalogue record for this book is available from the British Library.

ISBN 0 406 50255 2

Printed by Butler and Tanner Ltd
Frome and London

Preface

The United States is a more attractive investment market now than it has been in years; this is borne out by the flood of UK acquisitions of US public and private companies in the last three years – $14 billion in 1986, and $29 billion in 1987, with 1988 totals estimated at $32 billion despite the meltdown of international stock markets. While there are megadeals in these figures, the average size of the reported acquisitions was $61 million in 1986 and $93 million in 1987; in reality, many of the deals involve purchases of $25 million or less, and this is the segment which continues to grow most strongly in the post-crash environment.

The type of UK company making the $5–10 million acquisition is typically one which relies heavily on its professional advisers to assist in all stages of the acquisition: identifying candidates, negotiating a deal, integrating the company afterwards, etc. Unlike the behemoths making the $500 million deals, the companies seeking smaller targets usually lack full-time acquisitions departments. The ones going after their first US acquisition often have little or no experience of the US business climate other than as a buyer and seller of goods, and therefore little or no familiarity with the legal structure, system of taxation, companies reporting requirements and such. They also lack the contacts in the States which an experienced hand can provide for doing research, making contact with target companies, and performing adequate investigations prior to negotiating a deal. The acquisitions of this size are almost always of private US companies, or divisions of much larger public companies. Since there is no statutory audit requirement in the US, it is often difficult to obtain information about such entities, especially without the full co-operation of the target; accounts are not automatically available, and often full financial information is not prepared. Therefore, an adviser must be ready to take a much more active role in obtaining (or even preparing) and evaluating information about such targets. Someone familiar with the stages and rituals of courtship in the United States can be an invaluable asset in effecting a timely and beneficial combination.

The adviser can be of even greater assistance if he or she can push the company to analyse its motivations for seeking an acquisition in the States. Ultimately, even the largest acquisitions require the involvement of both solicitors, especially in drafting agreements, and accountants, for consultation on both accounting and tax matters. However, the prepared adviser can take a much more active role from the start, if he or she has the expertise and resources to contribute. Gaining the necessary expertise and learning how to tap into resources is not difficult; it involves preparation more than arcane technical knowledge. The most important preparation is in learning what questions to ask, and at what point. These questions must be based on a basic familiarity with the US environment and the course of acquisitions in the US, especially typical stumbling blocks.

The aim of this book is to provide the necessary familiarity with the business climate of the United States, and to provide a leg up in anticipating the typical stages and stumbling blocks. It also identifies the primary resources for research in the US, to provide a basic set of contacts to be drawn on. The hope is that this book can serve both as an introduction and reference to speed the trip through the steepest and most basic part of the US learning curve, which is often the most frustrating and time consuming. By providing the basic information, it should also smooth communications with other parties, especially legal and other professional colleagues in the US, and should help overcome many of the typical barriers which slow the start of any acquisition process.

The specific concerns of making an acquisition in the US are a blending of points and experiences from two more general categories of activities: (a) making acquisitions, and (b) investment and doing business in the United States. To the extent that peculiar characteristics of the US business environment constrict choices, or make certain options more attractive, it is best to begin any analysis with a broad overview of the US and its structures and systems. This overview addresses, in particular, legal and taxation concerns which normally surface throughout the entire process.

There are far too many generic acquisition concerns to make it worthwhile repeating all of them in a book which is meant to have a narrower focus; however, certain basic principles are emphasised, as the distance introduced by an overseas relationship heightens the need to address fundamental concerns, such as formulating an acquisitions strategy. Forms of investment in the US, other than acquisitions, also are discussed, albeit briefly, but with a view to demonstrating the strengths and weaknesses of the acquisition option, rather than providing a detailed introduction to the various investment options in the US. The main focus of the second part of the book is the acquisition process as pursued in the US, particularly in regard to sources of information, differences in reporting practices and regulatory requirements.

Completing the acquisition is the focus of the last portion of the book, including guidance on structuring an offer, negotiating the final terms and financing the purchase. Last, certain post-acquisition concerns are raised which must be considered throughout the process, even if technically they arise only after the deal is complete.

The appendices are meant as ongoing reference documents containing details of contact names, sources of data and information and a case study which surveys the experience of one company, Thermal Scientific plc, which has been a successful acquiror of US companies.

In addition to allowing us to present this information, Hugh Sykes, the Chairman of Thermal Scientific, provided a number of insights into the whole process of making a US acquisition, which are reflected in the text of this book.

Unless otherwise indicated, the source of US company law requirements and other American legal concerns is material supplied by John S.D'Alimonte and Christopher E. Manno, London-based partners with the New York law firm of Willkie Farr & Gallagher and their associate Steven J. Gartner. Their invaluable contributions to this project have been integrated into the text and constitute a significant enhancement of the information provided in this book.

The material covering UK legal concerns included in Chapter 2 – 'The Regulatory Environment' – was prepared by two partners in the UK firm of Richards Butler. Hew Goldingham (corporate) and Stephen Sayer (competition) have highlighted the concerns a UK company must address in its home country, an area all too often ignored during the acquisition process.

The authors would also like to thank Mary Tokar, a manager from Peat Marwick Main seconded to London, for her assistance in the preparation of this book. A great contribution, especially in regards to the research work and compilation of reference materials, has been made by Kristy Gillmann, a student from Nijenrode University, The Netherlands, whose efforts were part of the completion of an MBA degree.

Last, it is important to recognise the efforts of other members of the international firm of KPMG. The authors were able to draw on the expertise of people from both the US and the UK, including Melanie Goody from London's professional practice department, Ken Crawford, a US tax partner resident in London, and many dedicated members of the support staff around the world who provided assistance throughout the project.

In addition to providing basic information about the structure of the business environment and acquisitions in the US, the text emphasises differences between common practice, and even vocabulary, in the US and UK. This contrast would also apply for countries with legal and business systems based on the UK, such as Hong Kong, Australia, and New Zealand and other Commonwealth countries.

Christopher Sneath
Herbert Adler

Contents

Appendices

Part 1
Background

CHAPTER 1
Overview of the US

The US marketplace

The United States of America is a nation with a landmass larger than Western Europe. Located in the northern part of the Western Hemisphere, the continental US is bordered on the north by Canada, the south by Mexico and the Gulf of Mexico, the east by the Atlantic Ocean and the west by the Pacific Ocean. As the fourth largest country in the world in both area and population, the nation consists of approximately 3.6 million square miles in 48 contiguous states, plus Alaska, northwest of Canada on the Arctic circle, and Hawaii, 2,100 miles west in the central Pacific. It also has independent territories under its jurisdiction, including Puerto Rico and Guam, which enjoy privileged trading relationships with the United States. There are about 6,000 miles between the nation's most distant points, with 2,800 miles between the East and West coasts of the continental US, and 1,600 miles between north and south. The country enjoys climate ranges from Arctic to near-tropical and the landscape offers diverse terrain such as rugged mountains, broad prairies, sandy coasts, and vast river basins.

Within the continental US there are four different time zones: Eastern, which is five hours behind Greenwich Mean Time, Central, Mountain, and Pacific, which is three hours behind Eastern Standard Time. Central Alaska and Hawaii fall within the same time zone two hours behind Pacific and ten hours behind GMT.

The population provides a marketplace of over 245 million people, with an annual growth rate of approximately one per cent. Approximately one quarter lives in the northeast region; a second quarter resides in the Midwest; California, Florida and Texas together hold a third quarter, and the balance is located in the southern and western states. The South and West have been the areas growing most rapidly in recent periods, although the population is gaining in the midwestern industrial states as their economies strengthen. Today, the fastest growing age sector is the 35-44 age group. The national language of the US is English; however in New York, Los Angeles, Miami and the Southwest there are substantial Spanish-speaking populations.

In 1987 the gross national product of the United States was 4,488 billion dollars, an increase of approximately six per cent from the 1986 figures (these figures exclude the effects of inflation). The country's civilian workforce numbers over 121.5 million people, of whom approximately 44 per cent are women. In general, the labour force is highly skilled and enjoys a high standard of living. The median family income in 1986 was $29,500; in 1987, the figure was $30,853. In addition, the unemployment rate was 5.4 per cent as of July 1988 and 5.8 per cent in December 1987. The inflation rates for the 12 month periods ending July 1987 and 1988 respectively were 3.9 per cent and 4.1 per cent.

Labour force

The labour force of the United States is highly appealing; foreign investors often benefit from the abundance, education and skill of the available labour. The development of rights for minorities and women has also aided in diversifying the composition of the current workforce. Labour unions have a strong economic impact on the country due to their size and influence, particularly that of the Teamsters, representing most of the transport workers in any industry, and the AFL-CIO (the American Federation of Labor-Congress of Industrial Organizations), representing most of the 'blue-collar' workers in industry. Traditionally, most large manufacturers have agreed to operate as closed shops, that is hiring only union members, but this has begun to change over the years, especially in the southern states. However, it should be expected that most industrial operations function in a unionised environment, usually with a single union representing most of the workforce and with some type of collective bargaining agreement in place. Recently, however, labour union membership has fallen dramatically as more companies look to non-union or at least open-shop arrangements as a prerequisite for new investments. The open-shop company is open on equal terms to both union and non-union employees. Simultaneously, previously unionised organisations are agreeing to greater flexibility demanded by management to improve productivity, including innovations such as Japanese-style quality circles. This creates a more flexible management/union atmosphere, but most established businesses, particularly those in industry located in the Northeast and Midwest, function as closed shops. Wages and working conditions are determined through negotiations between the two parties rather than by legislative order. The labour force is seldom represented directly on the boards of directors of corporations and fringe benefits are more costly and less extensive than in many European countries.

Education

The education system within the US differs somewhat from many European countries. For example, at the primary and secondary levels education is available free of charge in the public system, while the private system charges tuition fees. The education programmes vary from state to state with each local municipality responsible for the organisation and regulation of its own system. In the US approximately 12 per cent of all primary and secondary students attend private institutions, and total primary and secondary school enrolment is estimated to be 45 million.

All states require that children attend school until at least the age of 16 and a few states require attendance until the age of 18. The management of public schools is typically conducted by the localities themselves; commonly a local school board is elected to serve the public system. Private institutions are often church-related or can be non-sectarian. Most public systems are financed by local property taxes, but recently both state and federal governments have added support for the public education systems.

In the United States, approximately 34 per cent of secondary school (high school) graduates continue their education at the college or university level. These two higher level programmes refer to any institution which requires for admission a high school graduate certificate or its equivalent which often can be obtained through local community or night courses. There are both two and four year institutions available for university studies, the two year programmes typically referred to as 'junior colleges'. With a bachelor's degree, the common length of study is four years, normally between the ages of 18 and 22. Approximately 12.5 million Americans are enrolled in some form of college institution, and about 975,000 bachelor degrees are conferred each year. Unlike many foreign institutions, however, a tuition fee is charged at all post-secondary schools. The level of fees varies tremendously from nominal amounts for residents at state universities, for example in the excellent state system in California, to private universities having total charges in excess of $18,000 per year. Typically, the academic year is from early September to late May.

In many states, financial assistance is provided in the form of grants or student loans; often these are offered on a 'need only' basis, and loans typically have an extended pay back period. The federal government and the institutions themselves also have financial assistance programmes with varying terms and stipulations.

Post-graduate studies are necessary for many professions, including law (typically a three year degree) and medicine (usually a minimum of four years). Many business managers obtain MBA (Masters in Business Administration) degrees on a two year course of study, often following some amount of work experience. Approximately 24 per cent of the total masters degrees conferred in 1986 were in the area of business and management.

Perhaps in part due to the higher costs of post-secondary school degrees in the US, salary expectations are somewhat higher in the States than in the UK. The average starting salary offer in 1985 for graduates with bachelors degrees was $23,800.

Political system

The United States is a federal republic consisting of 50 states and the District of Columbia, each enacting its own laws and regulations. The political system is based on a separation of powers between the states and the federal government, which consists of three divisions: the executive, legislative and judicial branches. At the state level, governments have similar structures with distinct separation between the above three branches. Typically, there are also the following further levels in local governments: counties, townships, and municipalities.

In the federal government, the President heads the executive branch. A number of executive departments of the civil service exist under the President who appoints the head of each to become the collective 'Cabinet'. This body is responsible to the President and, unlike many democracies, its members are not also members of the legislature. In addition to the Cabinet executive departments, many regulatory agencies exist which are of concern to business. These include the Securities and Exchange Commission, the Federal Trade Commission, and the Federal Reserve System.

The legislative branch of the federal government is made of two separate chambers: the House of Representatives and the Senate. Known together as 'the Congress', the chambers are composed of 100 senators (two from each state, elected for terms of six years) and 435 representatives (the distribution dependent on each state's population and elected for terms of two years). For a bill to become a law it must be passed by a majority vote of both houses and then approved by the President. If the President vetoes the bill, however, it can still be made into law upon an override vote by a two-thirds majority of each house of Congress.

The political structure in the US is based on a multiparty system with the Democratic and Republican parties being the two dominant organisations. Other smaller parties also sponsor candidates, but to a limited extent. Only voters registered with a party can vote in the primary elections, held in each state to nominate party candidates. These primary elections are held throughout the year, in advance of the annual November election date (the first Tuesday of the month). Voting eligibility for the general election is by universal suffrage of adults 18 years and over.

A general election is held annually in November, combining local, state and federal elections. Every four years it also includes the Presidential election. Election of US representatives is every two years, while that of US senators is staggered, as are those of the state governments.

A system of courts headed by the Supreme Court constitutes the judicial branch of government. Rulings on the constitutionality of laws and appeals from lower courts are heard by the Supreme Court, and there is no appeal on any of the Court's decisions. In addition to this federal system, each state also has its own court system headed by the state supreme court. The legal system also includes federal courts which rule on cases involving federal laws. The decisions of both federal and state lower courts may be appealed to their respective supreme court; certain decisions of state supreme courts can also be appealed to the federal Supreme Court.

Governments at the state level have much the same pattern as their federal counterpart. Their chief executive, the governor, heads the state's executive branch, with additional powers being separated between the legislative and judicial branches. Unlike members of Congress, state legislators are frequently part-time rather than full-time politicians.

Attraction of the US market

In order to reduce their risks, companies and individuals often spread investments worldwide. In this respect, the United States offers many opportunities to the foreign investor, especially the foreign acquiror. Traditionally, the US government has openly encouraged investment in the United States and imposed few restrictions on foreign investors. There are no exchange control regulations or restrictions on the repatriation of dividends or investments. For many, the US business environment is considered the optimum climate in which to operate.

The political, social, and economic stability of the US has been a strong lure for many foreign investors, while another attraction is the large, reasonably homogeneous, readily available market. The US economy is enormous and the American consumer has a substantially greater capacity to pay for goods and services than many other consumers of the world. Furthermore, in some respects the US market is far less saturated than the European market. Tax and regulatory structures, although complex, are attractive; and while there are various state regulations, they are fairly well integrated and do not pose the same barriers as the international borders within Europe. Some special incentives for new business investment also exist, especially at the state level. Energy costs are seen to be substantially lower than in many other countries, and the advanced transportation and communication networks allow companies to take advantage of the entire coast-to-coast marketplace with relative ease.

Many companies are interested in the US for technological reasons. For years, the United States has been the leader in the development of labour-saving and mass production technologies as well as modern management techniques and practices. Foreign corporations who may wish to benefit from these technologies often invest in ongoing concerns in the US in order to obtain and adapt this know-how for use in their own markets.

In general, both federal and state government legislation remain neutral to foreign investment and although potential investors may be wooed by government officials, some controversy has recently emerged with calls for a certain degree of protectionism. In effect, American and foreign investors enjoy equal positions with regard to the political system as each is equally subject to most state requirements and federal restrictions. Significant bars to foreign investment exist only in certain strategic areas such as broadcasting facilities and public utilities, and there are restrictions on the ownership of defence contractors. However, most Americans realise that for them to maintain their standard of living, economic growth and employment is essential; therefore, if investors continue to bring money into the economy and continue to pay stable wages, they will continue to be welcomed.

The pro-business attitude within the United States makes it an attractive field for expansion. Perhaps more visibly than anywhere else, the successful businessman is a highly regarded figure in the community. Businesses themselves are also typically held in high regard in the communities in which they operate. Rates of taxation also create an attractive business environment; the top rate for corporate profits in the US is now 34 per cent. Furthermore, while there is no longer capital gains relief, certain favourable tax treatments are available to sellers. These rates help ensure a liquid market for entire companies and not just publicly traded shares. The introduction of inflation indexing in 1986, which will reduce taxable gains in the future, should help maintain and encourage this liquidity.

British investors also are attracted to the US by the efficiency and size of the capital and equity markets. The abundance of capital resources and high degree of market liquidity attracts foreign investors to the US and offers them opportunities to increase their own capital position. At a recent CBI conference, Gerald Dennis, Deputy Chairman of BAT Industries, indicated that for his company, now considered the fourth largest investor in the US, America has offered 'better and more profitable business opportunities than almost anywhere else in the world'. He further ventures to extrapolate that the same opportunity exists for many UK companies.

An additional attraction of the US market is that it holds significant supplies of raw materials and natural resources. With the American market expanding over diverse areas, potential investors have access to a wide range of materials and resources. The American consumer is also an attraction for investors. In general, the US market is willing to pay a premium for many foreign products which often are perceived to be of higher quality, style, or both, than domestically produced items.

A further important consideration for foreign investors is that production in the US by a foreign firm helps to prevent import restrictions. Domestic production allows virtually all import tariffs and quota allowances to be by-passed in this fashion. In addition, the government has allowed free trade zones within certain geographic areas. These are supervised by the Foreign Trade Zones Board which is part of the US Department of Commerce. Within this system, particular areas have been identified for use by both foreign and domestic goods trade which are free from customs restrictions for storage, manufacture, and assembly. With this allowance, the products hold no tariff for export and often have very limited quota restrictions. For additional information about the trade areas and their operations, contact:

> Executive Secretary
> Foreign Trade Zones Board
> Washington DC 20230

Government incentives to invest

At present, the federal government supports an 'open-door' policy for foreign investment; there are no general restrictions on direct investments in or the acquisitions of equity or loan stock securities by foreigners, apart from specific restrictions in certain circumstances. For example, federal law prohibits aliens and foreign-owned corporations from owning radio and television licences (a firm is considered foreign owned if more than 20 per cent of its capital stock is owned by aliens). Generally, while certain approvals at the federal level must be obtained (eg to satisfy antitrust regulations), only publicly traded companies are subject to ongoing reporting requirements. It is necessary to note that the rules and regulations concerned with formation, operation and dissolution of corporate entities are written, altered and enforced at the state level. A foreign investor should therefore keep in mind that because there are 50 states and the District of Columbia, these rules can and do vary considerably from state to state. From the federal perspective, however, there are requirements for SEC filings which only apply to transactions involving publicly traded companies.

The federal government issued an official statement on its policy towards international investment in 1983 which clarified the views of the current administration. The statement included the following points:

- Foreign investors in the US are accorded the same, fair, equitable, non-discriminatory treatment under international law [as US investors];
- The US opposes government intervention that impedes or distorts investment flows, that encourages retaliatory use of intervention measures by other governments and that may precipitate a downward spiral in global investment flows;
- A major objective of the US investment policy is to foster a domestic economic climate which is conducive to investment, ensures that foreign investors receive fair and equitable treatment under our statutes and regulations and maintain only those safeguards on foreign investment necessary to protect our security and related interests, and which are consistent with our international legal objectives;
- [The administration] will continue to work multilaterally within the OECD, GATT and similar bodies, and seek to conclude bilateral investment treaties and agreements with international countries.[1]

1 US Department of Commerce 'US Government Policy on International Investment' 18 November 1985.

A recently enacted federal statute authorises the President of the United States or his designee to prevent acquisitions of US companies by foreign persons if such acquisitions might jeopardise 'national security'. Section 5021 of the Omnibus Trade and Competitiveness Act of 1988 permits the President or his designee to investigate an acquisition by or with foreign persons to determine the effect, if any, such an acquisition might have on national security. The investigation must be commenced and completed and any decision to take action must be announced according to the statute's schedule. The process could take as long as 90 days from the date the President or his designee is notified of the acquisition. The President, upon finding credible evidence that the foreign person might take action that threatens to impair national security, may suspend or prohibit the transaction. The statute contemplates that regulations will be forthcoming which would clarify certain mechanical problems (eg who must notify the President and what form of notification is required). Parties should consult with legal counsel on this issue early in the planning stage of any acquisition of a US company. However, early indications from the current administration are that they do not plan to utilise these powers to restrict foreign investment activity in the US.

Both federal and state government agencies exist which regulate investment (for domestic and foreign companies alike) in specific industries, such as insurance, banking, utilities and transportation. Nevertheless, compared to many developed countries, regulations and restrictions are much less burdensome.

State investment incentives

Local and state governments do not follow the federal government's position of neutrality; about 6,000 economic development groups spend hundreds of millions of dollars annually in order to attract foreign investment into their areas. They do so in the belief that investment (domestic and foreign) helps enlarge the tax base, aids in employment, reduces welfare costs, and improves local economic situations, and they are therefore willing to offer various incentives to encourage investment in their areas.

The states use a wide range of recruitment techniques in order to lure foreign investment; some even conduct national and international promotion campaigns. To some degree there is competition between the individual states. This allows the investor to investigate many possible locations. These incentives are usually more important when starting a new business or making a significant new investment. The lures used by local agencies often include tax exemptions, various forms of directed revenues, and an ample supply of loans. Authors Martin and Susan Tolchin outline five categories basic to the incentive wars in their recent book, *Buying Into America*. These include the following:

(1) *Easing the tax climate.* To varying degrees, all states offer foreign investors some relief from tax burdens. However, as any political environment is subject to change, so is the applicable tax structure. Investors should therefore be cautioned against making a long term investment and commitment based on tax implications alone, but rather should integrate this factor into their overall long-term strategy.

(2) *Specific tax concessions.* Property tax exemptions are often granted to new

businesses, both foreign and domestic. Some property tax reliefs can extend up to 15 years on land and buildings. Some states also offer the opportunity for accelerated depreciation on plant and equipment in state tax computations.

(3) *Industrial development bonds (IDBs)*. State and local governments can offer municipal bonds with low interest rates in order to finance industrial projects. These IDBs are offered in two forms: (a) revenue bonds which are to be repaid from the project's revenues, and (b) general obligation bonds which make the locality responsible for repayment. Normally, the state or locality purchases or actually builds the industrial facility and then arranges to lease it back to the investor. In this way, the company has helped reduce its initial capital outlay and minimise some of its tax obligations.

(4) *Infrastructure and special services*. Some incentives are designed to assist foreign investors after locating in the state. These involve transportation links, specialised road connections, and water and sewage services. By obtaining these concessions, companies reduce capital expenditures and operating expenses. Some states offer specialised services in the form of research facilities through local universities, state-supported job training programmes, relocation assistance for expatriates, and various social assistance programmes.

(5) *Public-private sector agreements*. In some states, for example California and New York, the state has initiated various agreements with private entities in foreign countries. In some instances, the state assists in matching the domestic firms with their foreign counterparts on the basis of common interests and feasibility studies.[2]

While the states continue to battle for investment into their areas, further investigation and understanding of the alternative programmes is essential. Appendix 1 provides a listing of some of the various state agencies located in Europe, and shows the individual state trade/development offices in the US, any of which can offer more detailed information on these incentive programmes. Nevertheless, it is important to remember that most incentive programmes are geared toward supporting new investment to raise employment levels and tax bases. There are fewer incentives available to a new purchaser of an existing company.

2 Martin and Susan Tolchin *Buying into America*, copyright Times Books, a Division of Random House, Inc.

CHAPTER 2
Regulatory environment

Legal concerns and background

Although a significant number of legal concerns must be considered when acquiring a company, they should not be thought of as barriers to the investment. An acquiror should, however, seek sound legal advice and guidance when approaching an acquisition in order to understand any changes in the regulatory environment.

1 Acquisition vehicles and corporate structure in the US

Potential acquirors must decide upon the form of acquisition vehicle to be used in the transaction. Because this decision may impact upon several other aspects of the acquisition, it is usually made in the preliminary stages. The choice of business entity most advantageous for a particular transaction requires consideration of many factors, both non-tax and tax related. The most common vehicles – the corporation and the partnership – offer distinct characteristics from both these perspectives.

I CORPORATIONS
The corporate form is by far the most important – in terms of both business and capital – of the organisational forms in America. The most important legal advantage of the corporate form is the insulation from personal liability that is afforded to the shareholders. Shareholders of a corporation are, with some very discrete exceptions, not personally liable for the debts of the corporation. Thus, a shareholder's entire responsibility for the obligations of a corporation is limited generally to the amount actually invested in the business. Exceptions to this general rule are sometimes found. In particular cases where the corporation serves only as the 'alter-ego' or 'mere instrumentality' of the controlling shareholder, a court may 'pierce the corporate veil' to find shareholder liability. 'Piercing the corporate veil' runs counter to the accepted theory that the corporate form completely insulates individuals from liability. Hence, the step is somewhat drastic and one not taken lightly by the courts.

The corporate form also facilitates future resale of the acquired business because corporations are largely perpetual in duration and share certificates (if not restricted by the terms of a shareholder agreement) are easily transferred. If the purchaser plans to merge the acquired business with another operation or to resell to a third party or to the public, a corporate form will make the next transaction easier to accomplish.

Corporate earnings are, however, subject to two tiers of taxation in the United States. Earnings are taxed at the corporate level when earned and dividends are taxed when distributed to shareholders. Further, since the federal corporate tax rate is currently higher than the rate applicable to individuals, the corporate form is no longer a superior vehicle for accumulating capital. Limited exceptions to this dual taxation exist for federal tax purposes. Certain corporations with less than 35 shareholders (who must be individuals or specifically qualified trusts and may not be non-resident aliens) may elect to be taxed in the manner similar to a partnership (a 'Subchapter S' corporation), thus avoiding the first tier of taxation at the corporate level. Also, a portion of dividends distributed by a US corporation to a shareholder that is also a corporation may be excludable from the recipient's taxable income.

A corporation is a creature of state law and is formed by compliance with a simple and rather mechanical statutory process. The central step of this process is the filing with a state official, usually the Secretary of State or Commissioner of Corporations, of a short document usually labelled the 'Certificates of Incorporation' or the 'Articles of Incorporation'. State statutes vary, but generally any adult person with some minimum level of capital may form a corporation. Once this document is filed with the appropriate state official, the corporation technically and legally exists. The filing process usually takes about one day.

It should be noted that in the United States some terms differ from those used in the United Kingdom. In the US, the term 'stock' is used to refer to equity shares and a 'private' company is one which is unquoted. Therefore, a shareholder in an unquoted company would be referred to as a stockholder of a private company.

The Articles of Incorporation are usually very general, outlining only the contours of the corporation's capital structure and major governance mechanisms. They can be tailored, however, to the particulars of the acquisition transaction. The Articles can set forth terms and rights of various classes of shares such as special voting rights. In situations where the shares are to have preference over the entity's common shares upon the liquidation of the company, this may be designated as 'preferred stock' (preference shares) in the Articles of Incorporation. The Articles can be amended, as needed, with shareholder approval, to include preference shares in the capital structure, or to make other changes as desired.

Choosing the state of incorporation is a matter of some importance. American law will generally apply the law of the state of the corporation's domicile to controversies regarding corporate governance. By far the most popular choice for publicly held companies is Delaware, largely because of its relaxed attitude towards corporations in general. Since Delaware is so popular as a state of domicile, the Delaware law of corporations is generally more litigated, and thus more certain than the corporation laws of other states as a much greater body of precedents and decisions exists.

For smaller companies and companies that are privately held, choice of domicile may be more influenced by factors such as the location of business, the owners' convenience and a desire to avoid the imposition of multiple state franchise taxes. A company will be taxed annually by its state of incorporation and may be taxed by states where the company is qualified to do business as a foreign corporation. These 'franchise taxes' vary widely but are generally based, at least in part, on the number of shares of authorised and unissued stock and the value of assets of the corporation.

Within the constraints of the corporation's Articles and By-laws, the business of a corporation is managed under the direction of its board of directors. Directors are elected by the shareholders and perform their duties pursuant to the provisions of the corporation's Articles of Incorporation and By-laws. The corporation's initial By-laws are usually adopted by the incorporators and may generally be modified by the directors or the shareholders (as provided by statute, the Articles of Incorporation and/or by the By-laws themselves). Unless provided otherwise in the Articles of Incorporation, non-US citizens may be directors. An exception to this rule is where a federal statute prohibits such membership. For example, in certain situations, foreign individuals may not serve on the boards of companies that have contracts with the US Department of Defense. Similarly, a foreign individual may not be a director of a corporation that holds a fixed radio licence from the Federal Communications Commission.

Generally, the By-laws provide that all corporate actions may be taken by the directors except for enumerated actions requiring shareholder consent. Shareholders (and directors) act through meetings (annual or special) or by written consent, all as expressly provided in the By-laws.

Unlike the UK Companies Act, which contains many specific rules and restrictions, American corporate law is quite general, providing extremely flexible guidelines and leaving most governance issues to the principals (as embodied in the By-laws). The By-laws frequently establish when, and under what circumstances, shareholder meetings will be held and where the books and records of the company will be kept. Many states, however, do require that corporations organised pursuant to their statutes must maintain a 'presence' within that state. The purpose underlying such a requirement is to enable the state to serve the corporation with notices of litigation, levies, etc. in much the same manner as it serves individual citizens at their primary address. 'Presence' does not mean that the entity must operate or hire a staff in that state. Rather, the requirement is most often satisfied by retaining a registered agent in the state who will accept service of process in the company's name. There are companies that provide this service for a fee in every state and it is a widely practised method of satisfying the 'presence' requirement.

II PARTNERSHIPS

In a legal sense, a general partnership is simply an association of two or more persons to carry on a business as co-owners. The association may be express or implied, written or oral, but is generally embodied in a partnership agreement. In contrast, the creation of a limited partnership requires adherence to formalities prescribed by statute, including filing and sometimes publication of a limited partnership certificate. All states have partnership statutes, many of which resemble the Uniform General Partnership Act and the Uniform Limited Partnership Act.

In contrast to the corporate owner's limited liability, the general partnership form is characterised by the joint, several and unlimited personal liability of all general partners for the debts of the business. In the other form of partnership, the limited partnership, there is at least one general partner and the rest are limited partners. The general partner or partners of a limited partnership have joint, several and unlimited liability. The limited partners are liable only to the extent of their capital contribution but must remain 'silent' partners. If limited partners participate in the management of the partnership business they may lose their limited partner status.

Partners are not always individuals. Indeed, it is not uncommon for limited and general partners to be corporations. An individual can be shielded from personal liability by forming a corporation of which he or she is the sole shareholder and causing that corporation to become a partner in the partnership.

The earnings of a partnership are not taxed federally at the partnership level. Instead, earnings are factored out as income to the individual partners based on their share of those earnings which share is usually set out in the partnership agreement. These earnings constitute current taxable income to the partners, whether or not any cash was actually paid to them by the partnership.

For both legal and business reasons, it is advisable to express the partnership agreement in writing. The partnership agreement generally sets forth how and by whom the partnership will be managed, the distribution of profits and losses and the terms and conditions of dissolution of the partnership.

Another investment vehicle that parties should consider is that of a joint venture. A joint venture is functionally similar to a partnership: two or more parties agree to operate together and to share, in prescribed percentages, the profits and losses of such operations. The agreement reached is generally embodied in a document similar to a partnership agreement. A joint venture, however, is typically 'project specific'. It is often used in situations where the parties have separate operations but recognise profitable synergies should they join forces in a particular venture. To illustrate, a company that has a large amount of capital and a small presence in the United States may team with another company that is in the opposite position. The first company will infuse capital while the second trains managers and establishes a distribution network. The venture often contemplates a termination. In the above example the parties may decide that the venture will end when the second company achieves certain financial results or when the first company establishes an independent US distribution network.

2 Regulatory concerns when acquiring a US company

On the assumption that the investment method selected is the acquisition of an ongoing US entity, it is important to identify what regulatory barriers to investment might exist, especially with regard to certain sensitive industries. The discussion below is concerned with the acquisition of private companies, which are not subject to public filing and reporting requirements. The additional concerns of acquiring a listed company follow the discussion below, but are not addressed in detail, as quoted companies are unlikely targets for first time acquirors, and the complex US Securities and Exchange Commission (SEC) regulations are beyond the scope of this book.

As noted above, in the the United States, the term 'privately held company' refers to a company whose shares are not traded in the public markets. The legal concerns that underlie an acquisition of such a company, although numerous, may be divided into two major areas. First, there are regulations imposed by federal and state governments on acquisitions in general. For example, certain laws in the United States are designed specifically to prevent anti-competitive mergers and acquisitions. Other statutes ensure that acquisitions in particular industries are monitored properly. Secondly, there are somewhat narrower concerns peculiar to the particular acquisition and the parties involved. Such concerns include situations where the acquiring party wishes to own the acquired entity outright or where it seeks only to acquire certain assets. These concerns, which are more important in the consideration of the structure of an offer, are discussed in the third part of the book, which addresses completing the acquisition.

Many factors influence the degree to which these areas impact upon the transaction in question. For example, certain acquisitions are so small in economic terms that most government regulations do not apply to them. In addition, the structure of a transaction itself, eg, the purchase of assets rather than of a corporate entity, sometimes can mitigate or avoid certain of the concerns.

Acquisitions of companies in the United States, depending on their size and the acquisition participants, may be subject to a myriad of federal and state laws. Although a discussion of all the potentially applicable statutes, regulations and rules would be far too cumbersome for inclusion here, several commonly applicable statutes and a few helpful guidelines should be noted.

To best understand what regulations might be relevant, it is helpful to identify the participants and to set forth the nature of the transaction. A proper analysis would include a review of the estimated purchase price, the industry of the entity to be acquired, the form of consideration (eg, stock, cash, assets) and the nature of what is being purchased.

One federal regulation that affects numerous acquisition transactions is the Hart-Scott-Rodino Antitrust Improvements Act of 1976 (HSR Act). This statute, which is described below, is designed in part to prevent business combinations that would tend to lessen competition in the United States. The statute, which applies to most acquisitions that involve a minimum dollar amount or percentage of assets, focuses on the business activities of the participants.

The identity of the potential participants is significant and may be governed by regulations that subject the transaction to the jurisdiction of particular governmental bodies. To illustrate, if the acquiring party is a major shareholder of a bank, domestic or foreign, then an acquisition may require approval by the Federal Reserve Board of Governors of the United States if the acquired entity engages in certain types of activities, such as banking or securities. More commonly, the identity of the seller can be crucial. If the seller participates in a regulated industry, then prior notice and/or approval of the appropriate agency of the United States Government would normally be necessary.

The locations, ie states, where the seller transacts business must also be identified. As discussed in detail below, not every state where the seller has some contact is necessarily a state to be studied. The activities must be of a level where the entity is deemed to be conducting business in the state. For example, the fact that ABC Co's products are sold in a retail store in the state of Iowa may not rise to a 'doing business' level of activity, but if ABC Co has a sales force operating in Iowa, it may be deemed to be doing business there and, hence, be subject to Iowa's laws.

I FEDERAL REGULATIONS

1 ANTITRUST

The regulation most commonly applicable to acquisition transactions is imposed by the HSR Act. The HSR Act is a federal regulation administered by two agencies of the United States government, the Federal Trade Commission (FTC) and the Department of Justice (DOJ). The HSR Act is designed to prevent monopolistic combinations by allowing the FTC and DOJ an adequate period of time to review the antitrust implications of significant acquisitions prior to their consummation.

The HSR Act applies to transactions involving the acquisition of stock or assets where at least one party to the transaction has annual sales or revenues of at least $100 million and the other party has annual sales or revenues of at least $10 million and where the purchase price exceeds $15 million or the stock or assets being acquired represent more than 15 per cent of the acquired entity's voting power or assets. Parties to the proposed acquisition include, for the purposes of the HSR Act, the ultimate parent entity of both the buyer and seller.

The HSR Act is procedural – it merely imposes a waiting period during which the proposed acquisition is reviewed by the FTC and DOJ. During this period the transaction may not be consummated (ie title to the stock or assets may not pass). In consensual transactions, such as negotiated acquisitions of the stock or assets of a privately held company, both parties must file a Premerger Notification and Report Form (the 'HSR Form') before the waiting period begins. In non-consensual transactions, such as tender offers, the waiting period begins when the acquiring entity files its HSR Form. The acquired entity must file within a specified period (usually 15 days) after that date. The waiting period is 30 calendar days after the receipt by the FTC and DOJ of the required filing or filings (except where the transaction is an all cash tender offer to purchase shares, in which case the waiting period is 15 days). Early termination may be requested by indicating as such on the HSR Form. There is no filing fee associated with the HSR Form and there is no charge for requesting early termination.

The HSR Form is completed by the ultimate parents of both buyer and seller (or both parties to a joint venture). The HSR Form requests relevant information regarding the industries in which the parties participate as well as the particulars of the transactions. In brief, the initial review of the FTC and DOJ focuses on the dollar revenues of the reporting parties derived from activities in the United States, broken out according to product codes established by the United States Census Bureau. If both reporting parties derive revenues from the same code or codes then the HSR Form requests additional geographical information. The information is intended to facilitate analysis as to whether the proposed acquisition would tend to lessen competition in the United States or in any particular markets within the United States (eg the western states).

During the waiting period, the FTC and DOJ may request additional information from the parties. In that event, the waiting period is automatically extended for a period of time (usually 20 days) from the date on which requested information is supplied. If no request for additional information is made, the parties are free to consummate the transaction upon the expiration of the initial waiting period. Although the expiration of the waiting period does not preclude the antitrust agencies from subsequently attacking a transaction, no transaction to date has been attacked on antitrust grounds after compliance with the HSR Act.

Parties frequently ask whether they could close in escrow pending the termination of the HSR Act waiting period. To do this, all papers would be negotiated and executed and once the waiting period expired, the transaction would be 'released' from escrow and title and purchase price would be exchanged. Although not prohibited, in most situations, closing in escrow is not recommended. The primary fear is what happens if a disaster occurs? That is, if the buildings that constitute a substantial portion of the assets to be sold are destroyed by fire, can the buyer walk away from the deal? This is just one example of why the dangers of closing in escrow often outweigh the benefits. Especially in those situations where the parties' probable delay is often no more than 30 days, the preferred course is to close after the termination notice is received.

2 REGULATED INDUSTRIES

The federal government also regulates acquisitions in particular industries. Consequently, it is important to know the precise activities of the target entity. The potential acquiror should ascertain at the earliest possible juncture what, if any, federal licences and permits are held by the target. If assets to be acquired include a licence, then title to that licence is deemed to have passed when it is assigned. Government approval of the new assignee is often required. Even where shares are to be acquired and thus the licensee, ie the corporate entity, does not change, the federal regulation may deem the 'change in control' to be an assignment in fact. In some situations, federal licences are not assignable, and thus the licence cannot be included as an 'asset' to be sold. In such situations, the acquiring party generally applies for a licence directly and the transaction is not consummated until the licence is granted.

There is a broad range of federally regulated activities. Once the activities of the acquired party are ascertained, legal counsel should be consulted as to what, if any, agencies may have to be notified. Often, an officer of the target company should be able to pinpoint some if not all of the relevant agencies since licences have to be renewed with the supervisory agency in the ordinary course of business. The following is a list of some of the more typical examples of federally regulated activities and the agency of the federal government that oversees them:

Broadcasting (radio and television) and telecommunications	Federal Communications Commission
Banking and other thrift institutions	The Federal Reserve Board or the Federal Deposit Insurance Corporation (in the case of nationally chartered or federally insured banks) and the Federal Savings and Loan Insurance Corporation (in the case of federally insured savings and loan institutions)
Energy and natural resources	Nuclear Regulatory Commission
Air transportation	Department of Transportation
Public utilities and securities businesses	Securities and Exchange Commission; National Association of Securities Dealers; also state regulatory authorities for public utilities

The requirements imposed by each statute or supervisory agency vary but generally require advance notice, filing and/or prior approval. Each agency usually has specific forms and instructions that can be obtained free of charge by calling or writing to the agency's main office.

Depending on the activities conducted, it is also important to know whether the acquired entity is subject to any federal decree, or threatened to become so (eg environmental successor liability imposed through the Environmental Protection Agency Superfund authority and regulations). Environmental regulations cover many situations and can be quite extensive and complex. Parties to an acquisition transaction should be aware that federal and state regulations may impose liability on past and present owners for the cost of compliance with clean-up laws. Thus, even if the damage resulted from an action several years ago (eg subsurface leakage, use of asbestos) the cost of placing a facility in compliance or the fines attendant to such damage may be imposed, jointly and severally, on each owner of the facility from the date of the occurrence to the present.

II STATE REGULATIONS

Depending on the activities of the acquired entity and the laws of relevant states, certain state authorities may have to be notified prior to the acquisition and/or prior approval may be required. State statutes also are significant in the context of an acquisition of a publicly held company, inasmuch as state disclosure and anti-takeover laws may apply.

The buyer must ascertain which states are relevant to the transaction. The common factors to consider include:

(a) state of incorporation of the acquired entity;
(b) principal place of business of the acquired entity;
(c) principal executive offices of the acquired entity;
(d) states where the acquired entity is formally qualified to transact business as a 'foreign' (ie out of state) corporation (pays taxes, registers on an annual basis); and
(e) states where the acquired entity does business.

The response to each of the above items can be a different state. For example, many corporations are incorporated in Delaware but have few other contacts with that state. Although a corporation's principal executive office is generally in the same state as its principal place of business, this is not always the case. A manufacturing company may have its main factories in one state and executive headquarters in another.

An entity must register as a 'foreign corporation' with a state if it transacts business to such an extent that it is deemed to be 'doing business' in that state. It is difficult, if not impossible, to quantify the amount of business that would be sufficient for a company to be deemed to be 'doing business'. The presence of an office or a sales force or significant local advertising are examples of activities which would generally constitute doing business. 'Qualifications to do business' are granted by states (and renewed annually) to entities that complete the appropriate forms and satisfy certain minimum requirements imposed by the state (usually no more than an annual filing fee of about $100).

A company may do business in a state without being formally qualified. The level of its activities may be such as to subject it to the state's jurisdiction regardless of whether the company has formally registered to do business there. There is nothing uncommon or illegal in not registering where one's activities are minimal. Sometimes failure to register only prohibits a company from instituting an action in the courts of that state.

Some regulatory areas are, or for all practical purposes are, within the exclusive jurisdiction of the state governments while others overlap with the federal government's jurisdiction. Insurance laws, including those that apply to insurers as well as those that apply to agents and brokers, and real estate laws are examples of areas that fall within the states' domain.

State insurance regulators recently played a significant role in the bid by B.A.T Industries PLC (BAT) for Farmers Group Inc, an American insurance company (Farmers). To obtain control of Farmers, BAT had to notify the insurance authorities in nine states and solicit the approval of each. Not surprisingly, the regulators reacted differently to the BAT application (another illustration of the autonomy of individual states in certain situations). Before Farmers and BAT reached their friendly deal, three states had approved the BAT application, four states had rejected it, two states had not published a decision and one state court had overturned the initial rejection by the commissioner of insurance. (Currently, it appeared likely that the regulators would approve the applications since Farmers now favours the deal.)

Another area subject almost exclusively to state law is 'product liability'. Product liability is a growing body of law that deals with the injuries caused by defective products or products that do not contain adequate warnings of potentially hazardous characteristics. Depending on the particular state law, a person injured by such a product may be able to recover damages from several parties including not only the actual manufacturer, but also the current owner of that business if the manufacturer no longer exists or is unable to satisfy the judgment. Some states have even imposed joint and several liability on manufacturers and their successors. State law in this area varies greatly and is derived from statutes and prior judicial decisions.

Antitrust, food and drug and environmental protection laws are often regulated by both the state and federal governments areas. Many states have environmental protection regulations that may or may not resemble their federal counterparts. For example, the State of New Jersey requires advance notice of any sales of businesses within its boundaries that are engaged in the manufacture, storage, transportation or handling of hazardous wastes or hazardous substances.

Finally, local governments (city, county, municipal) may participate in acquisitions of businesses within their jurisdictions. The role, if any, is usually a minor one, such as requiring a local permit or imposing an annual fee for certain activities. However, the involvement, in some situations, is quite significant. For example, in order to build on a property or change an office building into a warehouse, a zoning permit or variance may be required. Zoning and many other types of land use regulation are the usual subject of local governmental authority and regulation.

3 Concerns particular to the transaction

The above discussion deals with its subject matter on a 'macro-level', by exploring pressures imposed by federal and state regulation. Other legal issues are generated by, for lack of a better term, 'micro-level' concerns – the particular needs of the individual buyer and seller. These concerns will influence the legal form and structure of the transaction as well as choices made with respect to the purchase vehicle and the mode of acquisition. See 'Structure of the offer' on p 117.

I TRANSACTIONS WITH TROUBLED COMPANIES

Other concerns which may be particular to the transaction arise if the target company is troubled – at, or near, bankruptcy. Acquiring the business of a financially troubled company poses particularly complex issues under either share or asset purchase methods.

For example, if the target company was part of a consolidated corporate tax group, it remains severally liable for all tax liabilities incurred by the entire group over the period during which it was a member thereof. Thus, acquiring the share capital of a subsidiary of a troubled parent company may produce surprisingly complex tax indemnification issues. As a further example, fraudulent conveyance law may affect either asset or share deals with a troubled owner. Under certain circumstances, the sale of assets of an insolvent company may result in a fraudulent conveyance which could be reversed by creditors of the seller or by a later trustee-in-bankruptcy of the seller.

Although a summary of US bankruptcy law is beyond the scope of these brief comments, a few observations are justified. American bankruptcy law is a system mixing both federal statutory and common law. The US Bankruptcy Code is divided into chapters, most of which deal with distinctly different types of bankruptcy proceedings. Chapter 11 deals with reorganisation proceedings, which are designed to preserve the debtor's business intact while restructuring its liabilities. Chapter 7 concerns liquidations, ie proceedings designed to marshall the assets of the debtor-entity and discharge finally all liabilities thereof without regard to preserving the debtor's business. Under both chapters, the trustee-in-bankruptcy is given extensive powers to pursue assets of the debtor, to rescind unfavourable transactions executed prior to filing of the bankruptcy petition and to control any on-going business of the debtor.

II PURCHASES OF US QUOTED COMPANIES

As stated earlier, one of the assumptions of this book is that the target company is likely to be a privately owned entity, and therefore not subject to the reporting requirements of the SEC. Compliance with the regulatory requirements involved to launch a tender offer for a quoted company are worthy of at least a book in themselves; however, some basic considerations are given here, to indicate the types of points which may arise.

Any domestic company whose securities (equity or debt) are listed on a national securities exchange or traded 'over the counter' are, with a few exceptions, required to file reports annually and quarterly with the SEC. Audited group accounts are due within 90 days of the year end in the 10-K filing; unaudited quarterly data is required within 45 days of the period end on a Form 10-Q. This information is available to the public as it is filed and is a valuable source of current financial information about a target.

If a company wishes to make either a full or partial bid for a quoted company, even an agreed bid, it must comply with the applicable rules of both the SEC and the exchange upon which the securities are quoted. At a minimum the offeror will have to file a Schedule 14D-1, which provides financial information about the offeror (including a reconciliation of the accounts to US GAAP amounts), information about the consideration offered, the shares of the target then owned by the offeror, its officers and directors, and the means of financing the offer. This document must be filed within five business days of announcing the offer. Meeting this tight time deadline is very demanding, and must be anticipated in the planning of any bid.

If the acquiror has a stake in the company prior to making a tender offer, it will also have to consider certain sections of the Securities Exchange Act of 1934 (the 1934 Act) which require that any 'person' who acquires 'beneficial ownership' of more than five per cent of a class of equity securities registered under the 1934 Act (which would include virtually all issues listed on an exchange as well as those traded over the counter) must disclose such ownership and other specific information within 10 calendar days after crossing the five per cent line.

The acquisition of such a stake is reported by filing a Schedule 13-D, which requires disclosure of the purchaser's intent to cause or effect significant changes in the target, including a change in control, the sale of material assets or a reorganisation or liquidation, etc. The interpretation of beneficial ownership is broad enough to capture all direct, and most indirect, affiliations. It is important to know about, and comply with, these reporting requirements to prevent censure, fines, and litigation if and when a full offer is commenced.

4 Company law impact of US investment on a UK company

Corporate law in the US is generally a matter of state law, except in the securities law field where there is in any event overlap between federal and individual states' securities laws. There is no US-wide corporate law, in the sense of an equivalent to the companies legislation which applies (with some exceptions) to the whole of Britain.

The choice of US lawyers may therefore fall into the chicken and egg conundrum since the evaluation process may well encompass more than one state before it results in identifying a target in a single state. This said, it may well be found that US corporate lawyers are quite happy to deal with acquisitions involving the laws of other states.

I REQUIRED AUTHORISATIONS AND CLEARANCES

The most pressing regulatory concern from a UK perspective is, normally, to determine what stock exchange report must be filed, if any, in connection with an acquisition made by a UK quoted company. The tests are based on the amount of the purchase consideration and other tests to measure the size of the transaction in relation to the size of the acquiror and determine, for example, if shareholder approval is necessary.

Other concerns, while they must be addressed early, do not normally create barriers to making investments in the US. The following sections provide a general overview of the more typical concerns when an acquisition is considered by quoted and unquoted companies.

Within the UK, the acquiror may, depending on its circumstances (including its status as a listed, public company or an unlisted, public company, or a private company), be subject to a number of statutory or regulatory (external or internal) imperatives, in respect of or arising under:

- its Memorandum and Articles of Association;
- if it is a listed company, the provisions of The Stock Exchange 'Yellow Book', Admission of Securities to Listing, relating to acquisitions;
- if it is an unlisted company whose shares are dealt in on the Unlisted Securities Market (USM), The Stock Exchange 'Green Book', The Stock Exchange Unlisted Securities Market;
- if it is a company whose shares are dealt in on the Third Market, the rules published by The Stock Exchange for the Third Market ('The White Book');
- competition law;
- banking law, if the target's activities include a deposit taking business carried on by a person authorised under the Banking Act 1987; and
- the City Code on Take-overs and Mergers, if the target owns shares in a company to which the Code applies and as a result of the acquisition the acquiror secures or consolidates control of such company;

and if the acquiror proposes to issue its securities in connection with the acquisition:

- if it is a public company, the valuation provisions of sections 103 to 111 of the Companies Act 1985;
- the authorisation provisions of section 80 of the Companies Act 1985 in relation to the issue of shares or securities convertible into shares;
- the pre-emption provisions of section 89 of the Companies Act 1985 when equity securities are to be allotted for cash for the purpose of the acquisition;
- the control exercised by the Bank of England over certain capital-raising activities pursuant to the Control of Borrowing Order 1958; and
- the statutory regime relating to issues of listed securities under Part IV of the Financial Services Act 1986 (FSA) and those relating to issues of unlisted securities under Part V of the FSA, once the regulations to implement this Part of the Act are established. Until this happens, sections 56 to 71 of the Companies Act 1985 and section 57 of the FSA will continue to apply.

II MEMORANDUM AND ARTICLES OF ASSOCIATION
Three questions should be addressed under this head, namely:

(1) Does the acquiror possess the necessary power under the objects set out in its Memorandum of Association to make the acquisition?
(2) If the acquiror will need to borrow to fund the acquisition, will this result in the limit, if any, placed on the directors' authority to borrow on behalf of the company being exceeded?
(3) If the acquiror proposes to issue shares in connection with the acquisition, is the amount of its authorised share capital sufficient, and do the Articles of Association of the acquiror empower its directors to allot the shares?

The capacity of a company registered under the Companies Act 1985 and its predecessors is limited to the purposes contained in the objects clause of its Memorandum of Association. Consequently a transaction which falls outside the company's express objects or powers, or is not reasonably incidental to them, will be ultra vires, that is, outside the authority of the company, void and incapable of ratification by its shareholders. Nevertheless, a person who enters into an ultra vires transaction with the company in good faith (which is presumed unless the contrary is proved) will be able to enforce the transaction if it is one 'decided on by the directors' because in those circumstances, section 35 of the Companies Act 1985 would prevent the company from relying on its ultra vires nature.

Most companies' objects are drawn up in such a way that the ultra vires rule seldom causes a problem. It is important to establish in any particular case whether the 'main objects' rule operates so as to make one object dominant and the others ancillary, or so as to result in there being more than one main object, subject to the next paragraph. If the former case applies, anything not done in pursuance of the dominant object will be ultra vires unless it is reasonably incidental to it, even if it is apparently within an ancillary object. However, the objects clauses are usually drawn so as to make each separate object an independent main object, by including a clause to that effect.

Despite lack of specific power to make the contemplated acquisition, the company may still be able to rely on the commonly found sub-clause enabling it to carry on any other activity which can, in the opinion of its directors, be advantageously carried on by the company in connection with or as ancillary to its main object, provided the directors have a genuine (even if misguided) belief that such other activity can be so carried on.

It is in practice likely that a US acquisition will be effected either through a subsidiary set up in the US for that purpose, or by the purchase of the shares of an incorporated company (a significant reason being that a UK acquiror will probably not wish to purchase a business, because of the possibility of product liability claims arising if the business operates in a field where such claims are likely). The requisite power here will be to acquire and hold shares. If the acquisition does take the form of the purchase of an unincorporated business, and it is one operating in a different field from that of the acquiror, particular attention needs to be paid to the question of whether an alteration of the acquiror's objects (necessitating a special resolution) is needed.

The power to borrow will normally be specifically included in the objects of a company, but if it is not, a trading or commercial company will in any event have implied power to borrow money for the purposes of its business unless such borrowing is expressly prohibited. An express power to borrow must be exercised for the purpose of an intra vires business object. However, failure to do so would not render the borrowing void unless the lender was aware that the borrowing was for an ultra vires purpose. The exercise of the power to borrow is delegated to the directors, either specifically or under a general management provision in the company's Articles of Association.

Where a limit is placed on the directors' authority to exercise the borrowing power, and borrowing to fund the acquisition would result in such authority being exceeded, the consent of shareholders will have to be obtained. Whether such consent will take the form of a special resolution altering the Articles, or an ordinary resolution, eg authorising an increase in the amount of debt permitted to be outstanding, will depend on the circumstances.

If the acquisition involves the issue of shares in the acquiror, an increase in the acquiror's authorised share capital may be necessary, requiring an ordinary resolution of the shareholders. Discussed below are the requirements relating to the additional shareholders' authorisations for the allotment of shares and, where the purpose of the share issue is to raise cash, the exclusion (or modification) of shareholders' statutory rights of pre-emption over shares.

Finally, it should be noted that the ultra vires rule is likely to undergo major reform to reduce or eliminate its restrictive effects in the near future – possibly by new clauses to be introduced into the current Companies Bill which is expected to complete its passage through Parliament in the summer of 1989.

III THE YELLOW BOOK

A company whose shares are listed on The Stock Exchange (properly, The International Stock Exchange of the United Kingdom and the Republic of Ireland Ltd, herein referred to as 'The Stock Exchange') is bound by a number of requirements concerning acquisitions which are set out in section 6 of 'Admission of Securities of Listing', known universally as 'The Yellow Book'. Having regard to the focus of this work, ie acquisitions of smaller US unlisted companies, only those requirements set out in Chapter 1 of Section 6 will be referred to below.

Under Chapter 1, transactions are classified (mainly on the basis of certain comparative values) into:

- Class 1 transactions (which may or may not be 'major' Class 1 transactions requiring shareholder approval as well as a circular to shareholders);

- Class 2 transactions (requiring only a public announcement of certain details);
- Class 3 transactions (requiring a public announcement only in certain instances);
- Class 4 transactions (where shareholder approval may be required irrespective of the size of the transaction, because of the interests involved in the transaction); and
- very substantial or reverse takeovers (requiring shareholder approval and a suspension of listing pending shareholder approval and publication of listing particulars as though the company were a new applicant for listing).

The criteria for establishing into which classification an acquisition falls, the information which must go into an announcement, the references to the section of the Yellow Book where the information which must be given in a circular to shareholders is contained, and the rules governing consultation with and clearances of documents by the Quotations Department of The Stock Exchange and the timing of shareholder approvals and making of announcements are set out in Chapter 1 of Section 6 of the Yellow Book. It is beyond the scope of this work to go into the detail of the requirements; however, it is perhaps worth remarking that a series of small acquisitions in quick succession may be aggregated for the purpose of classification, thus resulting in the requirement to provide details of all of them in a circular to shareholders.

Further noteworthy points are that because of differing reporting standards – a US private company is not subject to audit (except in relation to some so-called 'exempt' or private offerings, which are subject to audit requirements under, eg, Regulation D of the United States Securities Act of 1933) – the investigation process required to satisfy the Stock Exchange's requirements is likely to be considerably more extensive and expensive than it would be in the case of a UK private company acquisition, and that the acquiror's shareholders' approval may be required for an acquisition if the reporting accountants are unable to report without qualification on the profits and net assets of the company or business acquired.

The regulations governing the issue of securities by a listed company which will apply, for example, if the acquisition involves the issue of shares which could increase the shares of a class already listed by 10 per cent or more, or if debt securities of any amount are to be issued, are contained in Chapter 1 of Section 3 of the Yellow Book. These regulations integrate the further requirements of The Stock Exchange with relevant EEC directives concerning official listing of securities on stock exchanges, which were given effect to in the FSA 1986. An acquiror intending to issue its securities in connection with a US acquisition will have to observe the detailed requirements of Part IV of the FSA 1986 and Chapter 3 of Section 2 and Chapter 1 of Section 3 of the Yellow Book, if listed, or of Part V of the FSA 1986 if unlisted (the last, once regulations are issued).

IV THE UNLISTED SECURITIES MARKET

A USM company is bound by the undertakings given by it to The Stock Exchange in the form of General Undertakings entered into at the time of entry to the USM. In the case of an acquisition, these undertakings may require either that notification be given to the Quotations Department in the form of an announcement giving details of the assets acquired, how the consideration was satisfied, the value of the assets, and the profits attributable to these assets, or that a circular giving additional information as set out in Section D of the Green Book be sent to shareholders.

There are additional requirements relating to very substantial transactions or transactions which might result in a change of control, and to transactions involving interested parties for which prior approval of shareholders will normally be required.

V THE THIRD MARKET

A company whose shares are dealt in on the Third Market must have a Stock Exchange member firm as its sponsor and must give to the sponsor an undertaking, the model terms of which are set out in the White Book.

The model terms require the company to notify the sponsor of price-sensitive matters but do not refer specifically to acquisitions. The sponsor may however have required the company to give additional undertakings and the agreement with the sponsor should be reviewed to ensure that any requirements regarding acquisitions are complied with.

BANKING LAW

If the target's business includes an interest of 15 per cent or more, in terms of voting power, in an 'authorised institution', ie, with the exception of those institutions specified in Schedule 2 of the Banking Act 1987, a deposit taking business which is authorised by the Bank of England to accept deposits in the United Kingdom, it will be necessary to notify the Bank of England in advance to ascertain whether or not it has any objection to such interest coming under the control of the acquiror. The Bank of England will wish to be satisfied that the acquiror is financially sound and is a fit and proper person to have such an interest.

THE CITY CODE ON TAKE-OVERS AND MERGERS ('THE CODE')

If the target owns a controlling interest (which for the purposes of the Code means 30 per cent or more of the voting power) of a company to which the Code applies, ie, listed and unlisted public companies resident in the United Kingdom and certain private companies, or if the acquiror owns shares in such a company which when aggregated with shares in the same company owned by the target amount to a controlling interest, the Panel on Takeovers and Mergers must be consulted to establish whether any obligation arises under the Code to make a general offer for all the shares in that company.

The detailed provisions of the Code would need to be considered to establish whether or not the acquiror might come under an obligation to make a general offer either by virtue of the acquisition of the target or by virtue of subsequent acquisitions of shares in the company.

RESTRICTIONS ON DIRECTORS' ABILITY TO ALLOT SECURITIES

A company which proposes to issue shares as consideration for an acquisition may need to seek its shareholders' consent in one or more respects, apart from any necessitated pursuant to Chapter 1 of Section 6 of the Yellow Book, if it is a listed company. The requirement may arise in relation to:

● Section 80(1) of the Companies Act 1985, under which directors are not permitted to exercise any power of the company to allot 'relevant securities' – which expression includes rights to subscribe for or to convert securities into most types of shares – unless they are authorised to do so either by the

company in general meeting or under its Articles.
- Section 89(1) of the Companies Act 1985, under which, subject to at least one important qualification, a company before allotting any equity securities (which expression includes rights to subscribe for or to convert securities into most types of shares) must offer them by way of rights to its shareholders.

While the Memorandum or Articles of a private company may altogether exclude the pre-emption provisions of section 89(1), that does not apply to a public company. In their case, provided the directors have a section 80 general authority to allot, the pre-emption provisions of section 89(1) may be disapplied either by the Articles or by special resolution of the company. However, the pre-emption provisions of section 89(1) only apply to the allotment of equity securities for cash, with the consequence that if the shares to be issued are to be wholly or partly paid up for other than cash, eg as consideration for the acquisition for shares in a company or for a business, section 89(1) will be irrelevant.

Nevertheless, The Stock Exchange and the bodies representing institutional shareholders impose or attempt to impose their own further constraints on a listed company. Broadly speaking, the Stock Exchange will countenance the general disapplication of section 89(1) so long as the period of its validity is restricted to no more than 15 months from the date of the passing of the resolution or, if earlier, so that it expires on the date of the next annual general meeting. However, even where such a general authority has been given The Stock Exchange will still normally require that any issue of equity capital for cash, otherwise than pro rata to existing shareholders, must be approved by the shareholders in general meeting. The institutional investors protection committee has continued to insist on limitations even while recognising, inter alia, that the circumstances in which a company might wish to make allotments of equity securities for cash (otherwise than pro rata to shareholders) include small issues of shares in connection with a vendor placing in respect of an overseas acquisition where local legislation makes it impractical to issue shares direct to the vendors. These groups have sought to restrict the extent to which companies can exploit the disapplication of shareholders' pre-emption rights for the purpose of raising cash without giving existing shareholders the opportunity to subscribe for equity shares or stock convertible into, or warrants to subscribe for, equity shares.

A statement issued on 29 April 1987 by the Association of British Insurers expressed their views with regard to protection of pre-emptive rights:

> ... members of the ABI can be expected to oppose resolutions which seek to disapply pre-emption rights in respect of any amount of equity share capital in excess of two and a half per cent of the equity share capital in issue at the time such a general authority is sought and will expect companies requiring larger amounts for particular purposes to present a convincing case for their shareholders' specific approval ...
>
> It is also considered that in the related matter of vendor placings shareholders are entitled to expect a right of claw-back for any issues of significant size or which are offered at more than a very modest discount on market price. Members of ABI will therefore expect that issues involving more than 10 per cent of issued equity share capital or a discount greater than 5 per cent will be placed on a basis which leaves existing shareholders with a right to claw-back their pro rata share of the issue if they wish.[1]

---

1 Association of British Insurers 'Circular to All Members', London, 29 April 1987.

As already mentioned, the pre-emption provisions of section 89(1) of the Companies Act 1985 do not apply to non-cash issues. Frequently, an acquiror proposing to issue shares in connection with a US acquisition will follow the vendor placing route (where it is widely considered that because the US vendor takes no risk and is not responsible for selling the consideration shares in the UK, US securities laws and SEC regulations do not apply) so the section 89(1) provisions will not be relevant (although section 80 authority will be). Except where SEC public offering requirements do not apply because the shares are issued privately, unless the acquiror is prepared to undertake to fulfill the very stringent SEC disclosure requirements and continuing obligations, eg preparing financial statements which comply with US accounting practice, it will not wish to issue its shares to the US vendors.

Certain other provisions of the Companies Act may need to be considered by a public company when shares are to be allotted for a non-cash consideration. Where the consideration for the allotment includes an undertaking which is to be or may be performed more than five years after the date of the allotment (section 102(1) of the Companies Act 1985), such an allotment is unlawful in the case of a public company. If the consideration for the acquiror's shares includes, for example, covenants by the vendors not to compete with the acquired company or business for a period exceeding five years, the allotment will be unlawful. The penalty is borne by the person to whom the shares are allotted; he or she becomes liable to pay to the company (ie the acquiror, in this context) the value of the nominal amount of the shares and any premium thereon, attributable to the unlawful undertaking. A variation of an originally lawful contract to allot shares which, had it been part of the original contract would have made the allotment unlawful, is void. Even where the consideration for the allotment is or includes an undertaking which is to be performed within five years, similar consequences follow if it is in fact not so performed.

A second consideration arises (subject to exceptions) where a public company allots shares as fully or partly paid up otherwise than in cash; in such a case section 103 of the Companies Act 1985 may require the assets forming the consideration for the allotment to be valued and reported on by an independent expert. The expert must be a person who is qualified under section 389 of the Companies Act 1985 (which is likely to be superseded in the summer of 1989 by the provisions found in the current Companies Bill) to be the auditor of the issuing company, and this would, for example, normally rule out the US offices of the acquiror's UK accountants. However, the expert is entitled to obtain or accept specialist valuations which will probably be necessary in the case of a US acquisition, and it may be thought that the possibility for a close liaison between UK and US offices offers some advantages. However, this requirement does not apply in the case (inter alia) of a share for share exchange or a merger (ie where one company proposes to acquire all the assets and liabilities of another in exchange for the issue of shares or other securities of the first company to the shareholders of the other, with or without any cash payment). This means that if assets only, or only some of the assets and liabilities of a business are to be acquired, the foregoing valuation requirements will apply. Contravention of section 103 has much the same effect as contravention of section 102. In the context of section 103, the shares acquired on exchange, or the assets and liabilities acquired for the issue, may be those of any company wherever incorporated.

VI CONTROL OF BORROWING
The Bank of England's Capital Issues Committee exercises control over the timings of certain capital-raising activities, under the Control of Borrowing Order 1958 (SI 1958/1208). Timing consent is needed for issues of any listed or unlisted sterling securities to raise £3 million or more in Great Britain.

VII THIRD PARTY CONSENTS
An acquiror ought to be aware of any restrictions by which it is bound under contractual arrangements involving third parties, eg:

- banking facilities;
- Debenture Stock Trust Deeds or Loan Stock Trust Deeds or Instruments; or
- trading contracts

and consider carefully whether the proposed acquisition or the method by which it is proposed to be effected, eg borrowing, requires authorisation by any party – such as bankers, trustees for holders of Debenture Stock or Loan Stock or the holders themselves – in order to avoid a breach of contract (which may, in turn, trigger default clauses in other instruments). In particular, it is common form in Debenture Stock Trust Deeds not only to impose borrowing restrictions, but also to require that any charge over the assets of a subsidiary or any disposal of a subsidiary (or sub-subsidiary) shall require the sanction of an extraordinary resolution of the stockholders. Therefore, far in advance of making any acquisition, the company should compile a list of third party consents which may be necessary so that any limitations are recognised and allowed for.

VIII COMPETITION LAW

PREFACE
In making an acquisition of a US company it should not be forgotten that there are potential competition law implications, arising under either or both UK domestic and European Community (EC) law. The equivalent US laws – antitrust laws – are dealt with earlier in this chapter. The domestic competition law of other EC member states may also be relevant but is outside the scope of this work.

Competition law may affect the acquisition of a US company by a UK company in three ways. First, the acquisition itself may fall within either UK domestic or EC competition law. Secondly, the terms of the acquisition agreement may be proscribed by law. Thirdly, pre-existing circumstances may be caught and, if so, consideration should be given to dealing with them in the acquisition agreement by way of warranties. Last, it should be recalled that there is currently a risk of double jeopardy with the UK and EC laws. Conduct which falls foul of domestic law and also falls foul of EC law, and vice versa, can be penalised twice notwithstanding the fact that the acquiror may already have been punished for infringing the first set of rules.

Accordingly, it is important to consider the implications of competition law before entering into any binding obligations (although having regard to the focus of this work, it is likely to impinge only in very specialised areas). This is true even where the proposed acquisition may seem small: the tests for the application of some UK and EC laws relate to market share, rather than to size in absolute terms.

UK DOMESTIC LAW

In the context of UK competition law, a primary concern is the Fair Trading Act 1973 and its effect on the control of mergers. That being said, it would not be right to ignore wholly the Restrictive Trade Practices Act 1976 and, accordingly, brief reference is made to that Act later in this section.

THE FAIR TRADING ACT 1973 (FTA)

Certain mergers are subject to examination and control under the FTA to determine whether they operate or may be expected to operate against the public interest. The Director-General of Fair Trading, through the Office of Fair Trading (OFT), has the responsibility for monitoring potential mergers and takes a central role in the consideration of whether a merger, or potential merger, should be referred to the Monopolies and Mergers Commission (MMC). However, the final decision as to whether or not to make a reference to the MMC is made by the Secretary of State for Trade and Industry. The FTA provides a structure for the MMC's investigation and defines the powers which the Secretary of State may exercise if the MMC concludes that the merger would be contrary to the public interest.

A merger may be referred to the MMC for up to six months after the relevant facts have been made public but, in practice, almost all references are of proposed mergers. To fall within the scope of investigation, certain elements need to be satisfied:

(a) two or more enterprises (for this purpose a business or part of a business) have ceased to be distinct;
(b) at least one of those enterprises is carried on in the UK; and
(c) either the value of the assets (both tangible and intangible and wherever situated) taken over (without deducting liabilities) exceeds £30 million or the result of the merger is that a statutory monopoly is created or enhanced (for this purpose a monopoly is a 25 per cent share of the relevant market in the UK or a substantial part of the UK).

It is UK government policy that, normally, merger references will only be made on the grounds of a possible effect on competition. For these purposes, the definition of the 'market' is relevant, and the Secretary of State can in theory define this in any way he wishes. However, the present Secretary of State has indicated that, where appropriate, the international nature of a market will be considered. Nevertheless, it is ultimately the possible effect on UK consumers which is determinative.

It can readily be seen that the acquisition of a US company which exports to the UK, or which has a UK subsidiary, could satisfy the last test (known as the market share test).

Acting on a recommendation of the MMC, the Secretary of State has a wide range of powers to remedy or prevent any adverse consequences of a merger. These include, for example, the power to:

- regulate the prices to be charged;
- prohibit the acquisition of the undertaking or assets of another's business; and
- require the divestiture of a company, undertaking or assets.

In certain circumstances, the acquisition of a US company by a UK company may fall within the ambit of the FTA. Because of the potential consequences of this it is common practice for a company considering an acquisition to seek confidential guidance from the OFT as to whether such a merger is likely to be referred to the MMC. Because the guidance is confidential, it cannot be based on the comments of all interested parties, and therefore is not binding. Such guidance, if the OFT is prepared to give it (and in the majority of cases it is), may be 'positive' in the sense that on the facts available to him, the Secretary of State would not refer the merger to the MMC – or negative, where the opposite view is given.

Where an application for confidential guidance is made consideration should be given to making the contract for the acquisition conditional upon obtaining either the non-binding clearance of the OFT or the binding final clearance of the Secretary of State that no reference will be made.

RESTRICTIVE TRADE PRACTICES ACT 1976 (RTPA)
Certain agreements and arrangements need to be registered under the RTPA, namely those between two or more persons (including companies) who carry on business in the UK in the production or supply of goods, or the supply of services, under which restrictions as to certain specified matters are accepted by two or more parties. Such restrictions include negative obligations relating to matters such as the prices to be charged or quantities to be supplied or acquired (eg not to charge more than X or supply quantities in excess of Y). This may affect a UK company which acquires a US company if the vendor has other subsidiaries which are not part of the package being acquired and which operate in the UK.

It is not expected that the RTPA will be in force for very much longer. The UK government has published proposals for replacing the RTPA with new legislation more closely aligned with existing EC competition law and it seems likely that the new legislation will come into effect by 1990.

EUROPEAN COMMUNITY LAW
The Treaty of Rome superimposes EC law on the national law of each of the member states. So far as competition law is concerned, the two principal measures are articles 85 and 86.

ARTICLE 85 OF THE TREATY OF ROME ('ARTICLE 85')
Article 85 prohibits 'all agreements between undertakings, decisions by associations of undertakings and concerted practices which may affect the trade between member states and which have as their object or effect the prevention, restriction or distortion of competition within the Common Market . . .'. Unless exempted such agreements are void and a party giving effect to such agreements, unless the Commission of the EC has been notified of the agreements, is liable to a substantial fine.

The scope of article 85 is wide: it covers not merely legally binding contracts, but any form of agreement or arrangement whether or not legally enforceable. The agreement or arrangement must have an appreciable effect on the EC or a significant part of it, ie the UK or another member state. It was long thought that article 85 did not apply to mergers but recent cases have shown that, in certain circumstances, an acquisition agreement may fall within its scope.

So far as the acquisition of a US company is concerned, article 85 is only likely to affect an acquisition if the two companies are competitors. Quite apart from the possibility of an acquisition per se falling within article 85, there also is the question of whether any of the individual provisions of an acquisition agreement fall within the article. An example of such a provision is the restrictive covenant commonly given by the vendor of a business to protect the goodwill of the business being sold.

It is possible to approach the Commission in advance of a transaction to obtain its views as to whether, in the light of the information made available, the agreement or practice in question falls outside article 85. However, the relatively extended timescale involved in discussions with the Commission normally makes this course impracticable.

ARTICLE 86 OF THE TREATY OF ROME ('ARTICLE 86')
Article 86 provides that 'any abuse by one or more undertakings of a dominant position within the Common Market or in a substantial part of it shall be prohibited as incompatible with the Common Market insofar as it may affect trade between member states'. Article 86 includes a non-exhaustive list of 'abuses' including unfair prices or trading conditions, limitations of production, markets or technical development, discrimination and tied business relationships.

A company enjoys a dominant position when its relative economic strength allows it to prevent effective competition in a particular market. Such a position occurs when the company concerned is able to influence, determine or even disregard market conditions. The acquisition of a dominant position by a company may be an abuse if the acquiror is already in a dominant position.

It is by no means impossible that a UK company has a strong position in a given UK product market and that the acquisition of a US subsidiary with a share of that same market would fall within article 86.

The Commission has power to order termination of the infringement, to impose fines of up to 10 per cent of worldwide turnover, and in cases such as refusal to supply, to order the resumption of supplies. As with anti-competitive agreements under article 85, the guidance of the Commission may be sought in advance, but the same problems exist in terms of doing so on a practical timescale.

DRAFT MERGERS REGULATION
The Commission has published a proposal for an EC regulation on the control of concentrations (or mergers) between undertakings. If adopted the Regulation will give the Commission the power, subject to review by the European Court of Justice, to block mergers with an anti-competitive effect in a significant part of the EC and which have an effect in more than one member state.

Furthermore, mergers which give rise to a substantial change in the competitive structure within the EC could be prohibited even if they do not create a dominant position.

There is a considerable degree of overlap between this proposed regulation and the merger controls of some of the member states, including the UK. The extent to which this overlap may be removed remains, at this time, a matter of speculation.

IX GUARANTEES, CHARGES AND OPINION LETTERS
A typical acquisition in the US by a UK company, as has been seen, involves the setting up of a US subsidiary which may borrow from a US bank to finance

the acquisition. Although the lender can be expected to require that the facility be secured by charges over the assets of the purchased company (there being no similar constraints in the US to those which inhibit a UK company from giving financial assistance in connection with the purchase of its shares), the lender can also be expected to require a guarantee from the UK parent company of the US subsidiary's obligations.

It is the usual practice for the acquiror's UK lawyers to be required by the US lender to opine for the benefit of the latter as to the enforceability as against the acquiror of the documents to be entered into and as to their proper execution. The acquisition contract itself may also contain a condition that suitable opinions are received from the acquiror's US lawyers as to certain matters.

While it may be possible to modify the lender's initial requirements, whatever the rights and wrongs of the matter, the acquiror's UK lawyers may find that if they try to resist, the deal may not go forward.

The acquiror's UK lawyers will wish to frame the qualifications to their opinion with extreme care. By way of summary, they will wish inter alia to:

(a) confine the scope of their opinion so that it expressly excludes the effect of any law other than English domestic law as currently in force, and exclude any opinion as to enforceability outside the jurisdiction of the English courts;
(b) point out that English courts may not enforce an obligation to be performed outside England if its performance would be illegal or void or unenforceable where it is to be performed;
(c) point out the possible effect on enforceability of rights to set off or counter-claim, and limitations imposed by the law of eg insolvency, or principles of equity, and the general effect of laws affecting creditors' rights;
(d) point out that a recovery pursuant to legal remedies or in liquidation in England may be made only in sterling;
(e) point out that equitable remedies such as an order for specific performance or an injuction are discretionary and not available if damages provide an adequate remedy;
(f) draw attention to the English law doctrines relating to penalties, oral amendment of written contracts and the effect of terms relieving a person from a liability or duty owed independently of the contract;
(g) point out that an English court may stay proceedings if concurrent proceedings are being brought elsewhere;
(h) point out that a Companies Registry search does not reveal the presentation of a winding-up petition, and that there may be a delay in filing at the Companies Registry notices of orders or resolutions for winding up or an order for administration or notice of the appointment of a receiver, liquidator or similar person; and
(i) where the creation of a charge is involved, draw attention to the relevant provisions of the Companies Act 1985 relating to the registration of charges.

Finally, the acquiror's UK lawyers will wish to restrict reliance on their opinion to the direct addressee and prohibit the unauthorised publication of or reference to it.

(Note: if the acquiror is incorporated in Scotland or Northern Ireland, both parts of the UK, references to England and the English courts may need to be amended.)

X MISCELLANEOUS POTENTIAL PROBLEM AREAS

The foregoing short dissertation would not be complete without considering legal or practical pitfalls which may affect the acquiror or third parties as a consequence of or subsequent to the acquisition being effected.

One is that under section 765 of the Income and Corporation Taxes Act 1988, subject to certain specific exceptions, the acquiror may not without Treasury consent permit the US subsidiary to issue any shares (for example, for the purpose of an employee incentive scheme) or create any debentures – in effect debt instruments. It is not difficult to overlook these requirements, especially if the US subsidiary enjoys a high degree of autonomy.

Another is that if the acquiror has had the benefit of investment under the Business Expansion Scheme it would lose its qualifying status, which would have adverse tax consequences for the 'BES Investors', if substantially all of the business of the target did not consist of one or more 'qualifying trades' as defined in the BES legislation or if, following the acquisition, the acquiror and the target, taken together, no longer carried on their qualifying trades mainly in the United Kingdom.

Finally, an acquiror which contemplates appointing the proprietor or a substantial shareholder of the US target (or a person connected with such a proprietor or substantial shareholder) to its board or to the board of a subsidiary set up in the US for the purpose of the acquisition, should not make that appointment until the acquisition has actually been consummated, without considering sections 320–322 of the Companies Act 1985. In brief, the acquisition of non-cash assets valued at more than £50,000 or 10 per cent of the acquiror's asset value from a director of the acquiror or its holding company, or a person connected with him, is prohibited unless first approved by resolution of the acquiror (or its holding company) in general meeting. The consequences are less of a concern to the acquiror than to the individual seller, who may find himself liable to account for any direct or indirect gain he has made from the transaction and to indemnify the acquiror for any loss or damage resulting from the transaction, or even to find that the acquiror can treat the acquisition from him as voidable. There are de minimis provisions in section 320 taking out of the net acquisitions of non-cash assets valued at less than £1,000.

CHAPTER 3
Taxation concerns

As with the regulatory environment, there are many tax considerations applicable to an acquisition. The comments below are current as of the date of
publication; while there are no major US tax reform programmes proposed at
this time, there are continual changes from both 'technical correction' amend-
ments and tests by courts. Therefore the potential acquiror should consult his
or her tax adviser when entering into this type of investment to ensure that the
most beneficial tax treatment is obtained.

A company's taxable status depends on whether it is incorporated. Generally
a corporation is a separate taxable entity, taxed on its net profits at the corporate
level. No deduction is permitted for corporate profits distributed as dividends
to shareholders. Dividends are taxable to the shareholders as income, subject
to certain dividends received deductions allowable to corporate shareholders.
In contrast, partnerships, sole proprietorships, and S-corporations are generally
not separate taxable entities; items of income and loss are passed through and
taxed directly to the owners.

Corporations subject to tax

Domestic corporations are subject to tax on their worldwide taxable income. A
foreign corporation which is not engaged in a US trade or business is taxed
only on certain US source investment and other passive income. A foreign
corporation which is engaged in a trade or business in the US is taxed on net
income that is effectively connected with the conduct of that trade or business
as well as on certain US source investment and other passive income which are
not connected to such business. Gains from the disposition of US real property
interests are taxable (deemed to be effectively connected to a US trade) to foreign
corporations whether or not otherwise engaged in a US business.

Residency   A domestic corporation, for US tax purposes, is one created or
organised under the laws of the United States, or any state thereof (or the
District of Columbia). A foreign corporation, for US tax purposes, is one created
or organised in any other place. The situs of a corporation's management and
control does not determine its residency for US tax purposes.

Basic principles of federal taxation

Note that, while the following discussion outlines the broad principles which
are necessary to analyse a basic business structure, Appendix 4 has extensive
details of the general concepts raised below and certain other areas that are not
covered in this background section.

1 Domestic corporations

Income received by shareholders suffers taxation twice in the US: first, it is taxed at the corporate level and then, if and when the corporate earnings are distributed to shareholders, it is taxed at the individual level as dividend income. A domestic corporation is taxed on its worldwide taxable income.

Gross income is broadly defined as income from whatever source derived, including gross income derived from business, gains derived from dealings in property, interest, rents, royalties, dividends and compensation for services, including fees, commissions and similar items. Gross income is not, however, equivalent to gross receipts; gross receipts must be reduced by the cost of goods sold to arrive at gross income.

Gross income can be measured under several accounting methods, including the accrual method and, where appropriate, the cash receipts and disbursements method. Other accounting methods are available for special circumstances (for example, instalment sales, percentage of completion for long-term construction contracts, etc.). In computing cost of sales, inventories generally must be valued at cost. Several inventory costing methods are available, including the first-in, first-out (FIFO) method and the last-in, first-out (LIFO) method. The method of accounting used for tax purposes generally may differ from that used for financial reporting purposes, although where LIFO is elected for tax purposes, it must also be used for book purposes.

Once gross income is determined, allowable deductions are subtracted to arrive at taxable income. Generally, all ordinary and necessary expenses of earning income are deductible. However, determining allowable deductions is complicated because of the many possible deductions and alternative calculations allowed and because of the many interpretative gaps that exist in the law. For example, a deduction for expenses payable to certain related persons generally may have to be deferred until that person includes the item in gross income (for example, when received). Set forth below are a number of items that qualify as deductions from gross income.

DEPRECIATION (ACCELERATED COST RECOVERY SYSTEM – ACRS)

ACRS is a system of annual deductions for recovering the cost of a taxpayer's capital outlays. ACRS specifies the useful life and depreciation methods, based on the type of asset involved.

Under ACRS, as modified by the Tax Reform Act of 1986, property is classified into one of seven broadly defined classes, each with its own schedule of annual recovery deductions, which generally apply methods ranging from straight line to 200 per cent declining-balance to the property's cost. Most property would fall into the five and seven year category, which generally utilises 200 per cent declining balance method. The various categories and their depreciation methods are discussed further in Appendix 4.

OTHER ALLOWABLE EXPENSES

Other allowable expenses include:

Compensation   Reasonable salaries, wages and bonuses paid during the year.

Reimbursed travel and entertainment expenses   Generally these are deductible items, but only 80 per cent of meal and entertainment expenses is allowed.

Interest   Interest paid or accrued is generally deductible to the extent that it does not relate to indebtedness incurred to purchase or carry obligations on which the interest income is tax exempt. Special rules apply to original issue discount obligations. Interest is not deductible, however, on indebtedness that is treated as equity under the thin capitalisation rules. Prepaid interest is not currently deductible by a cash method taxpayer. Moreover the deduction for interest payable to certain related persons may have to be deferred until that creditor includes the interest in gross income.

Miscellaneous   Other ordinary costs of business usually include rent, repair and maintenance, research and development, advertising, employee benefit and bad debt expenses (the last under the specific charge off method, except for certain banks). Again, details are provided in Appendix 4.

Companies are generally allowed a deduction from income of 70 per cent of the dividends received from a domestic corporation. Where 20 per cent or more (by vote and value) of a company's shares are owned, this percentage is increased to 80 per cent. Where dividends are received from an affiliated (80 per cent or more of vote and value owned) domestic corporation, this deduction is increased to 100 per cent. The paying corporation, however, is not allowed a deduction for dividends paid. The corporate dividend received deduction reduces (eliminates for affiliated corporations) taxation of profits at each level of a corporate structure.

The resulting taxable income (gross income less allowable deductions) of a corporation is taxed at a regular rate of 34 per cent (see, however, the description of the alternative minimum tax, p 38), although for companies with less than $335,000 of taxable income, certain graduated rates apply which may reduce the rate to as little as 15 per cent. Capital gains are presently taxed at the same rates as other income.

2 Foreign corporations

The income of foreign corporations is segregated into two categories, each of which is taxed separately:

- Non-business income: certain types of US source investment and other passive income that are not related (that is, effectively connected) with a US business.
- Business income: net income that is effectively connected to a business carried on in the US.

A foreign corporation's worldwide income effectively connected with the conduct of a trade or business in the US is taxed on a net basis at the rates applicable to a US domestic corporation. US source non-business income is generally taxed on a gross basis at a flat 30 per cent statutory rate, unless double tax treaties apply to reduce or eliminate the 30 per cent statutory rate. The US/UK tax treaty applies to reduce this rate on certain categories of income. (Appendix 4 provides examples of those categories generally adjusted.) This treaty provides a number of benefits to companies operating in both nations.

However, to avoid being excluded from using it on a basis of treaty shopping or other disqualifying activities, it is advisable to consult a tax expert.

Non-business income is composed principally of 'fixed or determinable annual or periodical income', a term which indicates a class of generally passive income such as interest, dividends, rents and royalties. Other non-business income may include some original issue discount payments or gains arising from debt obligations, gains from the disposal of certain natural resources and gains from the disposition of patents or other intangible properties.

BUSINESS INCOME

While the meaning of 'engaged in a trade or business' is not clearly defined, it is usually taken to mean a degree of activity in the US that is regular and continuous, and not sporadic. The taxpayer's primary purpose for engaging in the activity must be for income or profit. Certain types of activities are statutorily excluded from the definition of a US trade or business. For example, trading in shares or securities through a resident broker, commission agent, custodian or other independent agent, whether for one's own account or for that of another, is generally not treated as engaging in a US trade or business, provided the transactions are not carried out through a US office or fixed place of business of the taxpayer.

Once it has been determined if a US trade or business exists, it must be determined what income is 'effectively connected' to that trade or business. For foreign entities, the determination of whether income is effectively connected is based in part on the type of income and in part on the source of that income. If it is demonstrated that the income is effectively connected it is, as stated before, taxed as the income of a US corporation would be (ie on a net basis at regular rates).

3 Other principles applicable to domestic and foreign entities

LOSS RELIEF

Net operating losses of the current year may generally be carried back three years and carried forward 15 years. Any loss not utilised within the carryforward or carryback period is lost. A net operating loss is generally defined as the excess of the deductions allowable for a taxable year over the gross income of the taxpayer for that year. The net operating loss for the taxable year is carried first to the earliest year to which such loss may be carried and then to each succeeding year, and applied to the extent taxable income exists for each of those years. The carried forward (or back) net operating loss is applied against taxable income for the relevant year, and tax is charged on the resulting taxable income, if any.

Limits are placed on the use of net operating loss carryovers of corporations after ownership changes whether resulting from taxable purchases of the corporation's shares or from tax-free reorganisations. Generally, if there is a change of more than 50 per cent of significant shareholder interest during a three year testing period, the loss limitation rules will apply. If the nature of the business changes significantly in the two years following an ownership change, no losses will be available. Limits are also imposed on the use of net operating losses generated by dual resident corporations.

4 Compliance

The US utilises a self-assessment system, where a return has to be prepared, the tax liability calculated, and any unpaid tax together with the return submitted to the Internal Revenue Service (IRS). The tax liability as calculated on the return is then open to review (audit) by the IRS normally for a period not to exceed three years after the filing of the return.

Tax payments, normally quarterly instalments, are required to be made toward a corporation's estimated tax liability for the revelant year, and the tax liability shown on the return reflects any such payments. Both foreign and domestic corporations are required to make estimated tax payments in advance of filing their tax returns. Estimated tax is defined as the expected regular tax and alternative minimum tax liability minus tax credits allowable. Payments are generally due on the fifteenth day of the fourth, sixth, ninth, and twelfth months of the taxable year. Failure to make such estimated tax payments when they are due may subject the corporation to penalties for underpayment of taxes.

Form 1120, US Corporation Income Tax Return, must be filed by domestic corporations on or before the fifteenth day of the third month following the close of the corporation's taxable year. Form 1120F, US Income Tax Return of a Foreign Corporation, must be filed by all foreign corporations that are engaged in a US trade or business. If a foreign corporation only receives US income that is not effectively connected with a US business, no return is required if the income tax liability has been satisfied by US withholding at the source.

Other taxes

1 Other income taxes

ALTERNATIVE MINIMUM TAX

The Tax Reform Act of 1986 expanded the application of the alternative minimum tax (AMT) to assure collection of minimum amounts of taxes from corporations which were reporting profits, but using tax preferences to significantly reduce or eliminate current taxable income. The thrust of AMT is to tax at a flat 20 per cent rate alternative minimum taxable income computed by adding back to taxable income certain tax preference items and adjustments. The AMT has proved a significant cash flow concern, as many corporations had previously utilised careful tax planning to minimise taxable income without impact on book income.

Some tax preference items and adjustments that are made in calculating alternative minimum taxable income include the following:

- accelerated depreciation in excess of allowable alternative depreciation amounts on property placed in service after 1986, with a few limited exceptions; and
- one half of the excess of pretax book income of the taxpayer over alternative minimum taxable income.

Only 90 per cent of any AMT liability can be offset by certain net operating losses and certain tax credits.

STATE AND LOCAL INCOME TAXES
Most states (and some local jurisdictions) tax corporate income through corporate income or franchise taxes. The tax rates range from as little as one per cent to 12 per cent. The taxable income computations for state purposes may differ from the computation for federal purposes. Once a corporation becomes taxable by a state, the state will generally apply an apportionment factor (usually computed using a three factor formula based on percentages of worldwide sales, payroll and property attributable to the state) to determine what amount of the company's income is subject to tax.

Certain states may impose capital or net worth taxes in lieu of or in addition to income taxes. Moreover, some cities (for example, New York City) also impose corporate income taxes. Most states tax each corporation separately. However, several states (including California) employ the unitary method and apportion and tax the income of a combined group of corporations conducting a unitary business and not just the income for the member with the local operations. Some states (including California) apply the unitary method to the worldwide activities of an affiliated group of corporations, while most unitary states limit the application of the unitary method to the US activities of an affiliated group.

State and local income tax expense is a deduction in arriving at taxable income for federal tax purposes.

2 Other taxes

PAYROLL WITHHOLDING OF INCOME TAXES
The federal government imposes several employment taxes on employers. Employers are required to deduct and withhold from the salaries and wages of their employees amounts to be applied toward the income tax liabilities of their employees. These amounts are periodically deposited with the federal government, and cannot be used by the company between payments; they must be deposited in a segregated account. Social security taxes and unemployment insurance taxes are also imposed on employers. State and local governments also generally require income taxes to be withheld from wages. Withholding taxes are not an expense of the company; rather, companies are required to administer the collection process for the government.

SOCIAL SECURITY TAXES
The US social security system provides a wide array of benefits to eligible individuals, and is funded by equal contributions from the employee and employer. The system provides old age and disability benefits to workers, benefits to dependants and survivors and medical benefits to elderly workers. These benefits are in addition to unemployment insurance provided by the states to compensate workers for loss of income during periods of unemployment (not more than one year of benefits is paid for each incident of unemployment). Workers' compensation programmes provide payment for employment-related injuries or death and are generally funded through insurance maintained by employers.

The social security tax is imposed on employers and employees under the Federal Insurance Contribution Act (FICA), with a similar parallel system for the self-employed. Social security payments are often referred to as FICA. The

FICA tax is a percentage of wages (7.51 per cent for 1988), paid by both the employer and employee at a combined rate of 15.02 per cent. These rates are scheduled to increase to 7.65 per cent each by 1990. The employer is required to collect the employee's portion of the tax by means of a payroll deduction and to remit this amount along with the employer's portion of the tax to the government. There is, however, an annually adjusted ceiling on wages ($45,000 for 1988); amounts in excess of this ceiling are not subject to FICA.

EXCISE TAXES
The federal government imposes excise taxes on the manufacture or sale of certain goods and services, the most common being an excise tax on most fuels, including gasoline, and on air transportation.

STATE AND LOCAL TAXES
More commonly encountered are state and local property taxes which are calculated as a rateable percentage on an assessed valuation (the valuation is periodically adjusted). Many states, and some county and city governments, also impose sales and use taxes on goods (and sometimes services) sold at the ultimate consumer level. These taxes are based on a percentage of the selling price, and are collected by the seller and remitted by the seller to the appropriate state government. Sales and use taxes are not normally included in the quoted price, as contrasted with VAT, which would normally be included in the marked price of an item.

OTHER
Other forms of tax, such as the environmental tax, accumulated earnings tax, and personal holding company tax, are discussed in Appendix 4.

Group structure concerns

As in any country or tax jurisdiction, the structure of the group formed to hold an investment can have a significant impact on the total tax liability. There are a great number of taxation considerations in the US, partly because of the multiplicity of taxation jurisdictions (federal, state and local), and also because of the number of possible organisational forms, including certain special purpose companies such as Foreign Sales Corporations (FSCs) and Interest Charge Domestic International Sales Corporations (Interest Charge DISCs). The brief discussion below is a broad outline of the types of considerations which should be made when planning the structure of a US investment; Appendix 4 provides some further details about particular points, including the purpose of Interest Charge DISCs and FSCs. Because of the complexity of this area, expert advice should be sought in advance to ensure that the most favourable treatment is gained. The purpose of this brief discussion is to provide enough background to formulate the correct questions, and to help understand why certain structures may be in place within an acquisition target.

1 Affiliated groups

Certain affiliated corporations may elect to file a single, consolidated federal income tax return for all members of the affiliated group instead of filing separate income tax returns for each member. Filing one return for all members of the group is simply a tax computation mechanism and does not convert the group into a single corporation. Each member of the group is jointly and severally liable for the entire tax of the consolidated group.

Generally, only US corporations are permitted to be included in an affiliated group. An affiliated group consists of a common US parent corporation, at least one other includable US corporation in which the parent owns at least 80 per cent of the voting power and total value of the shares, and any other includable US corporations that are connected to each other or to the parent under the same 80 per cent ownership tests.

The basic advantages of filing a consolidated return are:

- the ability to apply a member's losses against the income of other members;
- the full exclusion from taxable income of dividends from member corporations; and
- deferral of tax on gains from certain intercompany transactions.

The basic disadvantages of filing a consolidated return are:

- the consolidated return regulations must be strictly complied with as a condition to filing such a return; and
- each member must maintain an accounting period consistent with that of the parent of the group.

A foreign corporation that controls several US subsidiaries, some of which generate profits and others of which sustain losses, will often derive tax advantages by establishing a US holding company to hold the shares of its US subsidiaries, thereby allowing the group of US companies to file a consolidated return and offset any operating losses of members against the taxable income of other members. If a consolidated return is not filed, a foreign corporation may find its profitable US subsidiaries paying tax and its non-profitable US subsidiaries deriving no current benefit for losses generated.

The decision to file a consolidated return will depend upon many factors, including a corporate group's ownership structure and estimates of tax savings or tax costs. Once a consolidated return is elected, the group must continue to file consolidated federal income tax returns in future years unless it obtains the IRS's consent to discontinue consolidated filing. Such consent may be difficult to obtain. Certain state tax benefits may be obtainable as well by establishing a US holding company.

Corporations generally are required to file separate tax returns for state tax purposes, regardless of whether a consolidated return is filed for federal purposes.

2 Branch vs. subsidiary

In deciding whether to operate in the US through a branch or subsidiary domestic corporation, a foreign corporation must determine the deductibility of extraterritorial losses. If a foreign tax benefit can be obtained for the startup losses of an operation incurred by a US branch, consideration should be given to initially operating through a branch in the US.

When the US branch of a foreign corporation begins earning a profit, consideration can be given to incorporating the branch as a US corporation. The primary consideration is whether the country of the foreign investor would allow the use of a loss, incurred by the US branch from the conduct of its trade or business within the US, as a deduction against income not sourced in the US.

While the US has introduced a branch profits and branch level interest tax on a branch's effectively connected income not reinvested in the US, the US/UK tax treaty operates to make these taxes not applicable to the US branch operations of a UK company.

If a foreign company elects to hold its investment through a US subsidiary, and not a branch, the domestic company used would be taxed on its worldwide income at a maximum rate of 34 per cent, as described earlier. Generally, under the US/UK treaty, taxable dividends paid to a non-US parent would be subject to a reduced withholding rate of 5 per cent. Because reasonable management and advisory fees paid to parent companies would generally be deductible as expenses, and not subject to withholding, these may be used to transfer some of the profits to the parent in a tax efficient fashion. Economic substance to support the charge would be required however (see the discussion of allocation of income among related parties).

3 Advantages of a US holding company

As mentioned earlier, establishing a US holding company can provide benefits where a consolidated group can be formed for tax purposes to allow for group relief of all losses within the US. A US holding company can also be advantageous as regards funding an acquisition.

If borrowings are incurred in the US to finance the acquisition, the interest expense on those borrowings will normally be deductible from consolidated income (so long as problems such as thin capitalisation do not arise). Borrowing to finance the acquisition may also be attractive from a foreign currency perspective, as it matches the US dollar asset (investment in the acquired company) with the US dollar liability (debt).

4 Relief from double taxation

FOREIGN TAX CREDIT

A US corporation is subject to tax on its income from foreign sources as well as from US sources. However, a domestic corporation may elect annually to either deduct or take a credit, subject to limitations, for foreign income taxes paid or accrued during the year. If the corporation elects to claim a credit against tax, it is precluded from taking a deduction for foreign income taxes for that year. The foreign tax credit is generally limited to the US tax on the corporation's foreign source taxable income. Foreign taxes that cannot be currently credited may be carried back two years and carried forward five years. The foreign tax credit is also available to a US corporation for a portion of the foreign taxes paid by a foreign corporation in which it owns at least 10 per cent of the voting stock and which pays the US corporation a dividend. Even taxes paid by a second or third tier foreign corporation may be taken as a credit by the US corporation as long as certain direct and indirect ownership requirements are satisfied. Furthermore, the foreign tax credit is available to a US corporation for a portion of the foreign taxes paid by a controlled foreign corporation (a foreign corporation that falls within certain statutory US ownership requirements) when such US corporation is required, under the Internal Revenue code, to include in its gross income certain types of passive and other income earned by the controlled foreign corporation even though no distributions are made to the US corporation.

The foreign tax credit is also available to a foreign corporation for foreign taxes paid with respect to foreign source income effectively connected with the conduct of a trade or business within the US, but the credit cannot be used to offset the branch profits tax if such tax applies. There are also limitations upon the amount of foreign tax credits that can be used to satisfy an Alternative Minimum Tax liability.

5 *Thin capitalisation*

The classification of an obligation as debt or equity is of great importance in corporate taxation since the treatment of interest and dividends differs significantly. Both generally result in taxable income to a non-corporate shareholder, but only interest is deductible by the paying corporation. A domestic corporation, however, may deduct a percentage of dividends received from another domestic corporation. The retirement of a debt instrument is usually tax free but the redemption of shares is generally taxable to the recipient of the proceeds. Treating an obligation as debt or equity is often critical in determining which of several provisions of US tax law apply. Thus, in order to determine the federal tax implications, the nature of an obligation must be carefully evaluated before a transaction is consummated.

In 1969 Congress directed the Treasury Department to promulgate regulations that would provide a framework to resolve debt/equity issues. The Treasury has issued and withdrawn intricate and complex proposed regulations several times, but final regulations have yet to be issued. It is uncertain whether the Treasury will issue another set of rules in this area; however, at this time, objective rules do not exist to provide the much-needed guidance in this murky area. Judgments therefore must be made based on court cases. With respect to the debt to equity ratio, a rule of thumb (should one exist) is that a 3:1 or less ratio may be appropriate for related party debt, but this would have to be evaluated by taking into account the industry and particular circumstances of the parties involved.

6 *Allocation of income and expenses among related persons*

Foreign corporations that establish or acquire US subsidiaries should be aware of section 482 of the Internal Revenue Code, which requires arm's length dealings between related parties. Section 482 gives the IRS the power to reallocate gross income, deductions, credits or allowances among two or more related organisations, trades or businesses, whether or not organised in the US, if the IRS determines that such adjustments are necessary to correctly reflect income. Although section 482 is often applied to transactions between domestic parent corporations and their foreign subsidiaries, it also can be applied to transactions between US subsidiaries and their foreign parent. In addition to general guidance, section 482 and the regulations thereunder contain detailed rules for the appropriate pricing of loans, leases, licences, services and sales of goods.

Points specifically addressed by section 482 include:

- requirements for arm's length interest rates on loans or advances between members of a group of related entities;

- charges at arm's length amounts for marketing, managerial, administrative, technical or other services provided by one member of a group to or for the benefit of another group member; and
- transfers, sales, assignments, etc. of properties, both tangible and intangible, or interests therein, must include arm's length consideration and charges. Special rules apply to any transfer of intangibles (ie 'super-royalty' rules).

Of great concern to most groups of related entities is the intercompany pricing of sales of goods. In the case of sales by US corporations to related foreign corporations, the IRS is concerned primarily that the intercompany transfer price not be too low, resulting in a shifting of income away from the US. On the other hand, in the case of sales from a foreign corporation to a related US corporation, the IRS is concerned primarily that the intercompany transfer price not be too high, thereby resulting in an insufficient amount of income being realised subsequently in the US. However, the US Customs Service is concerned that intercompany transfer prices from foreign corporations on sales into the US not be too low for purposes of customs duties and antidumping considerations. Therefore, the Internal Revenue Code limits the transfer price on imports for income tax purposes, in transactions between related persons, to an amount not in excess of the comparable value claimed for US customs purposes.

7 Concerns specific to acquisitions

Tax considerations play an important role in structuring an acquisition as an asset purchase or purchase of shares. The requirements for each of those two methods are covered in detail in the chapter on 'Structuring the offer'. A few basic considerations are detailed below.

A purchase of assets is historically more attractive to an acquiror, since it generally (a) avoids a blanket assumption of all known, and unknown, liabilities; and (b) provides tax advantages because the basis in assets acquired can be written up to their fair value (to a maximum of the consideration paid) allowing these amounts to be tax deductible/recoverable at some point. This is a very important consideration as asset costs (other than land, goodwill and certain others with no determinable life) are deductible as depreciated or amortised in accordance with the tax code. In no circumstances (either asset or share purchase) is goodwill deductible in the US. Therefore, where purchased assets can not be revalued upwards, a greater amount of goodwill recognition occurs which cannot be written off for tax purposes.

On the other hand, the seller may want to sell shares. This might be the case, for example, where the proceeds from the sale of corporate assets are to be distributed to the individual shareholders, in which case the selling shareholders would suffer double taxation – once at the corporate level on the gain recognised by the corporation and again on the dividend received by the shareholders. Thus, in these circumstances, it would be preferable for the individual shareholders to sell shares of the US company and recognise and pay tax only on the capital gain on the sale of those shares (even though capital gains are presently subject to tax at the same rate as ordinary income). Therefore, the desire on the part of the purchaser to purchase assets must be balanced against the preference of the seller to sell shares.

Under the Internal Revenue Code, a share purchase may be treated (either when elected or deemed under law to be elected) for tax purposes as an asset purchase. Such treatment may be desirable when, for example, the target corporation has sufficient net operating losses to offset any gain triggered on the deemed asset sale, or under another special election where the old target group's losses can be used to offset such gain. The 'residual' method of allocating purchase price to assets is required to be used by the buyer and seller whether assets are purchased directly or deemed purchased. Under the residual method, the total consideration is allocated (to the extent of fair market value) first to the tangible and intangible assets with fixed and determinable lives, with the residual, if any, allocated to non-amortisable intangibles such as goodwill and going concern values. Although not binding on the IRS, it can be beneficial for the buyer and seller to specify the allocation in the contract of sale. This is because the IRS would be less likely to attack terms negotiated in an arm's length transaction.

Because intangible assets other than goodwill and going concern value are generally deductible for tax purposes, the exercise of allocating consideration to intangibles such as patents and customer lists is pursued more rigorously in the US than in the UK. It is not unusual to have a separate valuation performed to support the tax basis allocation, which usually aims for the fastest possible write off.

Part 2
Finding an Investment

CHAPTER 4
What form of investment?

A decision to invest in the US can be realised in several forms:

(a) an investment in US listed or unlisted companies with only a passive involvement;
(b) acquiring significant stakes in businesses or joint ventures that are actively managed;
(c) building US operations from scratch either as extensions of UK operations or as complementary operations; or
(d) outright acquisition of an ongoing US entity.

   While the focus of this book is acquiring existing businesses, it is worthwhile to consider some of the primary concerns of other options. 'Greenfields' operations and acquisitions are the most direct forms of foreign investment. A joint venture may be a suitable alternative to the acquisition since it can operate similarly to a purchased firm. It is interesting to note that many successful joint ventures often develop into an acquisition by one venturer or the other. Therefore, understanding the relative demands of different options will assist the investor to better evaluate the advantages, disadvantages, and potential costs of the target, as well as the options for entering the market as an able competitor.

Start-up operations

The decision to undertake a start-up, or greenfields operation, is one that demands a substantial commitment of resources not only of capital but also of management. Building an organisation from scratch in an unfamiliar business environment is fraught with hazards and uncertainties. Funding operating cost requirements and working capital needs may place an unnecessary, untimely strain on the foreign parent. With this in mind, investors should carefully weigh the benefits and costs of the start-up operation. On the other hand, it is this type of investment to which state agencies are most directed to serve new or additional investment into their areas because their mission is to promote economic growth and increase employment.

   For those companies which decide to follow the greenfields approach there are two vital considerations: securing adequate financial resources and offering a potentially successful product. A successful approach to these matters must consider the following stages and determine which are appropriate:

(1) establishing import and distribution facilities for finished products;
(2) importing component parts;
(3) assembling the work in process products; and
(4) manufacturing completed products.

Many foreign companies, however, encounter difficulties in the US which are the result of unfamiliarity with local business practices; therefore with the completion of each phase and the careful investigation of financing sources and market demands, the company is more assured of success. After all, it is only through proper planning and co-ordination that many of these potential pitfalls can be avoided.

The planning and development of a new company includes several basic but important steps. The following are considerations which should be included in the planning stages:

- site selection;
- determination of manufacturing and distribution system;
- determination of legal structure;
- identification of management needs;
- selection of accounting and reporting systems;
- cash flow forecasting and budgeting;
- identification of tax implications; and
- recruitment of staff.

Within each of these topics are further factors which become vital to the successful start-up; some of these include:

- availability and cost of labour;
- transportation availability;
- utility costs;
- market demographics;
- distribution facilities; and
- effective budgeting.

Foreign investors should therefore be aware of their importance as the greenfields operation gets underway. Insomuch as financial resources are key to the potential success of a business operation, without adequate planning of items such as these above, the entire venture may result in substantial monetary losses.

Joint venture and partnership

Investment entry into the United States market often occurs in the form of a joint venture, which is a type of direct investment that is increasing in popularity. Typically a foreign company agrees to share ownership with a local (US) entity, either public or private, and as a consequence, a different entity – the joint venture – is formed. Essentially, it is either organised as a partnership for a specific, limited purpose, organised as a corporation when a longer term relationship is anticipated or based on a contract form (project form) for the purpose of 'strategic partnering'. The laws governing partnerships and joint ventures are basically the same. Partnerships can be either general or limited partnerships, where the latter has at least one general partner and any number of limited partners. General partners have unlimited liability, while limited partners are at risk only to the extent of their capital investment, including undistributed earnings.

Within any of these options, the foreign company may hold either a majority, minority, or an equal investment position, and the joint venture can be started from scratch or by the foreign partner's acquisition of a partial ownership investment in an existing local firm. Generally, the two interests agree to share capital, expertise, products or other resources as a common endeavour is pursued. In addition, an essential element in creating the joint venture is the determination of management responsibilities of the respective parties. This includes consideration of the following:

• setting strategic goals;
• adoption of short-term business tactics; and
• evaluation of the performance of the joint venture.

Joint ventures, in general, are structured flexibly – some being formal creations of a jointly owned subsidiary, with others only an informal linkage to carry on a joint enterprise. As mentioned, ventures are typically limited in duration and scope, created for only one product; alternatively, they can be a long-term combination involving the development, manufacturing and distribution of certain goods or services.

An Atlanta, Georgia law firm, Hurt, Richardson, Garner, Todd and Cadenhead, surveyed UK/US investments. They made the following suggestions for planning to deal with US joint venture investments as a result of the study. Their summary suggested that an agreement among joint venturers should address the following points:

• type of local entity to conduct business;
• time limit within which the local entity is to be formed and remain in operation;
• conditions precedent (ie government approvals);
• government authorisation, including customs permits;
• liability for expenses incurred;
• financing of the local entity;
• contributions of venturers;
• decision making at the management level;
• pricing and manufacturing policies;
• compensation of management;
• transferability of interests;
• conditions under which a venturer can withdraw; and
• mechanisms to solve discrepancies or disputes.[1]

A vital concern to many investors is the question of control. Unlike start-up operations or actual acquisitions, which will be discussed in the following section, joint ventures may provide the foreign investor with less control than it wishes to have. In addition, the foreign partner may become frustrated if the local organisation's goals or practices conflict with its own. With this in mind, it is important to look further at the advantages and disadvantages of this type of investment vehicle.

The joint venture form of investment has many advantages to offer, including:

• risk sharing;
• information is often better shared;
• better access to market through an established players;
• established mechanism for settlement of disputes;
• economies of scale;

1 Daniel McRae, Hurt, Richardson, Garner, Todd and Cadenhead *Executive Summary – On US/Great Britain Investment* (Georgia, 1988).

- availability of technology; and
- availability of any combination of personnel, management and facilities.

However, the joint venture also has some significant disadvantages to be weighed against potential benefits, including:

- increased administration demands on management;
- requirement for a long term commitment;
- practical limit on the number of equity ventures;
- the need for compatibility of venturers (ie agreement on time constraints, expectations, profitability, and degree of commitment); and
- difficulty in obtaining timely financial information.

Although the investor may obtain immediate distribution, marketing or manufacturing capabilities, the compatibility of both parties' interests is of vital importance. How compatible are the managers and employees involved? What does the foreign investor hope to achieve? How does it fit into the overall corporate strategy? How much control/pressure can be applied to ensure receipt of timely, accurate information? Are delays in receipt of such material a minor inconvenience or a serious problem in the preparation of the acquiring firm's own financial information? These questions, although obvious to many, are often overlooked when the excitement of the deal is strong and time pressures may be great.

There are several important 'downside' factors to consider when evaluating the joint venture option. If a foreign company is sharing management responsibility, it must determine how to motivate its staff when it is not present on a daily basis; will it have sufficient information to evaluate a salesman's performance, for example? If the non-US partner is contributing the product, especially an established brand name, with the US partner assuming responsibilities for distribution and service, it could be giving away its trade name. Can it control the image developed for the product? And, can it ensure that it can reclaim the trade name when it desires? Certain industries have traditionally used some type of venture for brand-name distribution. For example, beverage manufacturers with non-US brands have often looked to American distributors to establish their market in the States. In this way, the foreign manufacturer gains the benefit of access to the US market, and builds recognition for its products.

Problems also can arise if a foreign company creates a product and participates in the creation of a new US brand name; who will have the rights to the name when the venture is dissolved? If it is the distributor rather than the foreign manufacturer, much of the investment may be lost, since a new manufacturer could supplant the original UK venture. This type of situation hurt Robot Coupe whose product was marketed in the US under the Cuisinart name. When the venture dissolved, the US distributor was left with the name, which it then attached to a new product and was able to build on the marketing Robot Coupe had helped to support. As a result, the manufacturer of the original machine was left behind further than before the joint venture began. They experienced overcapacity, a stronger competitor which it had helped to build and a loss of distribution channels. While this is not the necessary outcome of every product/distribution venture, it does illustrate several pitfalls which need to be avoided.

Joint ventures offer an easy introduction into the United States, allowing a foreign investor to 'test the waters' without embarking upon a full-blown

financial, operational and strategic commitment. However, while this can prove
a suitable initial launch into the market, a tentative approach can often hamper
the final results. Joint ventures must be considered very carefully in the planning
stages in order to identify goals, responsibilities and remedies to avoid the typical
failings of any half-hearted measures.

Acquisitions

Many foreign investors choose to acquire an existing entity rather than launch
a start-up or enter into a joint venture. This investment route presents a significant and potentially profitable decision for managers, and is the one on
which this book concentrates. There are important factors to be considered in
evaluating potential acquisitions which are general to all potential combinations,
domestic or international. Buying an established entity in the US offers certain
advantages to a foreign investor, including increased access to the US market
and reduced reliance on exports to the US. Kenneth Davidson cited several
reasons for acquisitions in his book, *Mega Mergers*. First is the attraction of
undervalued assets of the target firm. Second, acquirors see the purchase option
as a quick means to achieve growth. The third and fourth reasons cited by
Davidson are the increased access to new products or businesses and an attractive investment alternative for idle cash. Fifth, businesses utilise the acquisition
route as a method of responding to various changes in the business environment
such as demands for new technologies. A final rationale for pursuing a strategy
of acquisitions is that companies are seeking to take advantage of existing tax
and legal benefits built into the target company.[2]

Acquiring a company is somewhat similar to securing a marriage partner.
Assurance of a long-lasting, amiable relationship takes much thought, planning
and patience. The more both parties know and understand each other, the
greater the chances of success.

Although the appeal for corporate marriages has been strengthened recently
by the changes in the US dollar and the domestic financial markets, acquisitions
may end in disappointing divorces. Explanations for corporate marriage failures
range from insufficient planning to incompatible partners which could ultimately
lead to faulty business or organisational fits. Therefore to increase the potential
success of acquisitions, some general processes and guidelines should be carefully
examined. With international acquisitions some of these considerations take on
additional relevance and significance.

The key to a successful acquisition is the formulation of an appropriate
strategy, which is described in the next chapter.

---

2 Kenneth Davidson *Mega Mergers: Corporate America's Billion Dollar Takeovers* (Ballinger
Publishing Co, Cambridge, MA, 1985).

CHAPTER 5

Formulating an acquisition strategy

It is crucial for companies intending to engage in an international acquisition to be forward-thinking in their plans and to anticipate some of the problems that may occur. At the core of any successful acquisition programme is a sound and clear corporate strategy which is based on insight into the economics of the business, the competitive environment and the internal resource base. Prior to any acquisition of another business, the acquiring company must analyse thoroughly its own strengths and weaknesses in order to formulate a suitable strategic plan.

Corporate strategy

An overall strategic business plan is essential to the long-term management of any organisation and critical for a successful acquisition. Such a plan must be consistent with the managers' own philosophies, goals, criteria for success and measures of performance. Key elements of the plan should be discussed and also written, and should include a discussion of potential market segments, geographic targets and anticipated stumbling blocks. The chances for success are greatly increased if a formal strategic plan exists and if acquisition criteria are based upon the plan.

Before searching for the most suitable acquisition target, the acquiring company must complete two basic, but extremely important, steps:

1 Identify exactly who and what the company is

Acquisitions tend to amplify the acquiror's strengths and weaknesses; therefore, it is vital for the company to outline its own position prior to identifying target companies. This self-realisation process assists in anticipating any problem areas. Furthermore, by outlining the company's own characteristics, management can better co-ordinate the various acquisition processes involved.

The following is a brief list of factors which should be considered when analysing a company's own strengths and weaknesses. These are included to help management with the understanding and implementation of the corporation's long-term strategy and with the ultimate success of the acquisition process.

The factors which should be considered as an acquiror evaluates its position include:

- product/market share analysis;
- the basis of past successes and failure;
- management expertise;
- company objectives;

- company culture;
- financial resources;
- technological expertise; and
- physical plant.

By understanding what has brought the company to its current position and identifying those factors which have added to the success of the company, a plan for future growth through acquisition can be implemented more effectively.

2 Define the company's objectives

After evaluating the points above, acquiring management must complete the second important step: they must formulate clearly the overall objectives of the company. This step is absolutely necessary prior to any acquisition, but even more important in international acquisitions since these investments often are inherently more complex. In some cases, the excitement of the deal misdirects management or causes some oversight in the necessary processes; by outlining the company's objectives, management will have a clearer view of the direction the acquisition should take. Some of the questions which should be included are:

- what type of company does management want the entity to become?
- what industry position should the acquired company presume to occupy?
- what will the operating performance, facilities, and management of the acquired entity be?
- what crossover effects does acquiring management hope to achieve from the acquisition? what crossover effects does management want to avoid?

One of the main purposes of this analysis is to identify the type of growth sought; the most typical being horizontal or vertical expansion. A discussion of these two types of growth begins on p 57.

The last point to consider in developing a growth oriented corporate strategy is to evaluate the resources for expansion:

- what are the company's financial resources? what is available currently and what can be obtained?
- how capable is present management of dealing with the possibility of an international acquisition? What are the interests of management and employees, both long and short term?
- what are the marketing, distributing and people strengths of the company?

Having reached an understanding of what it is and where it seeks to grow, some companies will determine that a programme of growth through acquisition is to be a part of their corporate plan. To achieve this goal, a strategy for acquisitions should be formulated, with the goal of developing a profile of desirable targets to use as a benchmark for screening candidates. An acquisition strategy should specify the targeted industry, list the required criteria for an acquisition (eg size) and lay the framework for an analysis of selected candidates.

Formulating a strategy

Any expansion programme requires careful planning. The trauma of uniting two previously separate entities, especially across international borders, brings additional concerns and considerations. Therefore the need for a well-developed strategy cannot be over-emphasised.

If the strategic plan demands an acquisition in the international arena, the planning considerations are somewhat expanded. The significance of different cultures and nationalities introduces additional challenges into the acquisition process and the foreign investor is well advised not to dismiss their importance. One should never underestimate the magnitude of potential differences, even between the US and the UK. Oscar Wilde once stated: 'We have everything in common with Americans nowadays except, of course, the language.' But some UK businessmen would venture to disagree with even that statement. Michael Stallibrass of Shearson Lehman has been quoted in *Acquisitions Monthly* as saying: 'Anyone who believes that the US is the same as the UK is crazy. There is a real cultural difference between the two.'[1] It is for this very reason that no rationalisation of variations in management styles or business beliefs should be left to chance.

The strategic plan drafted should address the following additional questions.

- Who are you? What business are you in?
- How does an acquisition fit into your overall corporate vision?
- How will the actual acquisition process develop?
- Who will be in charge?
- How much time will the acquisition demand?
- How much effort will the integration require and how much is it projected to require on an ongoing basis?
- What are the goals for this acquisition – both short- and long-term (one, two, and five years)? Growth? Increased sales? Name brand recognition?
- What position will the acquired company hold within your organisation?

The answers to many of the questions above are dependent upon the basic goal of the acquisition programme: diversification, consolidation of market share, building economies of scale – all likely and attractive, but conflicting, types of growth that demand different types of acquisitions. Therefore, one of the principal challenges in formulating the corporate acquisition strategy is identifying the type of growth sought. The following section reviews the various types of expansion, not to provide a list of rationalisations for a shopping spree, but rather to highlight the differing and conflicting goals and options of various strategies for growth. Pursuing an effective acquisition campaign is dependent upon understanding and articulating its basic premise.

Purposes for acquisitions

The decision to pursue a route of acquisitions can be based on one of several strategies. The most typical is expansion within one's own market by building economies of scale and/or market share by an acquisition in related areas to achieve horizontal or vertical diversification. A more conglomerate oriented goal is to seek beneficial returns on capital invested, regardless of the industry. This second type of diversification does not anticipate significant synergistic benefits from other members of the group. Typically, companies acquiring in related businesses provide synergistic effects such as capacity/market expansion and economies of scale, while on the other hand, acquisitions in unrelated

1 Peter Osborne 'Hitting the Acquisitions Trail', Acquisitions Monthly, March 1988, p 18.

businesses seek financial stability and increased earnings potential. Each purpose of an acquisition, of either a related or an unrelated business, has certain considerations and characteristics, and each should be examined in relation to the corporation's long-term acquisition strategy.

Companies tend to be most successful in an international acquisition when they acquire companies in a similar business, where the understanding of marketing, production, management and capital requirements is made easier. A good example has been Ratners' acquisitions of several jewellery store chains in the US. The most important of these was its July 1987 acquisition of Sterling Inc, a situation where the company expected to gain from relying on Ratners' marketing abilities and financial strengths combined with Sterling's numerous locations in the US. Ratners identified an opportunity in a sector which was familiar to it (retail distribution of jewellery on a mass market basis). It had determined that the US retail jewellery market was dominated by smaller, independently owned stores and small chains, a degree of fragmentation that had previously existed in the UK and provided tremendous growth opportunities for Ratners, which characterised itself as an 'aggressive, well managed store chain committed to a strategy of national expansion'. Ratners also looked to the advantages it would gain from being such a large player – second largest in the world after the acquisitions – stating that its buying strength would result in significant economies of scale worldwide.[2]

Acquiring in related businesses offers two main alternatives: horizontal or vertical diversification. Both of these acquisition alternatives provide foreign investors with the opportunity to gain synergistic benefits. Acquirors will typically hope to benefit both from a fit with the target's operations, and also from improving the management and hence the performance of the acquired company. Before the management can effectively participate in a merger or acquisition transaction, the reasons for the deal must be understood. The value of combining two businesses is calculated not by just adding the respective assets together, but rather by also factoring in the synergistic benefits. While these are not easily quantified, they should be considered. The following examples are provided in order to better understand some of the various forms of these benefits.

Horizontal diversification

Brand X Company manufactures and sells vacuum cleaners only to the commercial market. By acquiring Company Y, which makes similar products but sells only to the retail market, Brand X can now sell X and Y products to both the commercial and retail markets.

Vertical diversification

Although Brand X manufactures vacuum cleaners, it has to contract out for the manufacture of the electrical cords and vacuum cleaner bags. If Brand X acquired companies that supply these parts, the cost of the vacuum cleaner production could be reduced.

2 Morgan Grenfell, press release 'Ratners Group plc Proposed Acquisition of Sterling, Inc', London, 3 July 1987.

Value-chain

The 'value-chain' analysis was popularised by Michael Porter in his book *The Competitive Advantage*. The 'value-chain' concept is based on the premise that every business unit is a collection of activities which allow it to compete effectively. In an article titled 'From Competitive Advantage to Corporate Strategy'[3] he identified two types of interrelationships which may create synergistic benefits: the transfer of skills and the sharing of activities. The two relationships which create synergy are components of the value-chain and are summarised below.

In any diversification strategy there is a desire to gain a better competitive advantage. The opportunity for the transfer of skills arises when businesses have certain similarities. If the similarities among the businesses meet the following three conditions, synergistic benefits may be created.

(a) The activities involved must be similar enough that sharing expertise is meaningful. Broad or general similarities are not sufficient for effective diversification; they must be related enough to influence the competitive advantage.
(b) The activities must be sufficiently important to bring significant advantages from diversification. Combining skills far outside core businesses may be useful, but it is not a sound basis for diversification.
(c) The particular skills being transferred, such as marketing or promotional expertise, need to be a primary source of a competitive advantage if synergies are to be obtained.

If the skills transfer offers an advantage to diversification, it is a strong source of synergy. It may be either on a continuing or a one-time basis. In many acquisitions and for those in well-chosen businesses, the acquiror may share expertise in a number of different areas, and an acquisition will therefore significantly improve their competitive position.

In addition to the transfer of skills, sharing activities among businesses also may create synergy through diversification. This type of sharing provides benefits by lowering costs or increasing differentiation. Reduced costs will occur if, for example, economies of scale are achieved or if utilisation of facilities is improved. Differentiation improvements may occur if activities such as accounts processing are shared which may provide additional features of value to the customer.

In order to gain synergies, sharing activities must exist among activities which are significant to a business advantage. A costs and benefit analysis should be conducted to determine whether synergy is possible through sharing opportunities, as well as considering possible economies of scale. If the acquiror is not attentive to realising these economies, the cost may outweigh the potential benefits. Nevertheless, opportunities for diversification which allow business activities to be shared may create a means for synergies to emerge.

By diversifying horizontally, the investor seeks to limit competition or broaden the business base. In many cases, the additional capacity or opportunities for geographic expansion are the main purposes of a horizontal diversification strategy. Increased profits can be obtained from horizontal diversification through expansion of market power and presence, reduction of operating costs or a combination of the two.

---

3 Reprinted by permission of the Harvard Business Review. Excerpts from 'From Competitive Advantage to Corporate Strategy' by Michael E. Porter (May–June 1987). Copyright © 1987 by the President and Fellows of Harvard College; all rights reserved.

Pursuit of identified purpose

An acquiror following the horizontal acquisition strategy will seek to purchase another firm within the same industry or in a related business. This should expand the market share of the acquiror, thus allowing it to strengthen its competitive position within the industry. If operating cost reductions emerge as a result of the acquisition, barriers to entry also may be strengthened. Potential entrants will be deterred if faced with a large competitor whose costs are lower, because that firm would be better positioned to engage in a price war if the need arose.

Horizontal diversification was a driving force in the formation of American business at the turn of the century. Joseph McCann and Roderick Gilkey, in their book *Joining Forces*, describe the remarkable growth of that period as being driven by a desire to expand capacity rather than attempts to limit competition. Companies today still follow a horizontal growth strategy, but with less energy than in the early 1900s. Generally, horizontal expansion is most typical of industries which tend to be concentrated in the hands of a few large players, according to McCann and Gilkey. Examples of this type of expansion cited include such deals as Texas Air/Eastern Airlines and R. J. Reynolds/Nabisco Brands.[4]

Foreign investors might move into the US where they feel there are opportunities for this type of growth due to splintered markets. This is particularly true where they have had success in establishing national firms in the UK. Industries cited recently as candidates for consolidation of players include jewellery retailers and service industries such as advertising. It is important, however, to recall that a strong regional firm in the US may be the size of a national firm in the UK, and that acquirors should not underestimate the strengths, or desire for independence, of regional players.

For those companies wishing to diversify vertically, the driving force tends to be the creation of production economies. With the purchase of either upstream (backward integration) or downstream (forward integration) companies, the acquiring entity can potentially increase its profit base by reducing overall costs or at least increasing profit margins. For instance, by buying a company one step back in the production chain, the acquiror provides a captive outlet for the other company's products. In this way, the overall effective market power of the acquired company is strengthened. The upstream supplier's position is improved, because the acquiror should experience economies of scale. Likewise, in a downstream diversification, the underlying objective is similar: to reduce overall operating costs and increase economies of scale. By purchasing a customer and its market facilities, the investor acquires the potential to reduce operating costs.

This type of vertical combination also limits competition for those firms operating in the supplier market. Again, barriers to entry emerge as new competitors are faced with increased capital requirements needed to operate in the industry. Acquiring firms therefore enhance their overall industry position relative to potential competitors.

When companies acquire unrelated businesses (those not directly linked by technological, market or production processes), the main purpose is to seek financial benefits. Generally, the desire to stabilise financial performance and

4 Joseph McCann and Roderick Gilken *Joining Forces: Creating and Managing Successful Mergers and Acquisitions* © 1988, p 20. Reprinted by permission of Prentice Hall Inc, Englewood Cliffs, New Jersey.

build earnings is a strong motivation for this 'conglomeration' move. Limiting competition or expanding capacity are secondary factors for this path of diversification. Unlike diversification in related businesses, acquisitions outside the traditional core business look for the target's ability to carry additional debt and increase stock market performance. Risk reduction and countercyclical acquisitions have been popular in the past, but an increasing number of these have come full circle and been labelled as poor fits or unfocused group expansion, lacking a driving force or vision. Many organisations built through acquisition have been forced into restructuring or divestitures as a result.

Diversified conglomerates may be a holdover from days when the function of capital allocation rested with corporate entities rather than financial markets. As markets have grown more sophisticated in the past 25 years, especially with the influx of substantial pension funds and other more flexible capital, investment bankers and the financial instruments they have created have asserted control over the market and the role of corporate finance divisions within companies has been reduced. Shareholders are requiring that companies maximise return on capital and become market leaders rather than diversified behemoths.

Part of the difficulty with the conglomeration type of acquisition is the hardship management encounters when dealing with the complexities and size of the structure. Integration and co-ordination between the varied entities is almost impossible without a clear understanding of the long-term objectives of the group. In many cases the individual businesses are considered part of a portfolio, each challenged to achieve specific goals and optimum returns. Management tends to be decentralised with each company operating relatively independently and with little transfer between companies. Performance of each component part will tend to be evaluated on fairly objective measures – return on investment, cash flow, etc., allowing the portfolio to be managed and evaluated from afar. Management must therefore consider these objectives if co-ordination between all efforts is to be optimised. A company pursuing a broadly based diversification policy should examine its motives and long-term goals carefully.

The pursuit of a programme of expansion that seeks more than one of the above types of growth will be very difficult, as each strategy establishes a different set of basic criteria for the target acquisition. The process of defining a corporate strategy (discussed prior to the above analysis of paths for growth) is based first on an analysis of what the company is, how it got there and what its needs for the future are. A formulation of its strategy for future growth must reflect the selection of one of the above routes, which can then be reflected consistently in the development of an acquisition programme.

After formulating the broad corporate strategy which includes a directed programme of acquisitions, it is then necessary for the broader goals to be translated into a rough sketch of the type of acquisition target sought – the process of formulating an acquisition strategy.

Acquisition strategy

Following the thorough development of a strategic plan based on an acquisition programme, potential acquirors must define particular acquisition criteria. There are two general concerns for assuring success. First is the emphasis of strategic fit between the two companies and a determination of how the target will contribute to the acquiring firm's overall corporate strategy. The second factor focuses on the importance of organisational fit between management styles and beliefs. By examining these two broad areas, a workable, harmonious structure between the two parties is more likely to emerge.

By actually putting down on paper the criteria which should be met by the target, acquisitive management is better guided through the entire search and integration process. Unsuitable candidates are eliminated at an early stage with the use of detailed criteria and thus the process time may be shortened.

The profile indicates the type of company to be purchased by referring to such issues as:

- business;
- industry;
- ownership (public/private company);
- location;
- size (either in numbers of employees or annual revenues);
- turnover;
- minimum profitability;
- organisation structure;
- maximum purchase price; and
- key factors for success.

These are just a few items which must be addressed in a successful acquisition search. It is wise to initiate the search only after this information is in hand – written down as well as talked about and agreed upon. If the acquired entity will not support the corporate acquisition strategy, then the time and capital of the investment could prove to be inconsistent with management's philosophies and goals. The newly acquired company could be unfairly forced to adopt unrealistic goals or may be judged by inappropriate measures. Detailed criteria for the acquisition candidate therefore help to identify the most attractive target at the most reasonable price. It is important to recall at every stage that an acquisition programme is a tactic or strategy, and not a goal in itself.

Planning the acquisition process

There are additional factors beyond objectives, strategies and formulas which affect the success or failure of a potential investment. Acquisitions require much more consideration than merely determining who is involved or what price should be paid. The manner in which the acquisition process itself is conducted is critical to the successful outcome of the deal and of the future integration stages. With attention to the potential problem areas of the process, a smooth transition from strategy to implementation to integration will be seen; without it, failure is almost certain.

In general, there are four problem areas which should be considered in every acquisition, and which are of even greater concern in international transactions: task segmentation, accelerating momentum, expected ambiguity and mis-allocation of management systems. Historically these areas have been overlooked, as they are considered inherent to the process itself, but as the interest in and understanding of the entire acquisition environment grows, they have been recognised as factors to be examined and considered from the outset of the programme. These areas provide potential acquirors with the opportunity to examine closely the nature and path of the current acquisition programme and make adjustments where necessary. It is important to realise that these are only some of the basic considerations when implementing a structured acquisition programme, and that each individual company and transaction will carry its own specific requirements. The areas of concern are examined in more detail below.

1 Task segmentation

By dividing tasks and duties of the acquisition process, problems such as poor integration between various efforts or misallocated time may develop. It is vital, therefore, to segment tasks only where absolutely necessary. By keeping a careful watch on the progress and development of the tasks' completion, the acquiror should increase co-ordination and integration. The complexities of the various tasks may demand a certain degree of segmentation which could result in a misdirected focus, eg on strategy only, thus disregarding organisational or process issues. Therefore this separation should be chosen carefully and monitored by management. By integrating the tasks as much as possible, the potential for acquisition success is heightened.

2 Accelerating momentum

Behind the acquisition process itself are strong accelerating forces. The excitement, tension and involvement in the acquisition often drive the process stages – at times with unfortunate results. For instance, executives from both entities generally have a strong desire to complete the acquisition as soon as possible, and if the deal is even slightly contested, acquisitive management will push even harder to act quickly. By understanding that player commitment, ambiguity, secrecy, and, in some cases, decision-maker isolation add to the feeling of increased momentum managers can successfully move to prevent their possible harmful results. Some of these potential effects include premature solutions or decisions, inadequate consideration of integration issues and increased potential for an unsuccessful outcome. If managers regulate the momentum of the acquisition process stages, then the possibility of maintaining a workable speed is increased. In the 1982 Berkshire-Hathaway annual report, Warren Buffett explained the phenomenon by stating: 'For in many acquisitions, managerial intellect wilted in competition with managerial adrenalin. The thrill of the chase blinded the pursuers to the consequences of the catch.'[5] Therefore, if the acquisition is to be successful, it is essential for management to work through the process in a timely and directed fashion.

3 Expected ambiguity

To some extent and for a limited time, a degree of ambiguity is advantageous to the acquisition process. A major problem emerges, however, if this level of uncertainty continues ad infinitum. At the outset, ambiguous acquisition approaches seem to be non-threatening and allow manoeuvering room for negotiations; if unclear motives persist, completion of the processes will be all but impossible. The two parties 'test the waters' of expectations before laying everything out on the table and then as the deal appears to be more secure, the

5 Warren Buffett, Berkshire Hathaway 1982 Annual Report, p 39.

details of the expectations and interpretations of the transaction are revealed. For the international acquiror, the possibility of extended ambiguities is especially significant because cultural concerns often cloud relatively straightforward issues.

4 Misallocation of management systems

As the separate business entities each have individual capabilities and views, the potential for misallocation of management exists. If the acquiring firm has experienced success with its management systems, it may try to force those systems onto the newly purchased company. This may or may not prove to be the most efficient method of integrating the two entities and managing the new acquisition. In addition, the wider the disparity between the management styles of the entities, the more disadvantageous such imposed systems will become. Either firm may initially exert defensiveness toward the other's systems which could lead to a limited chance of success for the acquisition as a whole.

With an awareness of these potential pitfalls in mind, the actual target search can be conducted. There are four principal phases in the acquisition search, each requiring different levels of attention and supervision appropriate for the particular deal. Even though no two acquisitions are ever exactly the same, it is important for the management of the acquiring company to understand fully these four phases as the acquisition process gets under way and gains momentum, to allow them to take advantage of the natural cycle of a deal. These four stages, which are discussed in the following chapter, are:

Phase I: Agreement on a list of industry segments for investigation.
Phase II: Development of preliminary acquisition candidate screening criteria.
Phase III: Identification and ranking of potential acquisition candidates.
Phase IV: Contact with selected candidates and further analysis.

CHAPTER 6
Preparing for the search

Once it has been determined that international diversification is to be introduced as part of the long-range plan, and identification of target industries has been made, the foreign acquiror must face the need to bring together the best search team possible. This team will be instrumental in all phases, from the very beginning – identifying all potential candidates – to negotiating the deal and assisting with post-acquisition integration.

After the basic acquisition criteria have been defined by management, but prior to embarking on any search programme for target companies, the decision must be made about who will be involved in the process and what form the search will take. Whatever form the search programme follows, someone should be chosen as the focal point to help co-ordinate the procedures. This choice should be made on the basis of management capabilities and an understanding of the corporate direction. In addition, the person in charge of the project must be in a position to speak directly with top management in order to report on the progress of the entire acquisition process.

The most efficient way of conducting the search is to ensure that all possible candidates are identified so that they can be evaluated in a single screening process rather than raising new candidates throughout the process and having to return to the screening stage. After the industry has been selected in Phase I and criteria for an acquisition target outlined in Phase II, the step which follows is the actual search for the particular company which meets those criteria. One of the most important things to remember is to take enough time! Nothing is gained by rushing into an acquisition choice if the choice does not fit with acquiring management's objectives. The search process will take time and may involve different players, such as lawyers, accountants and investment bankers; but the key point to remember is that the actual acquiror is embarking on the acquisition and not the outside players. It is the acquiror who not only is making the outlay of funds for the transaction, but also will have to live with the candidate after the deal is made.

An inexperienced or first time acquiror in the US market should work more closely, if possible, with experts than their seasoned counterparts. Normally, there are both internal players from within the acquiring company, and external players from various firms of advisers with a limited interest in the deal, participating in the acquisition process. Careful attention should be given to the selection of internal players to give the acquisitive management the opportunity to utilise its own resources effectively. The array of external advisory experts, mentioned briefly here and discussed in more detail later, provides acquirors with a more objective and critical view of the transaction and its potential effects on the company. The outside players include investment banks, commercial banks, accountants and tax experts and lawyers. Brought in early and utilised properly, these investment experts can provide additional guidance and lend experience to the search programme, rather than merely assisting in the completion of the deal once the target is identified. Acquisition advisers are a valuable source of data about both industries and individual candidates; they can provide practical experience in negotiating the structure of the agreement, securing the deal and examining the detailed items often overlooked by newcomers to the acquisition process.

Assembling the team

Internal players

As with any capital investment, the number and variety of players involved differs with each individual business. In the international acquisition arena, cultural complexities and geographic distance often add to the sheer size of the group of participants; however, the investor must be careful that this group does not get out of hand. More importantly, foreign acquirors should maintain a clear view of time and costs involved in undertaking a search process, while prudently identifying those players who will contribute accurate, relevant and timely assistance to the process. Whatever form the programme takes, whether active or passive search, the focal point for the process must be identified.

Acquiring management should determine which of their own internal senior members will 'spearhead' the target search and the entire acquisition process so as to ensure co-ordination and integration of the various contributions. This responsibility should not be viewed as an occasional digression from mainstream responsibilities only to be attended to between other pressing engagements, but rather it should remain foremost in the manager's tasks. After all, the ultimate impact will have long-lasting and corporate-wide effects.

The internal players often appear at different points of the acquisition programme. These participants typically include senior management and representatives from the various functional areas of finance, marketing, human resources and strategic planning. (If more than one of these roles is filled by a single person, proportionally more of his or her time will be required.) Some may participate at only one point in the process while others may be involved on a recurring basis.

One factor which determines the degree of involvement of any one person is the level of importance the company attributes to the acquisition. This determines the calibre and number of the internal members used and the extent of their contributions. For those companies not highly experienced in making acquisitions, upper management may fail to recognise the importance of active involvement and actually may dismiss the idea of acquisitions as a future investment alternative. Until upper management is willing to support a progamme of acquisitions, it is unlikely that the process will proceed successfully. On the other hand, the more acquisitively active company will at times support an in-house 'acquisition team' to review regularly possible acquisitions and analyse their potential effects on the group. This type of situation is more likely to exist when the company has the acquisition alternative as a key component of its long-term corporate strategy.

One of the most significant internal players in the process is the chief executive officer, typically the managing director of the acquiring company. The level of interest and involvement by the managing director often sets the mood and attitude of the other internal participants for the remainder of the process. The process can be delegated to another executive or to a team, but ultimately, whether actively interested or not, the managing director must become involved in the final decisions. What is most likely is that the managing director may have an enthusiastic, active interest in making acquisitions. Although preliminary research will be conducted by others, the managing director may join in the planning, analysis and review of the team's progress. If the director is inexperienced in acquisition transactions the more experienced members of the team may have more influence towards the completion of the deal. If the executive is well-seasoned, however, the team may only hold a supportive, consultative position. Alternatively, as the experience of the team develops, the managing director may delegate more and more responsibilities to them, holding himself in reserve to iron out final problems and direct long-term strategies. In either case, the chief executive's involvement is essential.

Wayne Boucher from the University of Southern California conducted in-depth interviews with merger experts as part of a study into mergers and acquisitions. All the experts agreed on the role of the chief executive:

> If a company is to be successful in its acquisition programme, the CEO must be personally involved. Because of the importance of timing in these deals you need a negotiator who can cut through the red tape and make whatever concessions and accommodations may be necessary to close the deal.[1]

It is important to recall that the use of time must be properly planned. For instance, larger acquisitions which may require restructuring or management reorganisation will demand much more time and more closely focused attention by the director than would those deals which cause few wide-reaching changes. In general, however, managing directors should be careful to avoid pulling out of the process too soon; if implementation and co-ordination are delegated prematurely to others, the entire programme may prove to have been conducted in vain.

The stages in which the chief executive should participate also must be identified. In *Joining Forces*, authors McCann and Gilkey outline five key areas where the managing director's contributions are vital to the acquisition process:

- determining acquisition screening criteria;
- selecting the best choice of a target;
- outlining the price and terms for structuring the offer;
- making initial contact with the target company; and
- actively negotiating the completion of the deal.[2]

In addition to the managing director, other internal players should also be involved in the acquisition programme. Senior management should be the focal point for the acquisition process and should oversee the search efforts. The leadership and practical experience of the senior management will play an important role as the group moves into the implementation stages. Presumably the top manager involved will have strong financial experience and will be an effective leader.

Additionally, this senior member of the team will guide various functional and support groups. The personnel department along with the financial and legal groups will participate in the acquisition process, in some cases from the beginning. If the group has a corporate research and information services

1 Kenneth M. Davidson *Mega Mergers: Corporate America's Billion Dollar Takeovers* p 217 (Ballinger Publishing Co, Cambridge, MA, 1985).
2 Joseph E. McCann and Roderick Gilkey *Joining Forces* © 1988. By permission of Prentice Hall Inc, Englewood Cliffs, New Jersey.

department, it can be used effectively for the preliminary research and screening.

In addition to key internal players, there are a few others inside the acquiring company with a supportive role. The board of directors and the middle management are two main examples. In the case of the board, their degree of participation varies significantly from company to company. Furthermore, in many cases the board's involvement is restricted to advice on specific candidates or approval of the deal structure; since many of the details are handled by the managing director prior to submission to the board, the directors' involvement is quite often limited.

Like the board of directors, middle management also have an interest in the acquisition process and its ultimate success. They are typically the group most affected by any acquisition, although they are rarely consulted before the deal is made. Realistically, it is the continued commitment of these managers which is a crucial ingredient to the success of the acquisition. It is important to realise that acquisitions should not disregard the potential influence of middle management since they run the daily operations of the group. In a service industry, this issue is exacerbated because they are the assets as well as the management of the company.

Often middle management cannot be brought into the process too early, or perhaps even before the deal is completed. However, an immediate priority should be to inform middle management of the deal in order to use them to sell the acquisition to the other employees; they should be brought into the process as early and as fully as possible.

External players

Foreign acquirors must realise early on in the acquisition search programme that it is important to put together a team whose mandate is to evaluate potential acquisitions objectively. As mentioned, the head of the team should be the company executive responsible for acquisitions, with other players assisting from the financial, accounting and legal sectors. These external advisers should be well versed in how business is conducted in the US and should hold an important role in the transaction. The major external contributors involved in the acquisition process should include, as necessary, members from the following professional groups:

- investment banks;
- commercial banks;
- accounting firms;
- intermediaries; and
- lawyers.

Each group is examined further in order to understand their possible involvement in the acquisition process. In addition, it should be emphasised that the acquiror normally chooses only one of these players to assist in the search process; the full team is usually brought together only after the list of potential candidates has been narrowed to specific targets.

Before hiring advisers, the costs of using them should be negotiated and agreed. The impression may be conveyed that fees are not negotiable – but that is rarely the case; as with any other cost in the acquisition process, fees are negotiated. A typical proposal on smaller transactions from bankers and intermediaries is that the 'Lehman Formula' be used as the basis for fees. (This formula is: five per cent of the first $1 million of purchase price; four per cent of the second million; three per cent of the third million; two per cent of the fourth; and one per cent of any amount thereafter.) While it is typical to base the fee on a per cent of purchase price of a completed deal, an additional monthly retainer may be charged. It is important to note that the formula is not sacrosanct.

Detailed descriptions of each of the advisory groups follow.

Many of the other advisers, particularly lawyers and accountants, bill based on time and expenses incurred. The acquiror should ensure that there is a clear understanding of the brief for these advisers and require realistic estimates of the time expected (and therefore expense which will be incurred). To keep track of costs being incurred, it might be worthwhile to arrange a schedule of billings at regular intervals.

Another important consideration in assembling a team of advisers is the selection not only of firms to be used, but also individual players. It is not unreasonable to ask for a presentation and to use the opportunity as an interview mechanism. Assembling the team means fashioning a group that works well together, with complementary personalities. Therefore, it is also important to obtain commitments from the firms about who will actually be doing the work; if the selling point of one group is a highly respected, expert partner with broad-based contacts, ensure that he or she will be around for more than the sales pitch. The amount of time spent by someone of that level is obviously expensive; however, the acquiror should have a firm commitment that key figures will be available and involved in more than just the presentation.

I INVESTMENT BANKS
By far the largest and most important participants in mergers and acquisitions activity in the United States, especially for larger deals, are the investment banks, the US counterpart to the 'merchant banks'. They are the storehouses of expertise, resources and contacts and serve as the focal point of the major deals. The investment banks are normally retained only on the largest sale situations; they prefer not to expose themselves to a transaction that may not come to a close. In representing a purchaser, their fees typically involve a monthly retainer plus a success fee; but as the investment bank is able to handle all aspects of the transaction, from structuring the deal and providing the financing or the access thereto, many acquirors feel that the service of the investment banks is unsurpassed. In practice, investment banks must be used in an offer for a publicly held company.

II COMMERCIAL BANKS
The second group commonly participating in acquisitions are commercial banks. They are another important centre of merger and acquisition activity, although considerably less so than the investment banks. These institutions have traditionally focused on providing financing for acquisitions. The commercial banks service this area primarily because it has become an important source of fees and because of the prestige attached to merger and acquisition activity. Historically, they have been brought into acquisition deals by investment banks to provide the necessary short- and medium-term financing. However, the commercial institutions are starting to expand their advisory capabilities to compete head to head with the investment banks.

A difference is seen between the investment and the commercial banks when the specific deals handled by each are analysed. The commercial banks tend to exhibit somewhat less of a concern for quality than the investment banks; tied to a particular corporate customer by virtue of an overall banking relationship, the commercial bank will agree to become involved in a merger/acquisition situation with the corporation as a logical extension of (and to prevent erosion of) the banking relationship already established between the two. Even if the specific situation may not be of the highest quality, many commercial banks will not jeopardise a long-term relationship with an important client. Commercial banks will also handle transactions below the minimum dollar requirement of the investment banks. These circumstances may make commercial institutions more attractive advisers for acquirors seeking smaller acquisitions.

One of the advantages of employing a commercial bank as a key adviser is the fact that commercial banks typically have among their roster of customers a ready inventory of potential buyers and sellers. They also, by the very nature of their primary business activity, are able to provide financing for the proposed transaction.

III ACCOUNTING FIRMS

In the United States, and increasingly in other countries, all of the major accounting firms engage in some form of merger and acquisition advisory activity to varying degrees. Although they are normally willing to work on deals of any size, the principal niche for the accounting firms is the smaller transactions, ie those under $50 million. Furthermore, two of the main advantages of working with the accounting firms are the availability of a worldwide register of clients and therefore a significant list of potential sellers, and the fact that most of the accounting firms charge fees on a time and expense basis only.

Unlike some external or internal members of the acquisition team, the accounting firms have expertise and experience in many varied areas. The professionals of accounting firms can perform any or all of the following tasks necessary in the acquisition process:

- help define the acquisition criteria;
- conduct the search by identifying, screening and analysing candidates;
- establish contact with selected candidates;
- develop a strategic review of targeted candidates;
- assist with negotiating a price structure of the deal;
- advise on various financing alternatives.

Professional advisers from accounting firms can also perform independent valuations of non-public entities, either under existing conditions or under planned acquisition or divestiture scenarios. These valuations can help clients resolve issues including decisions on whether to acquire or divest specific businesses, where to set asking or bid prices, and how to structure the overall financing of the deal.

In addition to the items already mentioned, accounting firm advisers are critical in the tax structuring of transactions. With the tax experts involved in the planning of the acquisition, they may be able to effectuate significant savings to both the seller and the purchaser. Savings for the seller may help in the price negotiations whilst the benefits for the buyer may appear in the future, thereby improving the overall financial return for the purchaser. Tax advisers can have significant input into the structure of the deal in order to ensure that current and future tax liabilities are minimised. This influence holds particular significance when the choice of investment vehicle is made.

IV INTERMEDIARIES
The fourth major advisory group and by far the most prolific sources of smaller merger and acquisition opportunities are independent intermediaries. These intermediaries are normally firms of only one or two principals, which vary in qualification from highly professional to rather dubious, so potential acquirors should investigate credentials prior to contracting for their services. Although intermediaries will handle deals of any size, their primary niche, similar to the accounting advisers, is in the small transactions with a purchase price of between $1 and $25 million.

V LAWYERS
The last group of advisers discussed is usually one of the most important: attorneys, especially those working in the US. While they might not be involved in the search process, they typically provide essential assistance in progressing the transaction, assisting with determining such matters as what type of filing requirements the investor will have to fulfill, what various state regulations will need to be investigated, and which, if any, regulations will apply (eg environmental protection laws) to the foreign company's operations. Given the overwhelming complexities of and the wide variations among the different state laws, attorneys' advice is essential.

Lawyers are critical to the transaction insomuch as they are the parties responsible for drafting the actual acquisition agreement. It is essential that they know and understand the goals, plans and concerns of the acquiring company so that they will be able to advise correctly and effectively on what legal protection may be required.

There is no substitute for sound legal advice when undertaking an acquisition in the United States. Generally, the role American lawyers play in this respect is somewhat broader than their foreign counterparts; when embarking on an acquisition in the US, investors commonly seek legal advice fairly early in the process. The legal advisers are in a unique position not only to assist in the areas already mentioned, but also to hold discussions with appropriate governmental authorities and agencies when necessary. Additionally, in the US, attorneys often act as the centre of activity in connection with an acquisition by co-ordinating investigations, negotiations, legal filings, etc. It is important to determine which of these activities can be most profitably conducted by the lawyers so that the process may move foward with maximum efficiency but at minimum cost.

Once all the members of the acquisition team are chosen and briefed on the objectives and goals defined by acquiring management, it is important that the responsibilities of all external and internal players be extremely well co-ordinated and that the company's expectations of each adviser should be defined in writing at the initial stages of the acquisition. A mechanism for communications should be established within the acquisition team and between the supervising management involved. This avoids duplication of effort and, most importantly, provides a link to ensure all vital information is communicated quickly. Acquiring management must feel comfortable working with each of the advisers and various members of the search team.

If the company is to do an active search, it should consider hiring one of the previously mentioned advisers to assist in the search. When management narrows its list to specific targets, the team should be assembled and brought together to develop a suitable programme for contact with potential sellers. Following these two critical stages of the process, the acquiror may embark on the subsequent financial evaluation of the candidate.

The search approach

There are two alternative search programmes which may be followed, depending on available time, resources and management preferences. The two types of programmes available to acquirors are the passive search and the active search.

The passive search

The passive approach to identifying potential candidates can be accomplished almost totally from outside the United States. It involves informing investment bankers, merchant bankers, business brokers, accountants and lawyers of acquisition requirements. The goal is to uncover owners who have already decided to sell, or at least are considering doing so. The intermediary representing the potential seller will then reveal information about that company to the acquiring management, usually on a 'no-names' basis. However, this type of process will usually involve some type of fee, either a contingency or retainer fee, or a combination of the two. The potential acquiror therefore must analyse fees involved, and would be wise to ensure that any fee obligation for the identification of potential candidates is in writing.

The passive approach usually produces candidates of wide-ranging quality. Many of these companies may have been 'shopped around' for a while and may have lost a great deal of their appeal. Also, if an investment banker is handling the sale, an 'auction' may be held to sell the client to the highest bidder, rather than identifying the optimal buyer. Additionally, under the passive approach, the amount of 'deal flow' will be limited to those companies which come close to meeting the investor's acquisition criteria and known to be for sale, thus eliminating those companies not already on the acquisition 'market'.

The active search

The active approach to acquisitions can take two forms. A company can perform this search either from outside America or by assigning an executive to be resident in the US. If a company decides to perform the active search from outside the US, it is likely to engage an investment bank, merchant bank, accountancy or consultancy firm to do the initial search. This type of commissioned search usually attempts to identify which companies meet the acquisition criteria set by the potential investor, as described in Phase II of the acquisition programme, regardless of whether or not the owner is planning to sell the business.

If the active approach is taken, co-ordination and communication between the different members of the acquisition team can be enhanced by assigning a company executive to be present in the US to oversee the acquisition programme. While this may be costly, the expense of assigning the executive to the US may be offset by reduced professional search fees. In either case, it is important to be aware of the costs of the search before it begins. This will allow acquisitive management to compare the expected costs and benefits of this type of search against those of the passive search and the reasonableness of fees charged by third parties to conduct the search. Many firms who conduct target searches on behalf of foreign acquirors require a monthly retainer for a certain period of time, but this outlay can usually be offset against a total fee due upon the completion of the acquisition. Therefore it is important for acquiring management to clarify with the outside adviser the possibility of an additional fee being required upon the closing of the acquisition.

An active acquisition strategy calls for the acquiring company and its advisers to identify methodically and thoroughly all companies meeting a set of purposefully broad and preliminary acquisition criteria, whether or not these companies are known to be for sale. Fortunately, there are a number of systems in the US for translating acquisition criteria into a selection of corporate information, extending even to the identification of tens of thousands of privately held companies. This is possible although information on these types of firms is usually much less reliable and complete. As noted previously, there is no requirement for privately held companies in the US to have audited statements or to file financial reports with any credit agency. As a result, information on many private companies or divisions of publicly held companies may be limited.

The key to successful hunting is to isolate the following general characteristics, which facilitate the initial screening process:

- size, preferably expressed as a range of revenues or a number of employees;
- location;
- ownership status (publicly or privately held, division, or subsidiary);
- breadth of activities; and
- primary line(s) of business.

The US government has created a highly convenient method for defining this last criterion. The SIC codes, explained in detail in Chapter 7, 'Commencing the search', can be used effectively for this purpose.

As the search phase for the particular target begins, there are three factors which should be stressed in order to proceed in a discerning and effective manner.

First, the acquiror's interest should not be indiscriminately announced. Whether the target is publicly traded or privately held, the intentions of the acquiror should remain within the confines of the search group until such time as the acquiring management determines. With a public company as a potential candidate, the worst case scenario of untimely public disclosure would be a strong upward movement in the target company's share price. Bid rumours circulating could force the acquiring group into either paying a higher price or cancelling the acquisition altogether. In the case of an unlisted target, untimely, unauthorised rumours could damage both parties' positions. Only strong, committed acquisition intentions should be publicised and only at a time carefully chosen by the acquiring management; therefore, the researchers and members of the acquisition team must be careful not to disclose prematurely the acquiror's objectives.

A second feature which should be considered relates to the efforts employed in the search for a target. If a company puts forth diligent and extensive efforts to identify a buyer of one of its own subsidiaries to be divested, so should an acquiror give equal attention to identifying a company to be purchased. Whenever an acquisition takes place from the view of one company, it is actually a divestiture for another. It is useful for acquirors to understand that the type of research they are conducting is, in a sense, being conducted on them by the other company. In both cases, one being the search for a seller (an acquisition target) and the other being the search for a buyer (the divestiture of a subsidiary) the basic research is the same. More specifically, the research attempts to outline the strengths, weaknesses, opportunities, and risks of entering into a transaction with identified candidates. The research in both situations (the purchase or the sale of an entity) must be thoroughly and strategically conducted, completed and analysed if the company is to realise fully its corporate strategy.

A second concern is the increase in costs from looking overseas. While attempting to perform an in depth search across national borders is interesting and exciting, the difficulties and costs associated with foreign acquisitions some-times present problems if the transaction is not analysed locally. Regardless of the amount of background work conducted or the number of business databases accessed, some portion of the research has to be completed in the country where the acquisition is to take place. Some of the local research will include an examination of internal labour relations and relationships with suppliers and customers. Inevitably, this additional investigation will require assistance from local professionals as well as the co-ordinated efforts of the acquiring manage-ment. Therefore acquirors should be aware of this factor when outlining man-agement cost and time requirements for the acquisition programme.

Whatever form of search is followed, it is essential for acquiring management to remember that the possibilities for identifying additional candidates never end. The search for target companies should not continue ad infinitum, but as the search process gets under way, the acquiring company should simultaneously continue a passive search for targets, at least those known to be for sale. The discovery of such a candidate may render misdirected extensive searching unnecessary.

Sources of information

In some instances, the acquisition search could be limited to merely evaluating information already obtained through previous associations with potential can-didates. Some historical and financial information may already be known, thus eliminating the need to investigate further; however, this approach should be followed only in rare situations. The prudent investor should use an unbiased approach in the research efforts to ensure that all unsuitable candidates are 'flushed-out' early in the game and all potential ones identified. Nevertheless, existing information should not be discounted or overlooked, but rather it should be examined carefully and used as part of, rather than the limit of, research and analysis.

When the team is prepared to begin the search phase, the methodical, sys-tematic process can get under way. Initially, those members of the team chosen to search for the most suitable candidates gather and investigate available information. Published information from various sources is available to provide the acquisitive management with a good overview and a strong understanding of trends in the industry. This process should identify a list of companies which may be approached at a later date for discussion and evaluation. The list will be narrowed as additional financial and organisational information is obtained, but at the outset the acquisition search team will have the task of identifying those entities which fit the acquisition criteria and appear suitable for closer evaluation. One of the first challenges to be faced is obtaining enough information about targets to narrow the field of strong candidates to a short list.

Published sources of information

All publicly traded companies listed in the United States are required by the SEC to disclose information to the public about their activities and financial performance. There are various sources for this type of information available to foreign investors, including certain databases which can be accessed in the UK (as discussed below). However, since the only companies which are required to file with the SEC or to provide financial information to the public are quoted companies, it is quite difficult to obtain relevant and reliable data (especially financial information) on companies which are privately held (unquoted). As previously mentioned, there is no statutory audit requirement and no requirement to disclose or make available information about private (unquoted) companies or subsidiaries of public companies. There is no US equivalent of Companies House except for quoted groups.

In this respect, if the target is an unlisted company, or a subsidiary or division of a quoted company, it is unlikely that any financial information will be available except from the target itself. It is then necessary to make an evaluation from information which is available; this is likely to be product sales literature and other marketing information. Another likely source of information is a credit rating check, which will usually include some brief financial data, often unaudited, supplied to the rating agency by the company itself.

Hugh Sykes, Chairman of Thermal Scientific plc, described the broad-based search process undertaken by his company as one based on product information rather than financial data alone. He supports the idea that as many product and general business brochures as possible be obtained from any company operating in a target industry, in order to get a feel for the operations of the candidate. The more detailed financial information can be obtained from only the particular target, but the opportunity to gain the insight which can be obtained from descriptions of products and general operations should not be overlooked.

Most published sources of information concentrate on quoted companies. Only a few publications regularly publish data about non-quoted entities, as they have no statutory reporting requirements.

The following is a list of basic sources of information for identifying companies, beginning with the sources which cover both public and private companies.

DUN & BRADSTREET (D & B)
Company guides from D & B are a collected series of publications relating to quoted companies. D & B also will issue a credit report on a particular company, whether quoted or not, for a fee. These reports tend to prove most useful when seeking details on unquoted entities because they are virtually the only source of financial information and other data for unquoted companies.

INFORMATION SERVICES
There are information services available in the United Kingdom which, for a fee, will provide basic and general data on many US companies, but principally quoted companies. Some of these have evolved from press liaison information services and have experience in different countries, as they are organised to

monitor various foreign stock exchanges. In some instances, these services act as clearing houses between financial information and the general public. Some of the internationally recognised news and information services include AP-Dow-Jones, Reuters and UPI. However, to use these information services effectively, initial research must be completed to determine if potential targets are monitored by such firms.

FINANCIAL NEWSPAPERS AND JOURNALS

For US information, the business sections of the *Wall Street Journal, Financial Times* and *The New York Times* tend to cover the American markets thoroughly. In addition, such journals as *Mergers & Acquisitions* and *Acquisitions Monthly* provide readers with extensive lists concerning acquisition activity. Other journals which may offer special surveys and should be consulted are: *The Economist, Euromoney, Institutional Investor, Forbes, Fortune, Wall Street Transcript* and *Investor's Chronicle*. An advantage of referring to these types of sources is that key industry participants will be mentioned, principally quoted companies. Many of these types of sources can be found in the British Library, London School of Economics Library, London Business School Library, Manchester, Birmingham and Edinburgh Regional Libraries, and the Commercial Library of the US Embassy.

TRADE JOURNALS

There are some industries which publish their own specialist journals, trade papers or magazines. Although somewhat limited in circulation, these periodicals provide acquirors with an in-depth look into a particular industry. They can be useful guides to which companies are acting aggressively in their industries and market areas or making advances in industry technologies. Many trade journals include 'directory' listings of companies supplying products and/or services. An attractive feature of this information source is that both quoted and non-quoted companies are covered. The British Library: Science Reference & Information Service publishes a guide, 'Trade Directory Information In Journals'. These special periodicals, both current and back-issues, can be located in the Library of Congress, Washington, DC or the British Library, London, in the Financial Times Library (a fee will be required), and in the City Business Library (London) (free of charge).

REFERENCE SOURCES AND GUIDES

There are a number of publications considered essential by many business researchers. These are specialist guides to company searches often used in acquisitions by analysts, investors and financial professionals. For potential acquirors, these sources will provide valuable information about corporate ownership of subsidiary companies and preliminary information about the credit-worthiness of US entities. The major reference sources include:

1 WHO OWNS WHOM (UK AND NORTH AMERICAN EDITIONS)
This book provides a listing of corporate owners of subsidiary companies. Although not broken down into industrial categories, the book provides two different views of business ownership. One section covers the parent companies, and the other deals with subsidiaries.

2 MOODY'S CORPORATE PROFILES AND MOODY'S CORPORATE NEWS (US AND UK)
Moody's offers these guides as an information source for publicly traded firms. Some of the items covered include business description, interim and complete financial results and new products being introduced.

3 STANDARD AND POOR'S (US AND UK)
Some of the information available from S & P includes industry surveys, stock reports and corporate records of quoted companies. Known in the US to be one of the most reliable sources of corporate information, S & P provides researchers and potential acquirors with data on specific quoted companies.

4 THOMAS REGISTER (US AND UK)
Another valuable source of information for manufacturers and more importantly for identifying potential targets is provided by the Thomas Register. It is a guide published to enable purchasing agents to identify product manufacturers. This book is an invaluable guide for identifying unquoted companies by the specific products they manufacture. This listing, by product, includes both publicly held and privately owned manufacturers. For acquirors seeking to identify potential targets in a manufacturing industry, it is a valuable source of names; it is also useful for determining the degree of fragmentation and competition in a targeted area. Unfortunately this Register does not give any financial information, nor does it indicate whether there is a public market for a company. In addition, the listing indicates only the major products manufactured by the companies, and may therefore fail to identify those companies who may be significant producers in a relatively small market. The Thomas Register is limited in availability, with only the larger libraries holding it. However, their listing is available on line on the Dialog database services.

STOCK BROKERAGE FIRMS
Many of the large brokerage firms which deal in equities on behalf of clients offer market reports prepared by specialist research departments on publicly quoted companies. These independent analysts' reports often examine a series of companies which operate in a particular industry. From time to time, a special report will be written covering only one company extensively. These general reports are typically produced at regular intervals, and therefore offer potential acquirors up-to-date information. Since these brokers' reports are prepared in conjunction with the companies in the industry, they provide more comprehensive and accurate material than general press releases.

Database services for information

Many sources are available on-line with access to various databases. A wide range of information is provided through the use of computers, and is up-dated more regularly than the published data. This feature often attracts potential acquirors because the availability of current information may help determine the outcome of the deal. The following sources give an overview of some of the databases available in the United Kingdom.

COMPUSTAT
Compustat is a computerised information service covering financial information on quoted companies. Corporate coverage provides for 200 line items of annual financial statistics and over 90 quarterly items. Compustat is updated weekly and the databanks are stored on a standardised accounting basis to allow for full comparability of information. Compustat is owned by Standard and Poor's and additional information concerning its features may be obtained through the S & P services.

REUTER TEXTLINE
Textline is an on line database which provides a telephone-connected service in the UK linking worldwide users to a main-frame located in Great Britain. This service includes informative abstracts of worldwide company and business news. It may be searched by key words and phrases, topic code, industry and product code. The database is divided by geographic source of the information (eg Europe, US, Middle East) and by subject. Some company accounts are included. Key words or phrases are used to assist in the search; special databases are also accessible in areas such as finance, aerospace and accounting. Textline also possesses the ability to reprint extracts of company accounts.

IDD INFORMATION SERVICES
IDD Information Services, a subsidiary of Extel, provides a new on-line database specifically designed for acquisition researchers. There are two databases currently available in the United Kingdom – one is for US mergers and acquisition activity, and the other covers UK transactions. IDD Services databases are updated daily and provide such useful information as financial data, pending deals and premiums paid.

Appendix 5 provides more detailed information on these services and also identifies a number of other information sources.

Other sources of information

Information may be obtained from many additional sources in order to identify potential candidates. Potential acquirors should exhaust all of the available resources, within their budget, before selecting the final targets for future negotiations. Therefore, it is important for acquirors to investigate the additional following areas.

PERSONAL AND PROFESSIONAL CONTACTS
Foreign acquirors should not ignore existing personal or professional contacts. Often these provide additional and specific information not easily obtained through published sources. Acquirors may be able to identify targeted candidates through employees, customers, suppliers and trade associations, for example.

PROFESSIONAL ADVISERS
Already mentioned as key figures of the acquisition team, professional advisers can also provide valuable information for the search process. Aside from the technical advice available from these outside professionals, they can also provide

general data pertaining to companies in the targeted industry. Often these professionals will have access to information concerning companies looking to sell or companies which may be for sale.

CHAPTER 7

Commencing the search

Phase I: Identify the industry

The first step in setting the acquisition strategy in motion is to identify the target industry for the acquisition. More specifically, where is the acquiror looking to grow? It is useful to frame the analysis of the industry in a form which considers the following major factors: (a) potential for growth, (b) access to additional technology and (c) increased strength of market span. Questions to consider within each of these areas include, but should not be limited to, the following points.

GROWTH POTENTIAL
- What are the historical and projected growth rates of the industry?
- Is the industry strongly dependent on other industries which may potentially decline?
- What is the outlook for growth rates or companies in the industry in the face of an economic recession?

TECHNOLOGY
- What opportunities and threats have developed due to changes in technology?
- How do these changes affect the industry and particular target, if known?
- Can the acquiror provide the necessary technological support for market advances?

MARKET SPAN
- Do companies within the industry compete regionally, nationally or internationally?
- Do opportunities for geographic expansion exist?
- Does the industry have the ability to replace declining products?
- To what extent will the targeted company secure an additional presence in the industry for the group?

These considerations, taken with the self-analysis previously undertaken as part of the strategy setting process, should be used to identify target industries for possible acquisitions. If cyclical performance is a problem, selecting a target with a similar problem would only exacerbate the situation; if a company has excess cash flow it can probably look for an industry needing cash investment with future earnings potential. These and similar problems and opportunities should be considered when selecting a target industry.

Once a broad industry category has been selected, it is possible to use a US government reference book to obtain a better understanding of the activities within that category and its major participants. The Office of Management and Budget (OMB) numerically classifies all US economic activity through the use of Standard Industrial Classification (SIC) codes, which can assist in the initial stages of the search. Specifically, all industries are divided into segments and each industry segment is assigned a four-digit code. The SIC codes are used to promote the comparability of data describing various facets of the US economy. The SIC classification system covers all economic activities and defines the industries in accordance with the composition and structure of the economy. The system is hierarchical, ranging from a two-digit major group down to a four-digit industry code, according to the level of industrial detail considered most appropriate. The Standard Industrial Classification Manual provides a complete listing of the codes.

The use of the SIC codes can be demonstrated through an example of Brand X Company, a company which has identified four SIC codes in three industry groups which may contain companies with the desired characteristics for a possible acquisition. The SIC codes identified are in the following two-digit major group areas: Major Group 34 – Fabricated Metal Products, Except Machinery and Transportation Equipment; Major Group 35 – Industrial and Commercial Machinery and Computer Equipment; and Major Group 50 – Wholesale Trade – Durable Goods.

For each of the SIC codes identified, a further breakdown into the three digit industry group number is necessary. For example, within Major Group 34 there is Industry Group Number 345 – Screw Machine Products, and Bolts, Nuts, Screws, Rivets and Washers. This additional clarification helps the acquiror define which industry groups should be further examined. Within the four-digit number of 3452, Brand X Company looks at the specific industry containing establishments primarily engaged in manufacturing metal bolts, nuts, screws, rivets, washers, formed and threaded wire goods, and special industrial fasteners. Rolling mills engaged in manufacturing similar products are classified in Major Group 33 – Primary Metal Industries; establishments primarily engaged in manufacturing screw machine products are classified in Industry 3451; manufacturers of plastics fasteners are classified in Industry 3089. The following shows an example of some of the items produced in segment 3452 – the first of the four identified SIC codes:

3452 Bolts, Nuts, Screws, Rivets and Washers

Bolts, iron and steel	Screw eyes
Cotter pins	Screw hooks
Dowel pins, metal	Screws
Gate hooks	Spring pins
Lock washers	Spring washers
Machine keys	Toggle bolts
Nuts	Washers, metal
Rivets	Wood screws

This list indicates the varied products which may be found under one particular SIC code; therefore it is often worthwhile for foreign acquirors to investigate carefully which items are included in the classification codes when the target search begins. By examining different codes the acquiror can better identify the targeted group, and better adhere to its objectives.

By examining the chosen industry codes and the products included, the foreign acquiror is more likely to stick to the agreed upon acquisition strategy as the target search develops. Referring again to the Brand X Company, the three remaining SIC groups identified by acquiring management are explained in more detail below.

3589 Service Industry Machines, Not Elsewhere Classified Within this industry segment, companies are primarily engaged in the manufacturing of machines and equipment, not elsewhere classified, for use in service industries, such as floor sanding machines, industrial vacuum cleaners, scrubbing machines, commercial cooking and food warming equipment, and commercial dishwashing machines. Some of the individual items included in this sector are:

Cafeteria food warming equipment   Pressure cookers
Garbage disposals, commercial   Ovens, microwave
Sewer cleaning equipment   Water conditioners

5087 Service Establishment Equipment and Supplies Companies included in this industry segment operate in the wholesale distribution of equipment and supplies for barber shops, beauty parlours, power laundries, drycleaning plants, upholsterers, undertakers, and related personal service establishments. Items within this segment include:

Barber shop equipment   Power laundry equipment and
Beauty parlour equipment   supplies
Car wash equipment   Shoe heels
Morticians' goods

3599 Machinery, Except Electrical, Not Elsewhere Classified Within this industry segment, companies are primarily engaged in the manufacture of machinery and parts, except electrical items, and items not elsewhere classified. Products such as amusement park equipment, pneumatic and hydraulic cylinders, and flexible metal hose and tubing are included here. Some of the items included in this sector are listed below:

Amusement machines   Leak detectors-water
Catapults   Sluge tables
Ferris wheels   Weather vanes

Once the targeted industry has been clearly identified, the first of the four stages is complete and acquiring management needs to continue to narrow the focus of its needs and the characteristics of potential targets. By outlining specific characteristics which suitable targets should possess, the acquiror is forced to re-examine corporate objectives and ensure that the acquisition programme supports them.

Having defined industries and probably captured several hundred names, the next step in the process is to develop screening criteria to narrow down the universe of entities in the industry to suitable potential candidates.

Phase II: Develop screening criteria

To further define Brand X's acquisition needs, it is necessary to develop screening criteria to rank how compatible potential targets are with the acquiror. In any acquisition search there may be thousands of companies in the desired industries and, as seen in Phase 1, many operations are located in broad industry groups.

These companies need to be further screened by various other criteria in order to narrow the list into a size useful for further analysis by acquiring management.

In order to perform acquisition screening and to evaluate potential acquisition candidates, it is important to establish acquisition criteria. A large portion of the criteria should emerge as a result of the self-evaluation of strengths and weaknesses described previously. Certain target company characteristics that always should be considered in establishing acquisition criteria are listed below.

Target company characteristics to consider

- Industry
- Size
- Market
- Competition
- Product pricing
- Product uniqueness
- Significant customers
- Technology
- Production requirements

- Management retention
- Personnel requirements
- Industry position
- Geographical location
- Geographical sales distribution
- Profitability
- Financial requirements
- Ownership

There are many different acquisition candidates available to a foreign investor in the US. For the acquiror, however, it is important to understand and identify those characteristics which separate an attractive, potentially successful candidate from merely another company. Donald Clifford and Richard Kavanagh, in their book, *The Winning Performance: America's Growth in Mid-sized Businesses*, identified five key factors which make mid-sized American companies successful. (The authors consider a company with turnover from $20 to $100 million a mid-sized company.) Although each point may not be appropriate for every acquisition, the combined list provides a prospective acquiror with a stronger grasp of characteristics of a successful US entity. The five factors are:

- the company exists in a specialised market niche;
- the company emphasises product value and product quality;
- the company is innovative and constantly developing new products;
- the company 'sticks to its own knitting': they stay in the business that they know well and they do not conglomeratise; and
- management are noticeably committed to their company working hard and closely together.

These factors should be used to help identify the leading candidates for acquisition, instead of relying only on analytical tools and techniques. Likewise, foreign acquirors need to understand the strengths and direction of the most likely targets to be certain that they are moving in accordance with the industry. An additional list for attractive acquisition characteristics offers another look at candidate companies. In the book *A Guide for the Foreign Investor: Doing Business in the USA*, editors Robert Cushman and Herbert Morey offer this selection of six characteristics:

- participation in growing markets;
- proprietary positions in those markets;
- a business in which the acquiring company can improve its competitiveness;
- a business which is product – rather than service – oriented;
- sales in excess of $50 million, in order to give it both market and manufacturing scale in the United States; and

- a good gross profit margin on sales as an indication that costs are under control and productivity is at competitive levels.

While both of these lists provide acquirors with the opportunity to examine their candidates from a different perspective and using different considerations, it is important for acquiring management to remember that these should not be considered in isolation, but rather they are to be used in conjunction with other identification and evaluation techniques.

Once relevant characteristics have been selected, each can then be weighted in terms of importance. For example, the acquiring company may decide that geographic location of the target company is more important than industry position. Geographic location would then receive a higher ranking than industry position when comparing targeted acquisition candidates.

In developing their acquisition strategy, Brand X has defined the particular preliminary screening criteria for potential candidates and weighted each one in terms of relative importance. By setting the criteria into a workable format, acquiring management can approach the search in a more organised and coherent manner. The following table is an example of a possible criteria weighting.

Preliminary screening criteria and weightings

Criterion	Description	Weight
1	Primary involvement in one of the four selected SIC codes	Necessary
2	Revenues between \$2 million and \$10 million, or employment data indicating such a scale	Necessary
3	Compatibility with Brand X's general diversification objectives and existing skills:	
	• likely	4
	• possible	2
	• unlikely	0
4	Existence of willing industrial demand:	
	• likely	2
	• possible	1
	• unlikely	0
5	Business generating an ongoing service relationship with customers:	
	• likely	2
	• possible	1
	• unlikely	0
6	Preliminary availability of detail as to activities:	
	• good	2
	• fair	1
	• poor	0
7	Focus on one or a few lines of business:	
	• highly focused	2
	• somewhat focused	1
	• diverse activities	0
8	Availability of revenue data on a preliminary basis	1
9	Location in the eastern half of the United States	1

Criterion	Description	Weight
10	Audited by a major accounting firm	1
11	Operations dating from before 1960	1
12	Degree of profitability (apparent)	
	• substantial and ongoing	3
	• ongoing	2
	• erratic	1
	• marginal or losses	0

Weightings represent Brand X's judgment of the relative importance of each criterion as the assessment of potential candidates continues. Brand X has determined that the minimum total points for a company to remain eligible for further consideration is 12. This figure should be based on acquiring management's judgment of their particular needs and objectives. A company with more specific needs may require higher standards, but a company with an unfocused view of acquisitions may inappropriately select a relatively low number.

By using the appropriate weighting techniques as determined by acquisitive management, foreign acquirors have the opportunity to examine potential candidates systematically and methodically. In this way, the identification of targets is eased and the misuse of time and resources is eliminated. Therefore, acquirors should take care to include this weighting process in the acquisition strategy and critically determine those criteria and weights to be applied.

Phase III: Identification and ranking of potential acquisition candidates

When an acquiror begins to identify potential candidates, the search must adhere to the outlined objectives and criteria. Returning to the example of Brand X Company and recalling the research efforts already completed (the identification of a target industry and the listing of acquisition criteria), the company is in the position to select the strongest candidate. If too many candidates have been identified, it is necessary to reduce the population by constricting the broadest criteria. For example, determine which business activity is the most important, and then focus on companies with the best chance of meeting this need by limiting the population to those companies with an emphasis on the SIC codes in the more narrowly defined activity; other companies having only secondary or tertiary involvement are eliminated. Alternatively, additional criteria are developed to screen the initial pool, eliminating these who do not meet size, profitability, or other requirements.

In an actual case, the company represented by Brand X from the example uncovered well over 2,500 companies whose activities meet, to some degree, the definition of one or more of the selected SIC codes (Phase I of the acquisition programme). To further narrow the list of candidate companies, Brand X utilised the preliminary screening criteria set forth in Phase II. Specifically, companies whose revenues or employment levels reflect an undesirable scale of operations were eliminated. Of the more than 1,000 companies originally subjected to this screening process, approximately 550 survived. Since management determined that the sample remained too large for their continuing efforts to be effective, the company reviewed their position and adjusted the total allowable points for a candidate. Brand X then established a cut-off level by deciding to eliminate those companies that failed to receive 11 or more points; this adjusted screen generated 58 potential candidates.

The table on pp 88–89 provides an example of the remaining potential candidates with their total points and point per criterion indicated.

After possible candidates are rated by the criteria, acquirors then must rank the companies according to preference. The ranking order should categorise those candidates with the higher total points at the top and the lower point companies appearing at the bottom end of the scale (in the example, the total points possible for any candidate is 19). Where candidates have an equal number of points, they would choose companies by looking for those which achieved higher scores on the most important criteria. Rather than taking into account only the total points for these types of rankings, Brand X can examine those candidates with equal total figures by considering the points per criteria.

Looking at the 58 candidates listed on pp 88–89 and applying the dual ranking technique, Brand X would list its preference for the 10 most attractive selections in the following order:

Name of company	Total points
(1) A – SESA Industries Inc	18
(2) Consumat Systems Inc	17
(3) Preferred Utilities Manufacturing Co	17
(4) Alken-Murray Co	15
(5) Barnstead Co Inc	15
(6) Instant Industrial Products Inc	15
(7) TSI Inc	15
(8) Cherne Industries Inc	15
(9) MCA Corporation	15
(10) Penn 25 Inc	15

One problem which occurs in the above example is the lack of financial information for most entities. Especially if a large number of candidates are being ranked, it would be impractical or impossible to obtain financial data for all entities especially since most of the companies are unquoted. Two options are available to prevent discrimination against companies – which might be most desirable – where data is not available. One is to estimate the score based on other information. The other is to make the range of points include negative ones. In the above example, a score of one would be used for very good results, zero for good or not known results, and a negative value for known poor results. This would penalise for identified poor results but not discriminate against ones where data was not available.

The purpose of all this analysis, ranking, etc., is first to ensure that all potential candidates are identified. A primary resource for this is the SIC codes; another may be more product driven, for example, reviews of the trade journals (including advertisements of products and personnel ads – see who is hiring!) and the Thomas Register. Names gained through contacts, meetings, etc., should also be thrown into the pot to be included in the screening and ranking process.

Screening and ranking is the second part of the initial search process directed towards reducing a large group of names to a manageable list of the best potential candidates. The next stage – a refinement of the ranking – is to make a more in-depth analysis of the attractiveness and availability of these choices. To do this it will probably be necessary to contact the names on the list.

A company will usually seek to develop a list of 10 to 15 candidates for both long- and short-term cultivation. They should be grouped to reflect both attractiveness and availability: for example, a '1' is both a strong company and one likely to be for sale. Therefore, it should be a top priority in terms of attempting to negotiate a purchase. A '2' might be an available but less attractive company, not worth pursuing now, but not worth discarding altogether. Alternatively, it could be an attractive company whose ownership is structured so that it would be difficult to negotiate a buy-out. These candidates are worthy of long-term development but not immediate pursuit. The low priorities might have some of the most desirable matches but ones with management not interested in selling. It would be foolish to discard these 'Priority 3' cases because owners' intentions can change. If these companies do represent a good, solid fit, it would be best to be at the head of the queue when a deal begins to happen.

This tri-partite categorisation is best accomplished through direct contact with owners. Hugh Sykes, in the Thermal Scientific case presented as Appendix 6, describes how he approached, in an open and direct fashion, management of companies identified by his staff as potential acquisitions. Informal discussions allowed him to understand the interests of management as well as to gain more of a feel for the company itself. He also points out situations to avoid: one of the least viable is a company with a number of different family members owning the shares. In this case, an acquiror is likely to be running five separate sets of negotiations where different shareholders have different objectives and demands. A company has to be very desirable to be worth this kind of effort, which places a great strain on management resources.

What is important to note is how early in the process contact is made – not after a bid has been prepared, but as part of the assessment stage. Of course another result of contact at this point may be the determination that what looked like a 'Priority 1' previously, now is closer to a '99'. This obviously is valuable information. In either circumstance, making the correct approach to a candidate is a delicate and important next step in the acquisition process.

POTENTIAL CANDIDATES FOR ACQUISITION

					Criteria[1]							
Company	*Points*	1	2	3	4	5	6	7	8	9	10	11	12
API Corporation	12	.	.	2	2	2	2	1	1	1	0	1	?
A – SESA Industries Inc	18	.	.	4	2	2	2	1	1	1	1	1	3
Aero Mechanism Inc	12	.	.	2	2	1	2	1	1	0	1	1	?
Alken-Murray Corp	15	.	.	4	2	2	2	2	1	1	0	?	?
Ano-Coil Corporation	12	.	.	2	2	2	2	2	?	?	?	?	?
Atlas Electric Devices Co Inc	13	.	.	4	1	2	1	2	1	1	0	1	?
Auric Corporation	13	.	.	2	2	1	2	2	1	0	0	1	1
Aviation Instrument Manufacturing Co Inc	12	.	.	2	2	1	2	2	1	1	1	?	?
Barnstead Co Inc	15	.	.	4	2	2	2	2	0	1	?	?	?
Bison Corporation	12	.	.	2	2	2	2	2	1	1	?	?	?
Bolt Associates Inc	12	.	.	4	1	1	2	2	1	1	0	?	?
Brookfield Engineering Laboratories Inc	14	.	.	4	2	1	2	1	1	1	0	1	?
Canton Stoker Corp	12	.	.	4	1	1	2	2	1	1	0	0	3
Cherne Industries Inc	15	.	.	4	0	2	2	2	1	1	1	1	?
Chromium Corp of America Inc	13	.	.	2	2	1	2	2	1	1	1	1	3
Consumat Systems Inc	17	.	.	4	1	2	2	2	1	1	1	0	3
Daedalus Enterprises Inc	15	.	.	2	1	2	2	2	0	1	1	0	3
M. J. Daly Co Inc	13	.	.	4	2	2	1	2	1	?	?	?	?
W. C. Dillon & Co Inc	12	.	.	4	2	1	1	1	1	0	0	0	?
Driaire Inc	13	.	.	4	2	2	2	2	0	1	0	1	?
E/M Lubricants Inc	13	.	.	2	2	2	2	2	1	1	1	1	?
Exley Control Processing Inc	13	.	.	4	1	2	2	2	0	1	0	0	?
Exomet Inc	12	.	.	2	2	2	1	2	1	1	0	1	?
FRL Inc	14	.	.	4	2	1	2	2	1	0	0	1	?
Formulabs Inc	12	.	.	4	2	1	2	2	0	0	0	0	?
Gillmann & Burg Inc	12	.	.	4	2	2	2	2	0	0	0	1	?
Hamler Industries Inc	13	.	.	2	2	2	2	2	1	1	1	0	?
Holobeam Inc	12	.	.	4	1	2	2	0	1	1	1	?	?
Hy-Cal Engineering Co Inc	13	.	.	4	2	1	2	2	1	0	0	1	?
Instant Industrial Products Inc	15	.	.	4	2	1	2	2	1	1	1	1	?

Company											
Korfund Dynamics Corp	14	.	4	2	2	1	2	1	1	0	?
Lewis Engineering Co Inc	14	.	4	2	1	2	1	2	1	1	?
Ling Electronics Inc	13	.	4	2	2	1	0	2	0	1	?
Liquid Controls Corp	14	.	4	2	2	1	2	1	1	1	?
Luster-Coate Metalizing Corporation	13	.	4	2	2	1	1	1	?	1	?
Manno & Gartner, Inc	14	.	4	1	2	2	1	1	1	1	?
MCA Corporation	15	.	2	2	2	2	1	1	1	1	?
Metalweld Inc	13	.	2	2	2	2	1	1	1	1	?
H. A. Montgomery Co Inc	15	.	2	2	1	2	0	1	0	1	3
Ohmart Corporation	14	.	0	2	2	2	1	1	1	1	2
Peabody Gordon-Piatt Inc	12	.	4	2	1	1	0	1	0	1	?
Penn 25 Inc	15	.	2	2	2	2	1	1	0	1	2
Platronics Inc	13	.	2	2	1	2	1	1	1	0	1
Preferred Utilities Manufacturing Corp	17	.	4	1	2	1	1	1	1	1	3
Pullman Berry Co Inc	12	.	2	2	2	2	2	?	?	?	?
Quantronix Corp	14	.	4	2	2	2	1	1	1	0	0
Rowden Engineering Inc	14	.	2	1	2	2	1	0	1	1	2
Shaevitz Products Corporation	12	.	2	2	2	2	0	1	1	1	?
Stan Sax Corporation	12	.	2	2	2	2	1	1	1	1	?
Stutz Co Inc	12	.	2	2	2	2	0	1	1	1	?
TSI Inc	15	.	4	2	1	1	1	0	1	0	3
Tenney Engineering Inc	13	.	2	2	2	2	1	1	0	1	3
Transmation Inc	13	.	2	1	1	1	0	1	1	0	3
Wallerstein Co Inc	12	.	2	2	2	2	1	1	1	1	?
Walters Manufacturing Inc	15	.	2	2	2	2	1	1	1	1	3
Western Tar Products Corporation	14	.	4	2	1	1	1	1	1	0	?
M. D. Wilson Inc	13	.	4	2	2	2	1	1	1	0	?

NOTES

1 See Phase II.

. Necessary criterion; met by company.

? There is often little preliminary earnings information available on privately held companies. For the items identified by a ?, complete information was not available. Therefore, criterion 12, which deals with profitability, has not been applied in many cases.

CHAPTER 8

Developing a deal

Phase IV: Contact with selected candidates and further analysis

Overview of Phase IV

In this stage, the acquiror begins to examine certain factors of candidates in more detail by investigating items not covered in the previous three phases. This last stage of analysis and investigation deals with gaining understanding of the target to learn how to make it fit within the group, what its value to the group will be, what the seller wants to take away from the transaction and what the necessary conditions precedent to acquisition are. These goals can be summarised as a desire to:

- identify the prime candidates;
- decide if acquiring management would really like to own them;
- determine if buying a particular company is actually possible (or if it could be made possible); and
- determine the price for completing the deal.

Desirability should not be based on price alone, although the final decision to buy or not may be based on price since overpaying will impair or ruin the logic of the acquisition. Also note that the decision as to whether the candidate is desirable should be separated from the matter of availability, as it is often within the acquiror's power to change the question of availability.

The objective at this point is to take the pool of possible targets and work it into a grouping of strong short-term candidates, medium-term prospects, and those needing long-term development. It also is to discard companies which are not attractive candidates despite initial high rankings.

This prioritised list, discussed in the earlier chapter, will have to be worked by the search committee. To accomplish that, members might each take total responsibility for a few candidates, particularly if the contact is to be made by someone other than the managing director. Alternatively, team members might take responsibility by area – one for obtaining financial data, another for evaluating products, a third for making contact with the company.

Usually the first method is more successful, even if the contact is to be made by the managing director. Having one person responsible for tracking all aspects of a candidate is usually simpler, even if it means collecting information from other team members. In any case, there should be a regular schedule established to discuss progress with targets and agreement on a ranking. For a company devoting a substantial amount of time looking for a match, this might mean weekly meetings. For one in an ongoing process, a review and evaluation of the list and rankings might be a standard type of a monthly board meeting. In any case, regularly scheduled discussions and evaluation of this list of candidates and reports of any contacts are essential.

Contacting the candidates

Contacting target companies is a delicate matter which must be performed graciously as well as tactfully. It is widely felt that people and their personalities are the key to most acquisitions and that the viability of the entire project may depend on establishing an amiable rapport during the initial contact. If that first contact fails, there may be no further opportunity to pursue an acquisition with a designated target.

A senior executive or a prominent member of the acquisition team (lawyer, investment banker, accountant) generally initiates direct contact with the target company in person or over the telephone. A confidential letter can precede this call, thus preparing the recipient for the discussions to follow. However, a face-to-face meeting is more useful and better received, and is the preferred choice for making contact.

If a senior executive has contacts at the most senior level within the target, it is useful to use this resource to initiate the discussions. Likewise, if he or she possesses a common background with key officers of the candidate, that would assist in 'breaking the ice' for discussions. Certain members of the acquisition team may be particularly helpful in this activity due to their experience with making such approaches and the range of contacts they have available.

The main objective of the first discussion will be to establish an attitude of co-operation and candour, while gaining the opportunity to pursue acquisition discussions and obtain more in depth information about the target company. When the anonymity of the acquiror must be preserved or the acquisition candidate is a competitor and might be naturally reluctant to admit interest in merger discussions, an acquisition professional should be relied upon to make the first contact.

Whether the representative chosen by acquiring management to make the initial contact is internal or external, the basic elements of the contact pro-gramme should be similar. The table which follows outlines some of the basic elements and related issues of the contact process.

Elements of a contact programme

Element	Related issues
Who will approach the target?	• Company executive? • Merchant banker? • Accountant? • Lawyer? • Intermediary?
Identification of whom to approach at each target	• Controlling shareholder? • Chief executive? • Board member? • Key adviser?
Method of contact	• Telephone call? • Letter followed by telephone call? • Personally through social or trade event?
Development of tactics for each target	• Should the prospective acquiror's name be used? • Should specific investment objectives be outlined at first?

Element	Related issues
	• How much should be mentioned about the prospective acquiror and its rationale for a merger before an interest is clearly expressed by the target?
Agreement on next step	• Expression of no further interest, based on new information obtained?
	• An exchange of financial data?
	• An informal meeting?
	• A meeting at target's headquarters, at those of the prospective acquiror or at a mutually agreed location?

The initial approach is usually to the chairman, chief executive officer or major shareholder of the target company. Board members or senior executives may be contacted instead if they are known to be influential within the company. It is crucial that the person to be approached is in a position to participate in acquisition discussions and to play a significant role in determining the outcome of the deal. If an approach is made to others in the candidate's hierarchy, it could raise questions regarding the suitor's judgment and degree of interest; it could also create fears that takeover rumours had spread among the rank and file.

The general tone of the caller can shape the receptiveness of the acquisition candidate towards further acquisition discussions. An aggressive attitude will tend to evoke defensive reactions, while an uninterested attitude may give the impression that the acquiror is merely seeking to gain privileged information. The attitude conveyed must be one of respect and sincerity when pursuing an arrangement of benefit to both parties. The acquiror or its representatives must make an assessment of the degree of interest evidenced by the contact at the target company. It is understandable that a 'cold call' by a prospective acquiror may catch a candidate by surprise and evoke an unconsidered response.

Once the initial discussions are complete, there will be additional time for reflection and evaluation on the part of both entities. Hopefully, a consensus for further conversations between the acquiror and the principals of the target company will be obtained as quickly as possible so that the detailed evaluations and negotiations may proceed. However, if initial comments about minimum purchase price or terms are made or if there is an expressed disinterest, the acquiror should be cautious before committing substantial time and resources to performing additional analysis evaluating a target company.

A positive conclusion to the initial conversation would be the arrangement of a meeting among the key representatives of both sides. At that time both parties may be more able to articulate their requirements for pursuing acquisition discussions. Meanwhile, the acquiror should try to obtain any financial information or descriptive material that can be secured from (or about) the target company in order to aid in the preparations for further discussions. It is important to remember that, after the initial contact, there is likely to be a cultivation period of six months to a year, or possibly even longer.

After establishing a basis for discussion with a target, the acquiror would normally seek to obtain detailed, confidential information, usually beginning with several years of audited financial information. Although there is no statutory audit requirement in the US, most companies prepare such accounts for creditors, banks, etc. The situation will be more difficult if the target is a division of another entity, since it might not have separate financial information prepared. However, if it is possible to split it out for the purpose of selling the unit, some sort of separate financial information should be available, if only management accounts. If a preliminary review of the information obtained from the target supports its selection, it is time to undertake a detailed analysis of the company as a preliminary to negotiations.

Prior to receipt of the requested information, a confidentiality letter may have been sent by the seller. In essence, this correspondence places the acquiror on notice that some information supplied by the target is of a sensitive and confidential nature. The acquiror agrees when signing the letter to the confidentiality points outlined by the seller and that the information will be used by top management only. This type of letter also helps to re-affirm the serious intent of the acquiror. It would be unusual for a company not prepared to pursue the acquisition to agree to such terms. However, before signing such a letter, the acquiror should have it reviewed by its legal adviser.

The depth of the analysis to be performed at this stage will depend upon the number of candidates and the resources of the company. If it is possible to acquire only one company at this time, enough work must be done to select the best choice. If there is instead a broad programme of acquisition in place, pursuit of more than one candidate is likely, although the work may have to be somewhat staggered to reduce strain on the negotiators. The in-depth investigation will follow on, perhaps indistinguishably from the second level analysis, with both directed to determining if any offer should be made. If it is perceived that the acquiror is making numerous offers without in-depth analysis, it is likely to damage its reputation as an attractive purchaser.

Evaluating the candidates

I OBTAINING FINANCIAL INFORMATION
The first hurdle is obviously gathering enough information to make a sufficiently detailed analysis of the top fifteen (or so) candidates with the goal of pursuing serious negotiations with one, two or perhaps three currently. It is at this point that discreet research is performed to obtain financial information, including credit checks, off the record calls to industry contacts, etc. Also, the list of reference sources discussed in Chapter 6 and Appendix 5 should be consulted; while they might not provide audited annual statements, a great deal of solid data can usually be obtained through basic research.

II FURTHER ANALYSIS
The second level analysis is likely to address most of the following topics which would allow the acquiror to open serious negotiations:

- history of the business;
- corporate objectives and business strategy;
- management and employee profile;
- typical markets and competitors;
- underlying accounting and reporting policies;

- income and cost analysis;
- unusual items;
- management compensation and expense basis;
- prospects for the future; and
- tax charges.

(The point about management compensation is important where the owners are key employees. This is because US tax legislation usually makes it preferable for profits to be distributed as compensation rather than income distributions as it avoids taxation at the corporate level.)

In any acquisition, particularly in the international environment, there are certain considerations which must be examined. Following are a few key factors which should be considered throughout the analysis process.

III MANAGEMENT

Good managers are critical to the success of any business. Acquirors should scrutinise the motivation of the candidate's workforce, especially its management motivation and the efficiency of its hourly workers; work climate, response to criticism and suggestions, and capacity for growth should also be evaluated. The ability to communicate effectively is crucial for the acquisition and business operation to run smoothly. Acquirors need to examine the information flow of the company and evaluate if it is a free-flowing, casual system or if it is a more limited, structured environment. Whether there should be a free flow of ideas and views or if only one (or more) people should dominate the decision making process depends on the acquiror's culture and objectives. Acquirors should also consider what incentive plans may be necessary to ensure retention of key personnel.

IV PRODUCTS AND SERVICES

It is extremely important for acquirors to know why products or services of a candidate have been added or dropped. By looking into such items as what new products (services) are contemplated and what percentage of sales is derived from products (services) developed in the last five years, investors can gain insight into the target's potential capabilities. In addition, this information may provide an understanding of the movement of sales and whether they are customised or repetitive.

V INDUSTRY

It is important to try to identify who the target's large customers are, and if possible to find out how they regard the company and what their future needs might be. Along with this information, the acquiror will find it useful to make other evaluations of the company's performance in its industry. In doing so, it is helpful to consider the following questions.

- What segment of the economy does this company serve?
- To what extent does it respond to seasonal, cyclical or economic trends?
- Is it labour or capital or technology intensive?
- What are the basic economics of the industry?
- What is the basis of competition: price, quality, service, products, technology, or a combination thereof? How vulnerable is the company to competitors on each of these points?
- How are prices set? To what extent are they set by cost, by demand or by competition?

VI FINANCIAL RESULTS

Two basic facts acquirors should look for when evaluating financial results are consistency in financial reporting and comparability of numbers. When examining the rate of growth in sales and earnings, it is important to learn if the growth rate occurred because of increased sales volume or because of higher prices being charged. This indicates if the growth is actually real or if it is artificial, due perhaps to price inflation. Next, acquirors should consider the company's potential for growth and how capacity compares to production. Acquirors also need to look at what new facilities may be needed for maximum growth and all probable costs associated with such a capital investment.

For all companies, however, acquirors are advised to check the balance sheets and earnings statements of the candidates to see how the major financial ratios compare with those of competitors. Try to determine if any excess assets are tied up, producing too few sales or low earnings.

The capital structure of the entity also should be examined in part to determine how much capital will have to be replaced. It also will give an indication of the minimum purchase price, since any owner will want to recover its investment. A careful review will help you understand if you can afford the company; not just its purchase price, but also its on-going working capital requirements, especially if it is seeking to expand its business significantly.

An investigation of the capital structure of the target company usually covers items such as bank credit arrangements. Aside from these, however, are additional matters which should be investigated to provide further insight into the target company's capital situation, including:

- current stock (inventory) and debtor (receivable) analysis: what number of days supply of sales or production are on hand? how old are some of the materials? how many days' sales are carried as debtors? are provisions for bad debtors adequate? what credit management exists and what type of collection efforts are made?
- tax considerations: through what period have tax returns been filed? are there any audits currently underway by the IRS? are there any actual or threatened examinations by the tax authorities? also, does the target have any outstanding liabilities as a collector of taxes, eg, in connection with state sales tax?
- litigation matters: are there any? how serious are they?
- pension funding: is it adequate? are ERISA filings up to date? does the fund have a surplus or deficit?
- warranties and indemnities: does the company give them on its products?

Virtually all of this information should be available from the financial statements if they are audited accounts, other than details of ongoing tax examinations. (Note, however, that if there are any significant outstanding examinations or disputes over taxes, they would normally be disclosed.)

The information gathered in this fashion will then be used to perform rather traditional financial analysis that will allow a quantitative comparison of the candidates. Additionally, qualitative information (reputation of the management, products, etc.) is likely to be gathered. Typical financial ratios and measures to be calculated with the information obtained would normally include:

- measures of growth: increases in turnover and income;
- measures of profitability: gross margins, net income as a per cent of sales;

- financial management: number of days' sales represented by debtors, number of days' purchases represented by creditors; and
- return on equity, and debt to equity ratios.

Significant US and UK accounting differences

Of course, the financial statements, and any other information obtained, will usually have been prepared in accordance with US generally accepted accounting principles rather than with UK guidelines. To fully understand the information obtained, it would be best to at least estimate the impact of the differences between US and UK accounting standards, particularly as they relate to the target company. While this conversion may be tedious, even in terms of rough amounts, it allows for a much more meaningful comparison to results reported by UK companies and should avoid finding unpleasant surprises after the acquisition.

The differences between US and UK accounting principles are, for the most part, on detailed points and in regard to reporting and disclosure requirements, rather than sweeping differences in approaches to recording transactions. Areas with true significant differences in recording items include accounting for goodwill and fixed asset valuation. Other areas that might yield significant differences include pensions, income taxes, and foreign exchange. All of these are discussed below, and other major differences are identified in Appendix 7.

I GOODWILL
In the UK, goodwill can be either capitalised and written off through the profit and loss statement or written off directly to reserves in the year of the acquisition. In practice, the latter choice is almost always selected. In the US, goodwill must be capitalised and written off through the income statement over a period not to exceed forty years. This obviously has a significant impact on the income reported in years following an acquisition for those transactions involving significant amounts of goodwill.

II FIXED ASSET VALUATION
In the UK fixed assets are typically carried at valuation and can be written up to fair value, with an offset flowing through a 'revaluation reserve' in the shareholders' equity section. Depreciation expense is then based on the revalued amount and not on the original cost figure. Furthermore, certain investment properties may not be depreciated at all, on the basis that any loss in value will be reflected in valuation adjustments. In the US fixed assets, like any other asset, are carried at cost (or written down value when there has been a permanent impairment of the value to be realised by the company). All fixed assets (other than land) are depreciated over periods usually not exceeding fifty years, including investment properties. Uplifts of asset values above cost are only possible in connection with fair value adjustments relating to purchase (acquisition) business combinations.

III PENSIONS
The US has a new, fairly rigorous requirement with regard to pension accounting and to the actuarial method used to calculate pension assets and liabilities. The requirements of this pronouncement, SFAS 87, are for the most part compatible with SSAP 24; however, in some cases the treatment of any surplus or deficit

might be flowing through the profit and loss statement in a fashion different from that which would be typical for UK presentation. Therefore, if pension expense is a significant item in the US company's accounts, it is worth pursuing this point further to determine if there is a significant difference in the treatment of pension costs.

IV INCOME TAXES
The US currently employs the 'deferral' method of accounting for income taxes. This method is very much biased towards the income statement and does not take regard of changes in rates or other potential reductions in liabilities. However, a new liability method has been published and must be adopted for fiscal periods beginning after 15 December 1989, but even that will be different from the one used in the UK, principally since it requires full rather than partial provision. Therefore, it is likely that some adjustment will have to be made in respect of income tax expense and liabilities.

V FOREIGN EXCHANGE
The US requires use of an actual (ie) average rate when translating the profit and loss statements of consolidated foreign subsidiaries, as opposed to the UK where average or ending rates may be used.

Other less fundamental differences are discussed in Appendix 7. Please be aware, however, that while these differences can be labelled 'minor', they may result in significant differences to the financial statements of any one entity if that difference relates to a significant line of operation.

Some remaining key factors in a thorough evaluation include an examination of the plans and motivations of the owners. The labour force also should be investigated carefully by looking at its size, composition, stability and availability. Questions to be answered include: what have labour relations been? what is the turnover of employees? and what accrued or continuing liabilities might exist or occur under current employee benefits (pension plan, etc.)?

The goal of the above examination and analysis should be to determine if any of the candidates remain attractive. A valid and worthwhile conclusion may be that the priority list did not include any candidate which remains attractive on further investigation, and the acquiror should not be afraid to walk away (politely, and with many thanks, but firmly) at this, or any other stage of the process. Having progressed this far it is necessary, though difficult, to remember that negotiations are not automatic and required. It may be hard to reject the several weeks, or months, of effort necessary to get to this stage, but it is preferable to forging on blindly and acquiring an unsuitable subsidiary because you could not see outside the acquisition process.

CHAPTER 9

Analysing a target

Preliminary to, or as part of, the negotiation of the price an acquiror will normally conduct an investigation or some sort of detailed examination, usually including one or more of its professional advisers. Points raised as a result of this last and most exhaustive analysis may affect the final price, or establish certain contingencies in the purchase contract. It is quite useful for management to utilise a formal, directed checklist for the final stage investigation. One such list appears as Appendix 8, providing potential acquirors with a useful example to review as the acquisition progresses. Although not pertinent to every type of acquisition, this type of checklist is valuable for management because it generates hard facts about the target upon which a thorough evaluation can be based. The checklist indicates those important items which often may be overlooked in the heat of the deal.

The final analysis

The detailed examination of the target will proceed beyond the financial statements, usually incorporating site visits and the active involvement of the managing director. The type of information which will normally be sought includes data in the areas listed below.

CASH FLOW AND OPERATING RESULTS

SALES AND OTHER INCOME

- Examination of geographic concentration and product demand
- Trend analysis – with seasonal changes identified
- Permissible discounts
- Contracts outstanding
- Royalties or service fees
- Rental and other investment income
- Technical support fees
- Profile of material, labour and production overhead costs
- Standard and unusual costing procedures
- Production/storage costs

TAXATION, PROFITS AND VARIOUS ITEMS

- Tax basis – evaluation of high/low charge rates
- Analysis of current and deferred taxes
- Profit analysis by division and product
- Profit margin on sales
- Margin variance analysis
- Dividends on all categories of capital

- Additional appropriations per period
- Remittability of profit from overseas

The factors above cover an important part of the financial investigation; the foreign acquiror looks at these to evaluate past and current performance of the target. In addition to this, however, is the key task of analysing forecasted performance. Therefore, since the direction of the acquiror is forward-looking, the following points should be considered.

PROFITS, CASH FLOW AND ASSETS

- Review of accuracy of previous forecasting
- Sensitivity analysis on such items as market demand, price changes, currency fluctuations and input costs
- Available financial facilities and external financing
- Cost and depreciation of all categories of assets
- Depreciation/amortisation analysis for different categories of assets
- Basis of capitalisation of labour and materials
- Patent and trademark details
- Analysis of goodwill

DEBTORS, CREDITORS AND INVESTMENTS

- Home and export debt analysis
- Credit control policies
- Bad debt profile
- Trade debtor analysis
- Permissible credit period
- Credit provision details
- Bank borrowing limits and provisions
- Profile of securities and guarantees
- Leasing agreements
- Repayment schedules
- Investment holdings and values
- Details of repayment/withdrawal

Consideration should be given to the analysis of the likely expectations and concerns of the target company and its management and employees. If the acquiror's investigation team begins to question the candidate in an indiscreet fashion, the sellers may be reluctant to co-operate. Furthermore, acquisitive management should take care to indicate to its target that any and all information obtained from the company at this stage of the acquisition will remain strictly private and confidential. Normally a target will require some type of signed confidentiality agreement to release information adequate to respond to the last round of questions detailed above.

It is also important to review any management letter prepared by the auditors of the candidate, noting any exceptions in their report; in fact, a prospective acquiror might consider speaking directly with the accounting firm, although this procedure may only be appropriate later in the acquisition process.

The information gathered through the analysis process will flow into the next stage, valuing the target company as a basis for negotiating the price.

The valuation of the target company is often viewed as the one critical stage of any acquisition, as it is this process which underlies not only the determination of the price the acquiror should pay for the company, but also the potential profitability of the acquiror after the deal is completed. An important point to recall, however, is that the valuation is separate from the offer: the offer is the structure in which the agreed value will be conveyed.

Throughout, it must be recalled that these are methods of establishing price guidelines, and not a substitute for business judgment about whether a company is a sound investment choice or not.

Valuation methods for acquisitions

There are several specific methods for business valuations using the financial statements of the target company. The methods are divided into the following three categories:

- asset methods;
- earnings/cash flow methods; and
- comparable share sale method.

Asset methods

One of the most basic methods used to value a business examines the balance sheet to determine the net worth of the entity. It is usually the lowest amount any seller would consider in selling his or her business. However, if it is an ongoing business with a reasonable potential for continued profits, it is unlikely to be an attractive or accepted offer. Net worth is the difference between total assets and total liabilities. However, the accounting definition of net worth, as determined by generally accepted accounting principles, usually differs greatly from true economic net worth. With US targets it will be based on historical, rather than revalued costs, and will ignore most if not all of the intrinsic value – the internal goodwill – of an ongoing entity. Accounting net worth will usually fall between tangible net worth – a measurement of net tangible assets excluding items such as patents, trademarks, brand names, goodwill, etc. – and economic net worth, which recognises values for all intangible assets, including those not reflected on the balance sheet. An acquiror should first identify tangible net worth. This calculation excludes any intangible assets, and is often used in bank loans and covenants to establish minimum financial performance requirements.

In computing tangible net worth, items such as goodwill and values assigned to patents, copyrights, or new product development costs, if carried on the books, are deducted from net worth. In some cases, tangible net worth may be further adjusted to eliminate assets which, while tangible and carried at fair value, are extraneous to the company's main business (for example, an investment in an affiliated company owned directly by management).

The procedure is particularly important when making industry comparisons. In measuring the value of the business in terms of its performance against competitors in the same industry, only assets employed in the actual business operation are usually considered.

For example, assume the following condensed balance sheet:

	$
Assets	1,000,000
Liabilities	(600,000)
Net worth	400,000

Following the analysis of the assets, the following intangible assets are identified:

	$
Goodwill arising from the acquisition of a small supplier	40,000
Deferred financing costs	12,000
Patent costs	1,150
Investment in an affiliate	10,000
Total intangibles	63,150

The adjusted tangible net worth is $336,850: $400,000 book net worth less the $63,150 of intangible assets. This, of course, still may not be the final determination of value. In fact, the patent valued at $1,150 could be worth significantly more than its carrying value on the balance sheet.

Using tangible net worth to determine a value may be very misleading; however, it is a figure that should be computed. Acquirors should keep in mind that it is merely a benchmark for valuation, and should not be considered the 'end-all' figure. It does, however, provide a rock bottom price – usually some indication of liquidation or break-up value, and is therefore an important baseline.

Note that tangible net worth, computed in the above manner, is very different from economic net worth. Here, the assets used in the business are adjusted to reflect higher market or replacement values. This adjustment to net worth is also referred to as 'tangible net worth at market'.

In the tangible net worth at market method, the tangible net worth as computed above is further adjusted. Tangible assets are restated to reflect their true economic worth. Intangible assets, however, such as goodwill, remain omitted. In the previous example, adjustments to the tangible net worth of $336,850 should be made for the following assets, which are understated from a market value point of view:

	Book value	Market value
	$	$
Stock (inventories)	85,000	109,000
Real estate	100,000	250,000
Equipment	62,000	85,000
Total:	247,000	444,000
Market value in excess of book value		197,000

Tangible net worth is also adjusted:

	$
Book net worth	400,000
Less: Intangibles	(63,150)
Tangible net worth	336,850
Excess values	197,000
Tangible net worth at market	533,850

Although not in conformity with generally accepted accounting principles, this method is another benchmark and usually gives a more meaningful representation of the tangible net worth of the business.

Earnings/cash flow methods

Thus far the discussion has been about valuing a business by analysing balance sheet assets. More important, however, is the determination of what the company's assets earn. The assets of a business are normally looked at as an investment – as an asset group which will generate a certain income stream into the indefinite future. (The only time when this would not be the case would be the situation where a company's assets were being purchased with a liquidation in mind.)

To value a business as an income and cash generator means analysing and evaluating the net income and cash flow of the company. There are a number of methods employed to do so including:

- capitalisation of income method ('interest cap');
- discounted cash flow method;
- price-earnings multiple method; and
- dividend capitalisation method.

CAPITALISATION OF INCOME METHOD

As previously noted, a business can be looked at as an investment rather than as just a group of tangible or intangible assets. The true value of a business as an investment is the income stream that it generates, usually expressed as a rate of return related to its determined value. Thus, valuing a business as an investment requires that (1) the return be compared to other available competing investments, and (2) an adjustment be made for the appropriate, additional risk being assumed.

In using this valuation method, the first step is to develop a list of alternative investments and determine their rates of return. These alternatives could encompass virtually any investment medium including art, antiques, and undeveloped land, but it is normally best to start with low-risk, liquid capital market investment alternatives. By doing so, an idea of the best return for the lowest risk currently available in the market can be obtained and evaluated. For example, the following is a list of yields on various financial instruments.

Type of investment	Yield
Day-to-day savings accounts	$5\frac{1}{2}\%$
One year certificates of deposit	$8\frac{3}{4}\%$
Five year treasury notes	$8\frac{5}{8}\%$
Twenty year treasury bonds	$8\frac{1}{4}\%$
AAA corporate bonds	$7\frac{1}{3}\%$
Dividend yield on 'low risk' common stock	$9\frac{1}{2}\%$

Note that the minimum yield on any of the above investment instruments is $5\frac{1}{2}$ per cent and the maximum is $9\frac{1}{2}$ per cent. Since these yields, or returns on investment, are actually available in the marketplace, the income stream that a business generates should be compared with them, in order to value the business.

After available yields in the marketplace are determined and analysed, the second step in this valuation method is to determine the degree of risk associated with the income stream of the business. This is done in order to select the appropriate rate at which to capitalise the income stream. For example, if the income stream is viewed as being as risk-free as that of the return on a twenty year corporate AAA bond, then the $7\frac{1}{3}$ per cent rate of return could be used as the capitalisation rate for the business's earnings. With regard to closely held companies, it is almost always true that there is additional risk due to the decreased liquidity of the investment. Closely held companies generally have certain characteristics which increase the risk of investment. These risks might include:

- lack of management depth;
- inadequate capital base resulting in high leverage;
- reliance on a few customers and suppliers; and
- regional rather than national market, and therefore reliance on a more restricted economy.

There are many more possible risk factors depending on the age of the business, personalities of its officers/owners and other characteristics. Thus, because of these risk factors, a higher return must be sought when investing in or acquiring a closely held company. To determine the desired rate of return (or capitalisation rate on any investment), three components come into play: (1) the basic return, (2) the inflation premium, and (3) the risk factor appropriate for the particular investment. By looking at the most risk-free, liquid investments available, the first two factors can be accounted for. For example, the return on a twenty-year US government obligation reflects the basic return and the inflation premium that investors are looking for in the market, since there is supposedly no risk premium applied to the 'risk-free' US government securities.

Since an investment in a smaller business is usually more risky or at least less liquid than an investment in a large corporation, a higher rate of return is usually sought. Given the alternative rates of return available in the market, as specified by the table above, the appraiser may determine that given the risk in the business, a 15 per cent rate of return (capitalisation rate) is required to compensate for this additional risk.

Once the desired rate of return is determined, the capitalisation rate multiplier can be computed. This is simply the reciprocal of the capitalisation rate. Thus a 15 per cent capitalisation rate is equivalent to a 6.7 multiplier (1.0 divided by .15). The company's net income is then multiplied by this factor to determine the value of the business.

For example, assume the following net income results for the last three years and projected results for 1989:

30 June	*Actual*			*Projected*
	1986	1987	1988	1989
Net income (thousands)	$50	$80	$120	$200

In applying the multiplier of 6.7 times earnings, it must be determined which earnings to use: 1988's? an average of last three years? projected 1989 amounts? All three are shown in the following table:

Method	*Valuation at 15% capitalisation rate**
I Last year's earnings of $120,000	$804,000
II Three-year average of $83,333	$558,000
III Projected earnings of $200,000	$1,340,000

* The earnings used multiplied by 6.7.

With these three calculations obtained, the next step is to apply subjective weights to each value or to take a straight arithmetic average.

For example, the following probabilities might be assigned as weights:

Method	Value	Weighting factor	Value
I	$ 804,000	50%	$402,000
II	558,000	25%	139,500
III	1,340,000	25%	335,000
Composite value			$876,500

The logic behind the above 'weighting factor' is the application of higher percentages for more known results, particularly the most recent year which has a 50 per cent weight factor. Note that the historical three-year average and projected results are given lower weights. Obviously the results of such a calculation will vary significantly based on the relative weights assigned; selection of the most appropriate weightings is a judgmental decision drawing on the expertise of the acquiror and its advisers. Their weighting may also be affected by the results of their in-depth analysis and determination as to the amount of 'play' in the figures being capped.

The average method is simply the total of all values ($2,702,000) divided by three, which equals $900,667. Basically, an equal weight ($33\frac{1}{3}$ per cent) is applied to each valuation method.

Note, also, that the higher capitalisation rate sought, the lower the multiplier used. For example, if a 20 per cent return is sought, the multiplier would be 5.0 (1.0 divided by .20). Thus, the various calculations of earnings would have been multiplied by 5.0 rather than 6.7. Under Method III, this would result in a substantially lower value of $1,000,000, versus the $1,340,000 achieved above.

The problem now is to determine which earnings should be used. In the case of an established company, current and projected earnings are used (Methods I and III). But when a company is young its future is far more important than its past. Thus, next year's projected earnings can be used, but this should be done with caution.

Only true earnings derived from the operations of the business should be considered, and it therefore may be necessary to adjust reported earnings. 'One time' or non-recurring items should be excluded from the calculation. For example, the company may have sold some assets, or perhaps a product line or division, for a substantial capital gain. Since this gain (and the operations of the division) will not continue into the future, the related income or loss should be excluded from earnings. In a similar manner, if the company has been utilising a net operating loss carryforward over the last three years, so that its pretax income has not been fully taxed, this should also be adjusted. Adjustments should also be made for unusually large debtor or stock write-offs and varying accounting practices.

DISCOUNTED CASH FLOW METHOD

An adjunct to the capitalisation of income method of valuation is the discounted cash flow method. In this method, a company's cash flow rather than its net income is determined and then valued. It is based on a variation of the capitalisation rate technique used in the above capitalisation of income method. The cash flow method schedules projected cash movements and discounts them at the capitalisation rate to determine the present value. Typically, however, the discounted cash flow method is used primarily for larger transactions and in special situations. Examples of situations where it would be preferable include:

- when a business is established solely to fulfill a certain project or contract; this is a typical arrangement for a joint venture;
- in certain start-up and other companies where cash flow is more important than net income;
- when a certain time frame is set where an investor in a business, because of the risk of investment, wishes to see his or her investment (cash paid out) returned; and
- when valuing a mature company where projections of future cash flows are viable.

Discounted cash flow is identical to the capitalisation of income method except that at the end of the specified time period, the remaining net assets of the business are also valued and included in the overall valuation calculation.

To use this method, the following information must be obtained:

- the projected cash flow of the business over the next five years;
- an estimate of the liquidation value of the company's assets at the end of the fifth year;
- the remaining liabilities of the company at the end of the fifth year; and
- the capitalisation rate to be used as the discount rate to be applied to the cash flows and to the liquidating value of the assets.

(Five years is used here as the assumed holding period for the asset.)

A key point to recall is that any discounting is only as good as the projections themselves, which should be carefully evaluated as to their accuracy.

Before proceeding to the example, an additional use of the capitalisation rate must be explained. As illustrated in the capitalisation of income method, the capitalisation rate (rate of return) specifies the percentage return that must be earned each year on an investment, taking into account competing investments available and assumed risk. The flip side of the capitalisation rate is the discount rate, which is expressed as a series of present value factors. The discount rate specifies the present value (the value today) of a future stream of income or cash flows.

For example, recall that a capitalisation rate of 15 per cent was used in valuing the company's net income stream in the capitalisation of income method. In effect, the calculated value of the company must reflect a 15 per cent return on the company's net income stream.

In other words, if $1,000 were invested today a total return at the end of five years would be $1,000 x $(1 + .15)^5$ or $2,011.36. An alternative way of looking at this capitalisation rate of 15 per cent is to determine how much must be invested today, at a 15 per cent rate of return, so that it will compound into $1,000 at the end of a certain time period. This discount, or present value rate, can be determined by referring to a present value table and locating the present value factors for 15 per cent. (These are available in any corporate finance handbook; typically, business calculators such as the HP-12C, and most personal computer spreadsheets, can also run these calculations.)

Year	Present value factor for 15% rate of return	Value of $1,000 today
1	.870	$870
2	.756	$756
3	.658	$658
4	.572	$572
5	.492	$492

As the above table illustrates, if $870 were invested for one year at 15 per cent, $1,000 would be available at the end of that year ($870 x .15 = $130, and $870 + $130 = $1,000). Similarly, if $492 were invested for five years at 15 per cent, at the end of the fifth year the investor would have $1,000.

The present value factors are used in the discounted cash flow method since the purpose is to determine the present value of the company. The firm's present value is based on the required discount rate and its future cash flow stream over the five years being analysed.

An example may prove more helpful. Assume the following for SZRA Incorporated, a company to be liquidated at the end of 1993:

- a discount rate of 15 per cent;
- a net tangible book value in 1993 of $300,000 – that is, tangible assets of $800,000 less liabilities of $500,000;
- the realisation of the net cash flows as shown in the following table:

Valuation of SZRA Incorporated

(Thousands)

	Value today	1	2	3	4	5	Total
				Years			
Net cash flow	$218.1	$–0–	$50	$75	$100	$150	$375
Tangible assets at end of fifth year	393.6	–0–	–0–	–0–	–0–	800	800
Liabilities at end of fifth year	(246.0)	–0–	–0–	–0–	–0–	(500)	(500)
Total cash flows		$–0–	$50	$75	$100	$450	$675
Present value factor (15 per cent discount rate)		.870	.756	.658	.572	.492	
Present value of net cash flow*	$365.7						

* To determine this amount, each of the total cash flows for years one through five are multiplied by the present value factor for that year and then are totalled.

As computed, the total value of the income stream (net cash flow from operations after all cash expenditures) is worth $218,100 today. This amount, when added to the net liquidating value of the business ($393,600 less $246,000), puts a value on the business today of $365,700. In other words, if the company were purchased today for its discounted cash flow value of $365,700 and the projected cash flows for the five years were generated, the investor (or acquiror) would realise a 15 per cent compounded annual return over the five-year period without assuming any benefits from improved performance, or from integration within the acquiror's structure.

If another discount rate were used, however, the value today would be different than the calculated $365,700. Assume a 20 per cent discount rate instead of the previous 15 per cent. It reflects a higher required return, leaving the value of the business today as only $307,200 – a decrease of $58,500. As indicated previously, an investor or acquiror placing money in the business may use the higher 20 per cent discount rate to compensate for risk and uncertainty assumed. The result is an illustration of how a higher target return rate results in a lower calculated present value.

THE PRICE/EARNINGS MULTIPLE METHOD

The most common method for valuing publicly held companies is the price-to-earnings ratio (p/e). The p/e is simply the price of a company's share in the public market divided by its earnings per share. For example, if a company has net income of $100,000 and 100,000 shares of common shares outstanding, the earnings per share would be $1.00. If the shares were selling for $10 per share in the market, the p/e multiple would be $10 divided by $1, or simply 10. Therefore, since the company has 100,000 shares outstanding, the valuation of the entire company would be 100,000 shares times $10 per share, or a total of $1 million.

Another way of looking at the price-earnings multiple in terms of valuing the entire business is to multiply total net income by the p/e or the p/e of a similar enterprise. Thus, in the previous example, $100,000 times the p/e of 10 equals a $1 million value on the company as a whole. Valuing a closely held business by the p/e method involves simply multiplying its net income by an appropriate multiple. The multiple can be determined by an examination of the ratios for publicly traded companies whose businesses are similar to the company being valued.

The primary benefit of the p/e method is its simplicity. It can have serious drawbacks, however, revolving around the derivation of the proper multiple to be used. These drawbacks are summarised below.

- First, and most important, the stock of a private company is not publicly traded. It is illiquid and actually may be restricted from sale. Thus any p/e multiple arrived at must, by definition, be subjective.
- Second, the stated net income of a private company may not truly reflect its actual earning power. Most business owners prefer to keep net income down to avoid paying taxes. In addition, the closely held business may be 'over spending' for fringe benefits, instituted primarily for the owners' benefit.
- Third, common stock that is bought and sold in the public market normally reflects only a small portion of the equity position of the business. However, when valuing the closely held business under this method, the entire ownership position is taken into consideration. Controlling blocks of shares usually attract a premium rather than a discount, and this control factor would have to be considered.
- Fourth, in reality it is very difficult to find truly comparable publicly held companies, even in the same industry. Growth rates, available markets, competition, the payment of dividends and the financial profile (liquidity and leverage) will rarely be exactly the same.

Notwithstanding these drawbacks, a comparison can still be made and still be valuable, but usually as a benchmark rather than a final price. For example, in today's market an examination of comparable companies may show that the average p/e ratio for typical smaller companies is about 8. However, back in 1968, at the tail end of the previous bull market in publicly traded common shares, the average p/e probably would have been double this level. Thus, it is important to note that the price earnings ratio gives an indication of value – but only within the context of current market conditions.

An additional word should be said about the price-earnings multiple before proceeding to the next method of valuation. Note that the reciprocal of the price-earnings ratio is the earnings-price ratio – and this is, in effect, the capitalisation rate or rate of return that has been used in prior valuation methods.

For example, assume the following:

Net income	$100,000
Shares outstanding	100,000
Earnings per share	$1
Market value per share	$8

Based on the above data, the p/e is 8; but when expressed as a capitalisation rate, it is 1/8, or 12.5 per cent. In other words, the company with a valuation of $800,000 yields a rate of return, in terms of its net income of $100,000, of 12.5 per cent. This is close to the capitalisation rate of 15 per cent that was used earlier. Thus, the p/e method can provide a ballpark check with the prior capitalisation rate methods discussed. (Note also that the capitalisation rate can be converted to a p/e multiple. A 15 per cent rate of return is equivalent to a p/e multiple of 1.0/.15, or 6.7.)

THE DIVIDEND-CAPITALISATION METHOD

The dividend-capitalisation method of valuation follows closely the price-earnings multiple method. Instead of using the p/e as the determinant of value, the dividend paying capacity of the company, in terms of comparable companies, is used.

As most individuals who are familiar with closely held companies know, the owners usually try to avoid paying out dividends. There is little incentive to do so, as dividends are subject to double taxation, being taxed at the corporate level and then again as income to the shareholders. The owners can withdraw cash from the business in a number of more tax-advantageous ways, sometimes in a completely tax deferred manner (such as through a qualified retirement plan). This fact, however, does not negate the use of this method since it computes the capacity of the business to pay dividends, if it elected to do so.

There are two steps involved in valuing the business using the dividend-capitalisation method:

(1) determine the dividend-paying capacity of the company; and
(2) determine the dividend yield.

Step 1   Dividends are paid out of after-tax income, so the starting point is net income. Dividends also represent distributed cash that is not required in the business. Thus, a number of factors determine how much cash, as a per cent of net income, should be retained in the company. These factors are:

- *Near-term capital needs.* Cash may be needed to support higher projected debtor (receivable) or stock (inventory) levels.
- *Expansion plans.* Capital may be needed to fund a new sales effort; for

investment in research and development; for the hiring of additional personnel; or for the acquisition of additional machinery, equipment or plant.
- *Cash flow flexibility.* No business can plan perfectly; therefore a certain amount of capital should be retained in the business not only as a cushion against unforeseen problems but also to take advantage of future business opportunities.
- *Contractual requirements.* Existing shareholders' agreements or credit arrangements may preclude the payout of more than a certain amount of net income in the form of dividends. For example, a long-term debt agreement may prohibit the payment of dividends in excess of 50 per cent of net income.
- *Dividend paying history of the business.* If the business has paid dividends in the past, this fact provides a guideline for its dividend paying capacity. The past dividend payments should be analysed in terms of the company's net income and cash flow for the years in which the dividends were paid.
- *Dividend payments by comparable companies.* As in the price-earnings method, the basis of the dividend-capitalisation method lies in comparison with comparable companies in the same industry. Such companies (ideally they should be the same businesses selected for price-earnings ratio comparison) should be identified and their past dividend payments studied in relation to net income and net cash flow.

After looking at the above factors, assume that a company named Tricia Apparel Inc has the capacity to pay dividends equal to 50 per cent of its net income, or 40 per cent of its net cash flow. In making the valuation calculation using this method, it is best to use an average of the past five years' historical results.

The following table illustrates the company's average dividend paying capacity for the last five years:

Tricia Apparel Inc as of 31 March (000's)

	1984	1985	1986	1987	1988	Total
Net income	$105	$120	$90	$140	$160	$615
Plus: Noncash charges:						
Depreciation/ Amortisation	30	33	40	45	52	200
Total cash flow	$135	$153	$130	$185	$212	$815
Dividend paying capacity:						
50 per cent of average net income of $123,000						$61,500
40 per cent of average cash flow of $163,000						$65,200

Step 2 The next step is to determine the appropriate dividend yield. Dividend yield is defined as:

(Dividend paying capacity) / (Value of business) = *Dividend yield*

As the above equation illustrates, once the dividend paying capacity has been determined and the appropriate dividend yield can be identified, a valuation of the business can be obtained by using the dividend-capitalisation method.

The best way to determine dividend yields is to analyse the target in relation to comparable companies. As in the price-earnings ratio method, this usually produces a subjective result since no two companies are exactly the same. However, it is possible to obtain a good feel for the value determined on the dividend yield basis by looking at it in comparison to the overall dividend yield levels in the market, ie what comparable companies are paying in dividends. If, after the analysis, it is found that the dividend yield should be about six per cent, the valuation for the business can be calculated as follows.

Valuation of business based on dividend paying capacity of:

$$50 \text{ per cent of average net income} = \frac{\$61,500}{.06} = \text{value of } \$1,025,000$$

$$40 \text{ per cent of average cash flow} = \frac{\$65,200}{.06} = \text{value of } \$1,086,667 \text{ value}$$

Note, however, that the dividend yield selected has a significant effect on the total valuation. If an 8 per cent yield is assumed on the 50 per cent of average net income capacity, then the valuation is $768,750 rather than $1,025,000. Thus, much care and comparable analysis should be completed prior to the selection of the desired dividend yield.

Although the dividend-capitalisation method can be a subjective method of valuation, especially if the business being valued has never paid dividends, it still can be used as a complement to other valuation methods.

Comparable share sales method

Another major method of valuing a business is the comparable share (stock) sales method. This method analyses (1) actual sales of stock in comparable companies, (2) recent offers to purchase the company, and (3) actual recent sales of stock in the company being valued. Moreover, as noted earlier, the purest indicator of true value is an actual transaction between willing buyers and sellers. Unless circumstances surrounding the company have changed radically since a recent sale, the valuation put on the business in such a transaction is hard to dispute.

The purchase and sale of shares in companies comparable to the company being valued is also a good indicator. Again, however, certain caveats must be considered.

First, as discussed previously, true comparability is difficult to find. The financial and operating characteristics of two businesses may appear to be the same, but the intangible aspects of a business – that is the quality of its management, its innovativeness, resourcefulness, response to problems as well as to opportunities – are rarely the same. It is these intangible aspects which play a large part in determining the true value of a business. In addition, if the comparable companies also are private, information about transactions may be difficult to obtain.

Second, as seen previously, sales of shares in comparable companies, especially shares traded in public markets, almost always represent only a small portion of the total ownership position and rarely even a controlling interest. Also, the shares in publicly quoted companies is a liquid investment, while in contrast, closely held shares are difficult, if not impossible, to sell. However, these problems should not preclude using comparable share sales as a valuation tool; it is, after all, another good device in the overall valuation process.

RECENT OFFERS TO PURCHASE THE COMPANY

An additional means of valuation is to refer to recent offers to purchase the company. If such an offer has been made within the last year, it can support the valuation being made.

Even here, however, such offers cannot be accepted at face value. For example, assume a closely held business is valued at $1 million, using a combination of the methods which have been discussed. Six months before the valuation was completed, a potential buyer offered $1.4 million for the company. The question arises as to how the valuation study generated such a low figure.

To answer this, the prior offer must be studied in more detail. For example, the $1.4 million offer could have been structured to provide a 20 per cent down payment with the remaining balance paid over ten years at a modest seven per cent interest rate. It is important to re-emphasise at this point that when a business is valued, the valuation objective is to determine what the business is worth today in exchange for cash today. Other factors such as deferred payouts, contingent payments, tax structuring of the deal and so forth should be taken into consideration only after a basic value for the business has been determined. Thus, if a tax adviser finds a method whereby substantial taxes can be saved for the seller by a particular structure that the buyer will accept, the seller may then consider lowering the purchase price by an amount equal to the tax savings. If price is an issue to the seller, he or she would consider such a modification simply because the basic valuation (and total price) for the business stays the same.

The $1.4 million offer described above must be analysed keeping in mind that the total proceeds will not be remitted to the seller for ten years. There is, therefore, an opportunity cost and a credit risk assumed by the vendor that should be factored in before comparing it to the new $1 million offer.

ACTUAL RECENT SALES OF SHARES

Another method to test a valuation is to analyse actual recent sales of shares in the company being valued. Again, however, caveats must be applied.

First, share sales to key management may have been made at a bargain value to provide incentives. In addition, these minority interests, especially in a closely held company, should reflect a discount to their true value since they do not convey control over the business and are illiquid.

Second, shares sold to an outside individual or financial institution to raise capital for the business can provide a more accurate picture of value. Again, however, a discount should be applied for a minority interest and for lack of liquidity.

Third, other capital transactions with outsiders need not be in the form of straight common shares to provide an indication of value. Many institutional investors, such as venture capital groups or small business investment companies, invest capital in smaller businesses through debt instruments with an equity feature. For example, a conversion privilege or warrants (options) to buy common shares at a certain price per share is a debt/equity investment.

Since a transaction of this type is negotiated at arm's length and between willing parties, a valuation results. It is fair since the owner will want to place a high value on the company while the investor will try and justify a low one to maximise investment return.

As an example, assume a small business investment company invests $500,000 in a business through a seven-year convertible note. The note is convertible into

25 per cent of the share capital of the company. If the note is converted, $500,000 will be exchanged for the 25 per cent ownership position. Thus, the implicit value on the company accepted by both the owner and the investor when the transaction was made was $2 million – $500,000 divided by 25 per cent.

OTHER BENCHMARKS

Another yardstick of value regarding share sales involves not an actual historical sale but a future obligation to make a sale. For example, an employment agreement with a key manager may provide that the individual must sell his or her shares back to the company, and that the company must purchase them if that employee leaves the company for any reason. The agreement can provide good support for determining the value of the shares, since it spells out the method to be used – multiple of earnings, book value, tangible book value, etc. Since both were willing parties to the buyback agreement, it provides an indication of value for the minority interest covered by the agreement.

A shareholders' agreement may also provide an indication of value. The agreement may contain a clause regarding the future purchase of additional shares by existing shareholders, defining a mechanism for setting the price to be paid. If a closely held business has more than one owner, an important aspect of planning for continuing management, as well as for personal estate planning, is an agreement between the owners.

The agreement, whether it is a binding obligation on the shareholders or not, will typically contain a means of determining the value of the company's shares. If it is a mandatory obligation for a deceased shareholder's estate to sell, and for the company to purchase, the price the agreement provides is a very strong indicator of an appropriate method for calculating value, since the company presumably would not want to pay an inflated price and the estate would not want to sell at a deflated price. Value determined in such mandatory agreements, as a matter of fact, lends support for estate tax purposes.

Private company valuations

It is imperative to realise that the valuation of the private business in almost all cases is an art, not a science, and that ultimately, negotiation between the parties offering and requiring the valuation will play a paramount role in the final result.

It is not hard to compute a company's sales volume, determine its debtors, and calculate its return ratios. But it is somewhat difficult to assess the true value of a private business, as most business owners and professionals would quickly agree. Posing the question to an owner and then to his or her accountant, lawyer, insurance agent, and treasurer will produce a range of responses which are likely to amaze the investor.

The problem of valuation is so tricky because it simply can be viewed from many perspectives.

- How will the IRS value the company?
- How do outsiders value it when private or public equity capital is needed?
- What's the value if the owners want to sell out?
- How should minority stockholders value it?
- What is its value as a going concern that provides its owners with income and valuable fringe benefits?

A last point to recall is that a good part of valuation obviously depends on goals and motives. For example, if an owner transfers shares to family members as gifts, a low value per share is desired in order to minimise gift taxes. In contrast, when selling the business, the owners want the maximum price per share.

The primary difficulty in determining the value of the smaller business is, of course, that it is typically controlled by a few individuals or a single family. Unlike large corporations, whose common shares are widely held and valued daily in the marketplace, the common shares of small business are illiquid, that is, they cannot be readily sold. Besides that, a privately held company may lack depth in its management. After all, the business worth may be quite different without its key, perhaps founding, management. Therefore it is difficult to assess such business entities.

Unfortunately, many business owners are far too busy coping with the increasing complexities of today's business world and the day-to-day pressures of meeting payroll to ponder the questions of valuation. Furthermore, many simply do not care; they see their business as a highly personal asset and both operate and value it in that way.

As many business owners say: 'My business is worth what I can take out of it every year in the form of a good salary and non-taxable fringe benefits.' The fringes, of course, can include use of a company car, medical and dental insurance, liberal pension and profit-sharing plans and the ability to split income and shares among family members to save taxes. However, it is important for owners to realise that they have a share certificate, and that it is worth something. The key to valuation is thus to define the purpose for the valuation and then to fit the valuation methods available to meet that end. The challenge then becomes how best to approach this valuation dilemma.

There is no absolute value for a business, although value must always translate to terms of money. A company's beauty – and its shortcomings – are in the beholder's eyes. So too, a valuation or appraisal of a business is a determination of the value of the business for a specific purpose. It is, in essence, a determination expressed in monetary terms of the rewards of owning the business, or owning a part of it. What many individuals fail to realise is the emotional and monetary value of a business to its owner. For example, a business could have a solid net worth of $500,000 and earn $50,000 after tax. From an outsider's point of view, a $500,000 cash price tag on the business is more than fair:

- the owner gets the book value in cash;
- the buyer is paying ten times earnings;
- the owner can diversify his or her holdings and get a good yield on the cash; and
- the owner can retire.

However, from the owner's point of view, the $50,000 annual aftertax profit is in addition to a personal annual salary of $75,000, a company car and other fringes. It is difficult to try to equate hard dollars with these considerations. Another point is that after paying taxes of about $150,000 on the $500,000 price, the business owner may only have $350,000 left; over the next five years, he or she probably would have made that in any event. While the purchaser may determine that $500,000 is a fair price, it may be difficult to convince the seller that $500,000 is the replacement cost in terms of benefits sacrificed.

Summary

In almost every valuation, the 'motive' for the sale affects the valuation and can be as important as the 'numbers'. In fact, in many cases, the motives determine the maximum and minimum price range. To prove this, try buying a business from an owner who does not want to sell and repeatedly turns down offers versus buying a business from an owner's estate which needs cash to pay estate taxes.

Also, as stated earlier, a valuation does not prove an absolute value; rather, it is a basis for pricing. The next chapter looks at how 'value', as measured by various valuation techniques, is translated into an actual deal. Just as value is in the eyes of the beholder, influenced by motives and other factors, price is not an absolute. Most importantly, it is affected by its form and timing: shares versus cash; cash today versus a stream of payments; an agreed fixed total amount versus an agreed basic sum and contingent payout. All these factors, and the needs of the buyer, must be brought together during negotiations to complete the deal. The options generally available to do so are discussed in the next chapter – 'Structure of the offer'.

Part 3
Doing the Deal

CHAPTER 10
Structure of the offer

The various valuation methods discussed in the last chapter can be used as a guide in establishing a price range for the target company. The next step is to structure an offer to convey that value to the seller. There are many possible forms such a transfer can take; resources would be wasted if anything less than the best fit for buyers' and sellers' desires was fashioned. Different structures have different costs, and the satisfaction of both parties is enhanced where the seller maximises value received while the buyer minimises consideration sacrificed.

The basic question to resolve in determining the structure of the offer is whether the acquisition will be one of assets, or of the shares of the target company. The second important decision is whether the consideration will be cash, shares of some sort (ordinary, preferred, convertible), share rights (warrants and options) or debentures. The last facet is the timing of receipt: lump sum up front, some form of instalment sale, or on a contingency basis. Of course, by taking a note, the seller is accepting a form of deferred consideration, but there are obviously a number of possible permutations available.

Probably the most significant influence on the structure of the agreement will be tax considerations. Many of the basic concerns were covered in chapter 3; recall that a purchase of assets (rather than shares) is generally necessary to allow a buyer to get a step up in value for tax purposes. This would normally be an incentive for a buyer to seek an asset purchase, something many sellers are reluctant to agree to.

The only means for completing an acquisition without triggering tax effects is to do some variety of a share for share deal which would qualify as a 'tax free combination'. In the US, the term 'combination' is a general term referring to either a merger or an acquisition. As the same transaction may be an acquisition for reporting purposes and a merger for tax purposes, or vice versa, 'combination' is used to speak of either type of joining together. Usually when an individual or small group of owners is selling out, they prefer fairly liquid capital in return, rather than shares which may fluctuate in value. Furthermore, realisation of the value of these shares would require selling them, which would raise the same tax considerations as would the original sale of the company's shares for cash. Shares in a company listed only in the UK may be less attractive than those of a US quoted company, because there are higher costs associated with dealing in shares listed only in the UK and foreign exchange risk to a US long-term holder. For these and other reasons, it is unlikely that the purchaser would be able to agree to a tax free combination. Therefore, this section focuses on taxable combinations.

Form of the combination

Typically, a US corporation can be acquired in various ways:

- purchase of the shares of the corporation from existing shareholders;
- purchase of the assets of the target company; or
- exchange of voting shares of the acquiring corporation for shares or assets of the target US company.

By purchasing share capital of the target company directly from current shareholders, the buyer acquires the target corporation intact. No change in the acquired entity is effected since only the identity of the shareholders has changed. However, the company may be party to contracts or leases that require consent prior to any significant share acquisitions or 'changes in control'. In share transactions, the selling shareholders incur all the immediate income tax consequences of the transaction.

In an acquisition of assets, the buyer purchases all or a part of the target's business directly from the target company. One virtue of this method is that it insulates the purchaser from a blanket assumption of all of the target's liabilities. Although some common law and statutory exceptions exist, each liability of the target is subject to express negotiation and agreement before it is assumed by the purchaser. Third-party consents are often required to effect assignment of material contracts, leases or licences of the target company. Tax consequences of the asset transaction are generally borne by the seller.

If a foreign investor purchases some or all of the assets of a US target company, the acquiror receives a tax basis in the assets equivalent to the purchase price. The purchaser may buy the assets directly or may create a new US or foreign corporation to make the purchase.

The term statutory merger is used differently for legal purposes – matters of corporate structure, etc. – and tax purposes. In the simplest statutory (in the legal sense) merger, title to the acquired entity's assets passes to the acquiror (or its subsidiary) and all liabilities of the acquired entity are assumed by the surviving corporation. Mergers generally require prior shareholder approval and a state filing. Dissenting shareholders are often afforded appraisal rights under state law. Appraisal rights allow the shareholder to sell its shares back to the corporation at fair value.

1 Share-for-share

If the only consideration exchanged by the target and buyer is shares, the arrangement is formally between the acquiring company and the shareholders of the target. (Technically, when the purchase of another company is carried out by an exchange of shares, a merger occurs.) This transformation will develop as the two separate groups of shareholders exchange shares to form a single – yet enlarged – corporate entity with only one single – enlarged – shareholder group. The transaction can be effected either by acquiring the target for an issue of its shares or by the shareholders of both entities exchanging shares in consideration of an issue of shares by a new, jointly managed company. Often, however, the distinction between a merger and acquisition for shares is extremely slight, only to be recognised by the relative size of issue by either company. (Recall, however, that the accounting for these two different types of transactions is significantly different. If it is important for the acquiror to use one of these two presentations – either merger or acquisition – in their accounts, the appropriate structure must be selected at this point.)

The dilution on equity effect of acquiring a company for shares may be one of the most pronounced effects of a share offer, usually more so than an outright purchase with cash.

2 Cash-for-shares

Generally, acquisitions which do not involve the issue of shares by the acquiring company are deemed to be some form of cash acquisition. This is the case even when actual cash is not paid; wherever the target shareholder receives no form of equity interest in the purchaser, a transaction is deemed to be 'for cash'.

The tax implications of the cash-for-share transaction are important. The US tax authorities hold to the premise that a sale of shares is taxable. The difference between the purchase price and the selling price indicates either a capital gain or loss.

Regardless of the tax concerns for the target shareholders, acquisition of a company with cash consideration often places a strain on the acquiror's liquidity. It is quite possible to defer cash payments in order to relieve some of the initial burden, but ultimately the cash will have to be paid. The specific concerns relating to the use of cash or cash-related financial instruments are addressed below:

I SHORT-TERM LIQUIDITY
Typically, cash offers require that payment be made on a fixed date and under agreed conditions. Failure to complete on the agreed date usually carries heavy consequences. A large immediate cash payment can cause a drain on the purchaser's cash reserves or its balance sheet.

II MEDIUM/LONG-TERM LIQUIDITY
Unfortunately, some companies never recover completely from an extensive cash depletion. Therefore, many companies examine pay-back periods or cash pay-back rates in determining the total amounts of cash which can be offered and then can be recovered from the ongoing operation of the acquired entity. The consideration offered is structured to try to pay out in step with the influx of cash from operation of the acquisition.

III EXPOSURE TO FOREIGN EXCHANGE FLUCTUATIONS
To avoid the risk of the purchase price increasing due to exchange fluctuations, any funds paid in dollars should be either: (a) held locally in the US; (b) converted into dollars at a specified date to fix the sterling acquisition cost; or (c) hedged with forward foreign currency purchase contracts if the funds are held in the UK.

IV BANK BORROWING – LOCALLY
Foreign acquirors are best advised to consider borrowing locally for short-term lines of credit. In the medium- to long-term, where the need to consider potential currency exposure looms large, it is necessary for international investors to match prudently assets and liabilities. Furthermore, as discussed in Chapter 3, borrowings in the US by a US holding company may provide tax advantages.

3 *Acquisitions of assets (cash or shares for assets)*

The acquisition of assets rather than shares, as discussed previously, gives certain ongoing tax advantages to an acquiror, and certain legal disadvantages, in terms of contingent liabilities, to the seller. Otherwise, however, acquisitions of assets for cash have the same implications as those discussed above; acquisitions of assets for shares is discussed at the end of the 'non-taxable combinations' section of this chapter.

4 *Tender offers*

A tender offer is a simple offer to purchase (for cash, shares, or other property) the shares of a 'target' company. In general, the term 'tender offer' applies only to those deals involving the purchase of a publicly traded company, and not privately held entities. It covers any one of the types of offers discussed above.

Analysis of the forms of offers

Any combination is either tax-free – in which case it must be a qualifying share for share (or shares for assets) transaction – or taxable – a purchase of assets or shares for cash or cash instruments. These two general categories are discussed below to review the advantages and disadvantages of their various permutations.

Taxable combinations

Taxable combinations include the purchase of the shares or the assets of the target company for cash, debt, shares or any mixture of the three. The basic tax issues to be considered in a taxable combination are:

- the extent to which the acquired company will incur a corporate income tax;
- the tax treatments available to the acquired company's shareholders and whether any recognised gain is ordinary or capital and taxed currently, or deferred through the instalment sale provisions; and
- the tax basis of the acquired properties in the hands of the acquiring corporation.

The resolution of each of these issues may depend ultimately on whether the taxable combination is structured as a purchase of shares or a purchase of assets.

TRANSACTIONS TO BUY SHARES

BUYER'S CONSIDERATIONS
In a purchase of shares, the buyer acquires an existing company complete with all of its liabilities, known and unknown. This factor alone is a strong motivation for the buyer to cast the transaction in the form of an asset acquisition. However, a purchase of shares is far easier in terms of legal documentation and requirements. Because of the procedural advantages offered by purchasing the entire company rather than its parts, buyers have normally swallowed this risk to be able to step into the seller's shoes. Also, because the seller has the parallel advantage from a share sale – no contingent liabilities – an offer for assets can

be less acceptable. This is particularly true where the seller is seeking realisation of his or her capital.

SELLER'S CONSIDERATIONS
As a general rule, the seller of shares enjoys numerous tax advantages when compared to the seller of the assets.

- Gain realised on the sale or exchange is generally treated as a capital gain.
- Avoidance of recapture items (eg the amount of gain on the sale of depreciable property which represents depreciation charges previously taken for tax purposes).
- Simplicity in transfer.

Thus, in the majority of cases, the seller will be strongly motivated to sell shares instead of assets. The purchaser would normally not be able to overcome the seller's strong inclination in this direction.

TRANSACTIONS TO PURCHASE ASSETS

BUYER'S CONSIDERATIONS
In such a transaction, the allocation of purchase price among the assets is a critical element. The buyer seeks the highest possible allocation to stock (inventory) and depreciable assets which will reduce income from inventory sales and increase future depreciation deductions. (This is because depreciation and cost of sales reduce taxable income, while goodwill and its amortisation are not tax deductible expenses.) Also, the buyer will seek an allocation to debtors of at least face value in order to avoid generating a taxable gain upon collection. The seller, in turn, seeks the highest possible allocation to capital-type items (eg goodwill). These often conflicting objectives and the inherent complexity in transferring assets make asset transactions time-consuming and expensive.

Previously, capital gains were taxed at a lower rate than ordinary income. This was the strongest incentive for the seller to seek to classify the sale as being of a capital nature. The Tax Reform Act of 1986 eliminated the rate differential between ordinary income and capital gains, so it is no longer possible to have general guidelines as to the preferability of capital or ordinary treatment for any income on the sale. Instead, the circumstances of the seller will dictate his or her preferences. For example, corporations can only utilise capital losses to offset capital gains and not ordinary income. Furthermore, capital losses can be carried forward for no more than five years. Therefore, if the seller is a corporation with capital loss carryforwards, it will have a strong incentive to try to classify the income from the sale as capital in nature.

The tax attributes (eg net operating loss carryover) of the acquired company in a taxable asset purchase do not carry over to the buyer.

SELLER'S CONSIDERATIONS
In addition to the process of allocating the purchase price among the assets, the seller of assets faces other decisions which could materially affect the tax liability.

One of the considerations for a seller of assets is the new requirement under the Tax Reform Act of 1986 for the buyer and seller of assets to make the same allocation of purchase price to the assets sold. As discussed in Chapter 3, this may be written into the purchase agreement; each party must also file a report to notify the IRS of its allocations. As the objectives of the seller and buyer may be at odds in the allocation process, this requirement may make assets sales less attractive, or at least more complex.

CASH MERGERS

The cash (taxable) merger technique (as an alternative to a direct taxable acquisition of shares or assets) provides a distinct advantage for acquiring complete control of a target company, since under state law the interests of the selling shareholders are automatically extinguished in accordance with the terms of the merger. In a cash merger, the acquiring company forms a subsidiary and transfers to it the consideration to be used in the acquisition, eg cash, notes, or other non-share consideration. The acquired company is then either merged into the new subsidiary ('forward cash merger') or the new subsidiary merges into the acquired company ('reverse cash merger'). In either case, the shareholders of the acquired company exchange their shares for the cash, notes, or other non-share consideration furnished by the parent.

The direction of a cash merger transaction generally determines whether it is deemed a share or asset acquisition. A reverse cash merger is treated as a purchase of the acquired company's shares, and a forward cash merger is treated as a purchase of the acquired company's assets.

FUNDING OF TAXABLE ACQUISITIONS

The choice to structure a business combination as a taxable transaction is only the first step in the decision-making process. The tax consequences vary depending upon the types of consideration used in the transaction. Two types of consideration (other than cash) are discussed below.

DEBENTURES

The use of debentures of the acquiring company may offer the seller the advantage of electing the instalment method for recognition of gain. The instalment method is not allowable, however, if the debenture is payable on demand or readily tradeable on an established market. The instalment method also may not be used with respect to the disposition of shares which are traded on an established securities market.

The instalment method allows the seller to recognise gains (taxable profits) in proportion to the amount collected to the total proceeds to be received. This will spread the recognition and settlement of the tax liability over the life of the debenture. Interest incurred by the buyer and received by the seller is deductible and taxable, respectively, in the period in which it is recognised (accrued for an accrual basis taxpayer, received for a cash basis taxpayer).

If convertible debentures are issued by the acquiring company, two important tax issues may arise. First, under complex debt/equity classification criteria, the convertible debentures may be classified as share capital if the convertible debentures have more of the aspects of shares than debt. Such a classification would eliminate the tax deductions for interest expense on such instruments and would eliminate the seller's instalment sale election. Secondly, if the convertible debentures are debt for tax purposes, the interest deductions on such instruments may be disallowed if the acquiring company runs afoul of complex 'corporate acquisition indebtedness' rules. These rules are designed to limit interest deductions on financing for certain leveraged corporate takeovers. Interest incurred on 'corporate acquisition indebtedness' is disallowed as a deduction to the extent the interest exceeds $5 million per year.

WARRANTS

Debentures with detachable warrants may be issued with an interest rate lower than that of a 'normal' debenture because of the value attributed to the warrant. Any value attributable to the warrant is taxable to the seller as proceeds of a sale in the year of receipt. If the warrantholders allow the warrants to lapse without exercise, the lapse of the warrants may result in taxable income to the acquiring company equal to the value of the warrants on the date of issuance (ie the value if forfeited and therefore 'contributed' to the entity). Moreover, if either the debentures or the shares for which the warrants are issued are traded on an 'established securities market', original issue discount deductions can arise to the extent of the issue price allocatable to the warrants and therefore deducted from face value. This rule does not apply to the conversion feature of convertible debt.

Tax-free business combinations

In practice, the tax-free business combination is a rare occurrence. Nevertheless, it is important to understand the characteristics of this type of transaction to ensure a clear understanding of the various options available to acquirors. Assuming the parties agree to structure a tax-free business combination, close attention should be directed to the statutory requirements of such transactions. There are three primary combination methods which qualify for tax-free status:

- statutory mergers or consolidations;
- qualifying share-for-share transactions; and
- qualifying share-for-assets transactions.

Each of the above categories has its own special requirements. In addition, the courts have fashioned three fundamental principles of tax-free combinations designed to prevent the provisions from being used to undermine the taxation of corporate earnings upon distribution to shareholders. These three judicial doctrines are discussed briefly below.

BONA FIDE PURPOSE

A tax-free business combination must have a bona fide business purpose other than the avoidance of tax. Generally, if a transaction's only purpose is the avoidance of tax, it will be regarded as a 'sham' and treated as a taxable transaction.

CONTINUITY OF SHAREHOLDER INTEREST AND BUSINESS ENTERPRISE

The continuity of shareholder interest requirement provides that the shareholders of the acquired company must have a continuing equity interest in the acquiring corporation. As discussed in the following section, this requirement is generally subsumed by the fact that the acquiring corporation must use shares as consideration in the transaction.

CONSIDERATION OF ALL RELATED TRANSACTIONS

A taxable combination can not be artifically broken down into two or more components to qualify for non-taxable status. Specifically, the courts and the IRS have often applied the provisions of the 'step transaction doctrine' whereby two prearranged steps or transactions will be collapsed and treated as part of a single transaction. Generally, three overlapping factors are considered in determining whether to apply the step transaction doctrine: (1) lapse of time between two steps; (2) parties' intent; and (3) the interdependence of the steps. For example, a share-for-share acquisition immediately followed by the complete liquidation of the acquired company will be tested under the share-for-asset rules. Such recasting of the transaction may be fatal to tax-free status. Thus, it is critically important to determine when a transaction 'begins' and when a transaction 'ends' for tax purposes.

Payment of consideration

Last, there are timing considerations in structuring the payment of consideration. A dollar or a pound today is worth more than one a year from today. Also, if the promise to pay a year from today is in the form of a note, a seller takes on a credit risk. In return, the seller may ask for collateral or some sort of security: either the shares of the company being sold, or the underlying assets. The latter is preferable to the seller because the seller becomes a creditor of the acquired company itself; when a seller receives shares as security he or she stands in the shoes of shareholders.

There are only limited benefits to the purchaser from borrowing from the seller as opposed to borrowing from a bank or other financial institution. In either case, interest on the debt instrument should qualify as a tax deductible expense. The possible benefits may be more favourable terms (eg rate, repayment schedule, less restrictive covenants). The advantages to the seller of deferred compensation arise when they are tied to future performance through some kind of contingency or earn out agreement.

In many cases, purchasers may seek to bridge the gap between the seller's asking price and what the buyer is willing to pay through an agreement on a contingent payout. In this case, a further amount will be paid based on future earnings, achieving target financial ratios etc. These agreements are particularly valuable in circumstances where the seller is going to remain in place as a key member of management, and the purchaser feels a need to provide a strong incentive for continued effort. In this circumstance, the contingent payout can be structured as a hybrid purchase agreement/employment contract, but one with a distinct advantage: any additional sums payable would be classified as purchase price rather than compensation. Therefore, they are part of the investment in the acquired subsidiary and not period expenses subsequent to the acquisition. Of course, any contingency agreements with former owners based on their continued involvement must be carefully structured to ascertain that they will be considered contingent purchase price amounts, and not compensation. This type of structure does, however, mean that such payments are not currently deductible for tax purposes but rather form part of the basis in the investment.

There is a wide range for the ratio of contingent payments to the initial purchase price. Usually the fixed amount will be two thirds or more of the total possible price, although in service industries the contingent payment might be equal to the original agreed amount. The conditions are usually set based on targeted pretax income levels, and generally do not exceed periods of three years beyond the purchase date.

A concern when using contingent payouts is the inherent risk that companies will then be managed with an eye to maximising short-term profits rather than long-term gains; be careful of agreeing to pay out too high a proportion of post-acquisition income. Contingent payments should be used more to bridge gaps between the highest price the purchaser is comfortable with based on the current performance and the maximum the purchaser is willing to pay if certain potential improvements are realised.

CHAPTER 11

The negotiation process

All of the accumulated impressions and analyses pertaining to the acquisition candidate and its principals will come to the fore during the negotiation process. Negotiating the agreement is critical. An initial proposal for the acquisition is usually put forward during the early stages; this type of proposal, however, is normally based on preliminary information stated in the broadest and most flexible terms. The purpose of the initial proposal is merely to provide a starting basis for negotiations and will understandably require numerous changes as additional information is obtained.

As the acquiror begins the negotiation process for an acquisition, there are certain techniques and tactics which should be kept in mind. These, along with standard business protocol, provide a means of promoting favourable and reasonable negotiations.

First, the acquiring company must know its own position as well as that of the target. Through investigations, analyses, and evaluations the acquiror has gained valuable knowledge and a clear understanding of the target. Both parties to the negotiations should outline and prioritise expectations and objectives, in order to structure the most amiable deal possible. Furthermore, by understanding the company to be acquired – its objectives, goals, and concerns – the investor helps lay the groundwork for later compromises.

A second point acquirors should remember is the importance of common ground and compromise. While both parties seek to reach an agreement which is mutually beneficial, there is always a need for some 'give and take'. It is important for participants on both sides of the table to understand that some things must go the other party's way. A very effective method often used is for each party to establish its own priorities privately for each objective and then agree time limits for individual negotiating sessions. Each party then gets an equal amount of time to raise its priority objectives, thereby preventing any one party or topic from dominating the meeting.

A third point, virtually overlooked in some acquisition negotiations, is the need for both negotiating parties to maintain a pleasant attitude. There is an art in negotiating and it is always helpful that there remain a degree of levity. In the best situations, good attitudes are a welcomed part of the process; in the most tense sessions, levity can bring some much needed relief to the table.

Along with an element of levity, both parties should recognise the other's successes and achievements. A little flattery never hurt any negotiating process, but buyer and seller should not let this tactic get out of hand, less intentions and sincerity are questioned. Practically speaking, if both parties are serious about closing the deal, reasonableness and sincerity will prevail.

A final technique to be incorporated in the negotiating process concerns the importance of honesty. Both companies must be prepared to disclose key matters and reveal all material facts pertaining to their businesses. A reluctance to be candid may damage the negotiations or lead to unnecessarily strong emotions at a later time. Considering also that some of the news may not be welcomed, parties should time their disclosure carefully – but they should disclose! The sense of honesty and sincerity which emerges from frankness may advance the entire closing procedure and the relationships that will continue after the closing.

Legal documents relating to the acquisition

Legal documentation for an acquisition is, for the most part, straightforward. Once the basic terms have been agreed upon, parties often execute a 'letter of intent', known in the UK as 'heads of agreement', in the early stages of discussion. The use of a letter of intent, however, is less popular as a result of the decision in the Texaco/Pennzoil litigation in Texas. The contents and scope of a letter of intent range from a simple paragraph to an extensively negotiated document; however, a few provisions are common. The letter of intent will set forth, in general terms, what is being purchased, by whom and at what price. If it is a purchase of assets, it is likely to touch upon the extent to which liabilities will be assumed. Key issues of concern are often highlighted. These provisions, for the most part, are non-binding statements of intentions and understanding. The purpose of a letter of intent is to focus on the key issues and to provide a framework for consummating the transaction. It contemplates that the deal may not happen and that further issues may arise. Such letters generally contain a date upon which, if the deal is not consummated, the letter of intent expires. By virtue of its non-binding effect, parties are generally more willing to establish the framework and narrow the issues.

The structure of such a letter varies widely, but generally the following points are mentioned:

- structure of the deal – buyer, seller, and what is being sold (shares or assets);
- intended form of consideration – (approximate) amount and form (cash, shares, loan notes, etc.);
- method of payment for determining the amount: eg p/e ratio, premium over book etc., so that the basis for adjustments is clearly stated;
- timing for closing the deal, or end of negotiating;
- necessary steps required for consummating the transaction;
- accounting and tax objectives for each party;
- executive contracts (may include a non-competitive agreement); and
- assumption or payment by the buyer of the seller's debt.

The letter of intent also protects the negotiation process by restricting publicity and imposing confidentiality requirements. Often, the potential seller is prohibited from soliciting competing offers and meeting with other prospective purchasers. These provisions generally are legally binding.

As discussed earlier, a confidentiality agreement usually precedes the exchange of any detailed financial information, or other proprietary material. This type of agreement governs not only the disclosures made prior to the closing but also the treatment of and access to documents during the negotiations. A confidentiality agreement should state that all documents will be returned promptly to the appropriate party in the event the transaction is not consummated for any reason.

The purchase agreement is the primary and most important document of an acquisition. It identifies, and is executed by, each party to the transaction, sets forth what is being purchased, the aggregate consideration to be paid and the form and manner of payment thereof. The purchase agreement will also express the conditions, if any, which must be satisfied before a party has the obligation to consummate the transaction as well as any contingencies in the purchase price.

The purchase agreement is generally drafted by buyer's counsel and contains representations and warranties by the seller. Sometimes a seller will offer to draft the contract; in that way, the seller's counsel can initially limit the various representations and warranties, a situation which then requires the buyer to negotiate for items not included. Obviously the reverse applies when the buyer's counsel drafts the initial agreement. Representations and warranties embody the assumptions made by a buyer in deciding to proceed with the transaction. They elicit material information from the seller and, depending on their contents and/or the seller's reaction to being asked to make them, may serve as the basis for a disappointed buyer's pre-closing rejection or post-closing rescission or damage claim against the seller. The buyer will require verification of all major assumptions leading to the decision to purchase. Common representations include statements as to the title and condition of significant assets, the status of significant contracts, patents, trademarks and licences, the validity of financial information provided by the seller, compliance with statutes and regulations, the absence of significant pending or threatened litigation, the presence of hazardous substances and the absence of material adverse change in the financial or operating condition of the company.

The purchase agreement will also include covenants by the seller to take some affirmative act or to refrain from certain material actions. Typical covenants protect the assets and the business that is being acquired from certain actions of the seller prior to closing. Some very significant covenants which may be required are those prohibiting post-closing competition by the seller for some reasonable period of time or promising best efforts to obtain some result post-closing, such as a necessary consent or a required name-change. Purchase agreements will often contain a 'catch-all' covenant that provides that each party will take reasonable necessary steps after the closing to effect the transactions contemplated by the agreement.

Buyers also make limited representations and warranties in the purchase agreement, as well as covenants in some situations, although to a much lesser extent than sellers. Generally the buyer must represent that it is authorised to consummate the transaction, that required consents, if any, have been obtained and that there is no pending litigation which might prohibit consummation. If the buyer is giving securities as part of the purchase price, it must make certain representations about the due authorisation and validity of those securities as well as about the financial condition of the issuer of such securities.

Typically, each party to the purchase agreement agrees to indemnify the other for any loss incurred as a result of a misrepresentation or failure to perform a covenant. Indemnification provisions are rare in the context of an acquisition of a public company since the shares are widely held and no effective means of enforcing the indemnification provisions exist. The indemnification section usually sets forth the procedures to be followed in the event an indemnifiable claim is asserted by a party. Depending on the size of the deal, the indemnification provision may contain a 'cap' on indemnity and/or a 'basket' for indemnification. The cap is the maximum amount an indemnifying party can be required to pay. In the case of sellers, the cap could be as much as the purchase price although the seller will always argue for a much lower amount. A basket provides that the indemnity pay-out will not begin until the amount reaches a certain minimum. The basket recognises that the indemnity provision is designed to protect the parties against significant monetary losses. Once the minimum amount is reached, the indemnified party may be eligible either for all amounts thereafter (up to the cap, if any) or may be eligible to collect all prior amounts incurred (which will be the equivalent of the basket). The indemnification provision should clarify the type of basket contemplated.

Several other documents may be relevant to a particular acquisition. For example, an acquiring party which is purchasing some but not all of the shares of a company may desire that a shareholders' agreement be executed by each party who is to be a shareholder after the acquisition. Shareholders' agreements may contain provisions that restrict the sale of such shares as well as agreements to vote one's shares for the election of another shareholder's nominees to the board. Additionally, a party that accepts shares of the buyer as consideration for a transaction may request future 'registration rights'. Common forms of registration rights agreements provide for 'demand' registration rights and/or 'piggyback' registration rights. A demand registration right permits the holder of shares to compel the company to register such shares with the SEC so that they may be sold to the public in compliance with SEC rules and regulations. Piggyback registrations occur when the company proposes to register its securities with the SEC for sale in a public offering. In such an event, the party to the piggyback rights agreement has the option of requiring the company to include his or her shares along with the company's in the registration statement filed with the SEC so that they may be sold to the public in compliance with applicable rules and regulations.

Finally, existing management is often seen as a key to the company's success or has knowledge of the business far beyond that of any third party. Thus, the execution of employment contracts with key personnel is often a condition to the buyer's obligation to consummate the transaction.

Counsel's role in the acquisition process

Legal counsel in the United States often assumes a broad role in the acquisition process, including the evaluation of suitable target companies and suggesting the financial feasibility of alternative structures for the transaction. Local counsel for the buyer will help identify and resolve the various regulatory issues related to the acquisition, including the establishment of the purchase vehicle and obtaining requisite state qualifications to do business.

Aside from drafting and negotiating the terms of the documents described above (including the letter of intent, the purchase agreement and any necessary employment or consulting agreements), legal counsel will be most heavily involved in what, as an American term of art, has come to be known as the process of 'due diligence'. Due diligence is the process by which the buyer and its representatives (including lawyers and accountants) conduct a detailed review of the legal and financial affairs of the company. The process often reveals problems or potential problems that may not have been apparent at earlier stages of the transaction. The following is a partial list of steps usually taken by counsel during the buyer's due diligence.

- Financial information, material contracts and leases, litigation documents and tax returns are reviewed.
- Qualifications to do business are reviewed and, in particular states, the company's standing is ascertained.
- The company's charter and by-laws are reviewed for possible prohibitions to the deal and to identify the steps requisite to consummating the transaction. The charter and by-laws may contain anti-takeover provisions but usually this is the case only with publicly held companies. In any event, where a transaction is friendly, such 'barriers' are easily removed by the party in control of them.
- Shareholders' agreements are examined for restrictions on sales of stock. For example, shareholders in privately held companies often depend on each other if they want to liquidate (there is no public market for the sale) and such agreements usually grant rights of first refusal to the other shareholders.
- Debt instruments are examined for provisions allowing for acceleration upon a change in control of the company.
- Contracts and leases are reviewed for clauses which may require prior written consent for assignment.
- Employment agreements are reviewed for severance terms and other material provisions.
- Title documents are reviewed for significant assets.

The role of legal counsel will vary depending on the transaction. Frequently, counsel assumes responsibility for ensuring that the transaction process moves forward on schedule and reaches a timely conclusion. This role may involve arranging and leading negotiation sessions, applying for permits and tracking the progress of such applications, co-ordination and input of the comments of accountants and other participants and ensuring that all necessary documents are prepared, circulated, discussed and properly executed.

The role of the accountant in the acquisition process

It is likely that the acquiror's accountants will be actively involved in several aspects of the acquisition process. The buyer may elect to have the accounting firm assist with, or even lead, the search and/or evaluation process. Additionally, from the time a target is selected, a number of financial issues will have to be addressed, many of which require or can benefit from the input of the acquiror's accountants. Some of these issues are discussed below.

- *Tax planning and structure of the acquisition.* The economics of an acquisition can be significantly improved by proper tax planning in both the US and UK. As discussed in Chapters 3 and 10, the method through which the acquiror holds its investment has significant implications, as does the structure of the consideration. These items are not only intrinsically complex, but also constantly in a state of flux as tax laws change and court cases establish rulings and precedents.

- *Participation in analysis of the target.* It is typical that, as part of the final evaluations and negotiations, an in-depth investigation of the target be conducted, perhaps as part of the due diligence work. This type of work is known in the US as a businessman's review. This usually involves the accountants assisting in gathering information, making inquiries and analyses and issuing a report to the directors of the acquiror summarising their findings; this is often referred to in the UK as the 'long form' report. Additionally, it may be necessary for stock exchange or other reporting purposes to actually conduct an audit of the opening balance sheet or perhaps even a full scope audit as of the acquisition date. The investigation, while often conducted at the same time, is a separate exercise.

• *Reporting matters.* If the acquisition is significant to the buyer, and the buyer is a quoted company, it may be necessary to file certain reports with the Stock Exchange. The typical filing requirements are discussed in the UK company law section of Chapter 2. Class 1 circulars must include audited financial information about both the acquiror and the acquisition, and also certain pro forma statements which must be covered by a reporting accountants' report, the 'short form' report. It may also be necessary to include profit forecasts if a rights or other offering is being made to fund the acquisition. While these documents may be prepared by the company, the accountant must perform certain reviews and examinations to be able to make the required reports.

Conducting negotiations

The negotiation process is not restricted to formal sessions where representatives from both sides are attempting to put together a transaction; it includes all interchanges between the principals. Since the co-operation and goodwill of all parties will be required, it is important that all interchanges be on a candid and amiable basis. An important service that professionals, such as attorneys and accountants, can provide is to ask many of the difficult questions, push for the desired concessions, and deflect any hostility away from the principals. The formal negotiating session should be an arena where the professionals are the warriors and the principals interact only as friends. After all, it will be the principals who must agree to the transaction and who may ultimately need to work together on an ongoing basis if the transaction is consummated.

Usually, two parties do not sit down together to negotiate formally unless there is a basis for believing a deal can be struck. Therefore, it is typical to reach an understanding as to the key features of a likely agreement fairly rapidly. The first goal of the negotiations is usually to reach a broad understanding of the terms of the sale, which are usually set out in a letter of intent. This letter then serves as a basis for final negotiations. This will help prevent making promises to sellers that cannot be kept and will provide guidelines for determining whether acquisition discussions can proceed effectively. If, for example, the seller demands an all-cash transaction but the buyer is only willing to pay by offering shares, further discussions may be fruitless unless alternatives can be developed in the early stages of the negotiation process.

The importance of the acquiror recognising and understanding the needs of the seller cannot be over-emphasised. With all the time and effort that goes into building a company, the sale cannot merely be viewed as a financial transaction with no concern for those who will have their lives changed by the transaction. The seller, especially the seller of a private company, generally has invested much of him- or herself in the company, and draws much of his or her identity from a role in the organisation, especially where the company is an important part of the local economy. Tokens of esteem, such as a company car or a position on the board of directors of the acquiror, may be small concessions on behalf of the acquiror but may be important in reaching a successful agreement.

The transaction should be structured so it can be represented as being in the seller's best interests as well as the purchaser's. Driving a hard bargain can prove to be a mistake if it alienates a seller whose ongoing support is required in maintaining the business operations.

For successful acquisitions to occur, good negotiating posture mandates appearing flexible and reasonable – appearing natural has more than superficial importance. One of the primary objectives of negotiating is to create credibility. This is not done to mislead the other party, but rather to demonstrate sincerity and build a foundation of trust. Items identified in the investigation should provide support for points of contention, and mutual understanding of a negotiating rationale can prevent a breakdown of discussions due to emotional discord. Sound reasoning can facilitate compromise by making it apparent why certain provisions may be untenable to one party or the other.

Both the buyer's and seller's concepts for the transaction consist of interlocking separable parameters, which can be viewed both as bargaining chips and needs. They should be broken down into individual points or issues and prioritised as vital, moderately important, and giveaways. These points and their priority are to be kept extremely confidential since they are the basis for the negotiating posture. It is important to communicate which points are necessary – the 'vital' classification. If negotiations reach a stalemate, a strategic tradeoff of the less important points revitalises the deal and helps it regain momentum by creating an atmosphere of co-operation and flexibility, and thereby enabling negotiations to continue. If a particular point is too contentious, it makes sense to defer discussion on it until later. If negotiations proceed to a point where nearly every issue is resolved, the remaining obstacles may become far less important.

CHAPTER 12
Financing the acquisition

Background of information on the US banking system

When it comes to financing an investment, foreigners entering the US market are faced with some significant advantages not found in many other countries. The US banking system consists of approximately 14,500 banks chartered either under federal or state law and it also includes hundreds of institutional investors. The United States provides the largest capital market in the world. Although there are numerous financing sources available in the US, the commercial banks are most commonly used for funding in acquisitions. Therefore, foreign acquirors would be wise to take advantage of the highly competitive banking environment and talk with a number of institutions to obtain the most advantageous arrangements. Generally, when financing business transactions in the US foreign investors may find that loans are priced relatively cheaper in the US than in most foreign markets. Recently, the prime rate in the US (the rate which banks lend to their most favoured customers) has been 2.9 percentage points lower than in the UK. When loan rates are tied to LIBOR (London Interbank Offer Rate) as they increasingly are, the spread above LIBOR is lower in the US than in the UK.

Financing the acquisition

As foreign acquirors initiate the financing process, they must first assess their desire and ability to obtain financing in the United States, and decide if that is preferable to obtaining their financing in the UK. There are no restrictions in the US on access to financing for foreign investors; therefore it is possible for companies with adequate credit ratings to finance the entire US acquisition from US sources, although this alternative may not be attractive for various business or tax reasons.

Before securing any form of financing for a US acquisition it is advisable to look at various factors which affect the financing package. The relative importance of the following considerations varies from acquisition to acquisition. Nevertheless, the acquiring company should weigh these factors in their financing decision:

- size of acquisition;
- level of interest rates;
- foreign exchange exposure;
- tax considerations;
- existing bank relationships;
- plans for future growth (and capital requirements);
- cash position;
- target company's cash flow;

- access to capital markets; and
- strength of target's asset base.

Within this broad list of points, assorted options for financing are possible, which often include some combination of debt, equity and available cash. Some acquirors engaging in relatively small acquisitions may choose the simplest form of financing – that is, the use of its own cash, a decision which is a function of liquidity, cost of capital, foreign exchange risk and the size of the deal.

In addition to the above considerations, the foreign investor is well advised to consider a few questions which influence the structure of the package. The most desirable structure reflects an evaluation of taxation, interest rates, exchange rates, securities legislation and any applicable foreign exchange controls. Since choosing a particular financing method is a complex process which attempts to balance key factors, investors are advised to address the following questions.

- *What is the earnings impact of the acquisition?* Since one of the key factors behind acquisitions is the desire to improve long-term financial results, acquirors should investigate two types of financial projections. One is the future growth potential of the target, and the other is an analysis of how the different financing methods might affect the operating results of the combined entity.

- *What form of financing will best complement the target's short-term operating performance?* This question requires a look into the industry's short- to medium-term projections as well as the actual target's projections. For instance, an exchange of shares might be appropriate if the target company requires substantial short-term capital investment; a cash transaction may be more suitable if the target is able to generate large short-term cash flows.

It is important for foreign acquirors to investigate the various financing alternatives available to them in the US market. In general, the US capital markets may be broken down into the following broad categories:

- commercial bank financing;
- public debt and equity financing;
- private debt and equity financing;
- private-activity financing;
- long-term leasing; and
- commercial financing.

This list of categories may highlight opportunities sometimes overlooked by inexperienced acquirors. One advantage of securing finance in the US market is the ability to tailor the financing to meet specific needs; the various securities within these categories offer financing flexibility often needed by the foreign acquiror.

The most popular and practical forms of US financing for foreign investors include commercial bank financing, debt financing (particularly privately placed debt), commercial loans, industrial revenue bonds and leasing arrangements. Typically, private and public debt and equity markets are long-term, and commercial banking, commercial finance, commercial paper and leasing are medium- and short-term. It should be noted, however, that commercial institutions are usually responsible for short- to medium-term financing, whereas long-term lending is handled by investment banking firms acting as agents with institutional investors. (Recently, however, this situation has changed; commercial banks have begun operating as agents in the private debt and equity markets.) This separation of responsibilities differs from some European countries in which all capital requirements are handled by full service banks.

Short- and medium-term financing – commercial banks

Foreign acquirors with a strong credit standing will have an array of commercial banking institutions available to them for short- and medium-term financing. In some cases, the US commercial banks extend loans for many business purposes, including acquisitions, to US-based operations of foreign companies, especially with a guarantee from the parent. Usually, in these financings they may establish restrictive covenants and/or ask for liens on the assets of the subsidiary.

Commercial banks in the US often offer short-term credit in the form of a 'line of credit'. This arrangement provides a commitment by the bank to allow amounts of money to be drawn (up to a specified limit) by the particular company assuming that no deterioration in the company's financial condition has occurred. This form of lending is subject to short-term repayment and may require payment of a commitment fee. A line of credit may also be subject to the bank's power of cancellation at any point, or may require a specific deposit equal to a set percentage of the credit line to remain within the bank.

Typically, there are two forms of credit lines – those extended on an advance basis and those granted on an acceptance basis. A line of credit in the form of a straight advance offers the company the opportunity to borrow on demand with fixed maturities. Credit on the acceptance basis is typically used for identifiable transactions only. Instead of issuing funds to the company, the bank pays a draft to the selected customer up to a set amount. For the bank, the acceptance credit is a safer risk, but since only identified transactions are involved it is used less frequently than the advance credit line.

Generally, US banks receive an up-front fee for guaranteeing to make a line of credit available for a fixed period of time. The terms of the agreement then specify the interest to be charged on any agreements, usually expressed as a spread over a variable benchmark rate (ie LIBOR or prime). Additionally, a fee is paid on the unused portion of the line of credit, typically on the order of a fraction of one per cent of unused amounts. Commercial banks also offer secured and unsecured term loans for acquirors. In granting these loans, the bank examines such items as present and projected profitability of the company, long-range prospects for the company and the industry and the company's ability to generate cash. Often set for terms of one to five years, the term loans may require a semi-annual payment scheme. The assigned interest rates may depend on factors such as company credit standing and the company's relationship with the banking institution. Today, even these loans tend to have variable rates.

Like the term loans, lines of revolving credit can provide financing for one to five years. In essence, the company borrows, pays, and re-borrows up to a ceiling amount set by the bank. The revolving credit arrangement stipulates maturity, interest rate and assigned collateral. In many cases, this type of credit may be re-negotiated into a term loan.

Another form of financing commonly used in the early stages of a foreign investment in the US is medium-term financing. This method of financing usually extends for periods from three to seven years and may require more negotiation or company requirements than short-term financing. Generally, the interest rate associated with medium-term loans is fixed in relation to the floating US prime rate but the actual rate may be influenced by the disbursement and repayment scheme of the loan. This type of financing arrangement is extremely flexible in order to meet the characteristics and needs of a company's particular situation rather than forcing it into a standardised format. Often the bank may demand certain operating criteria for extending revolving credit to a company with various restrictions.

If there is a possibility of entering the US capital market, certain important characteristics of the environment should be understood by foreign investors. For example, debt placed 'privately' (unquoted), usually with institutional investors, may be arranged for as little as $1 million, but public offerings are seldom made for under $20 million. Foreign borrowers' interest rates for debt facilities in the US are dependent on numerous factors. Historically, however, private debt financing has had interest rates averaging between 25 to 100 basis points (.25 per cent – 1.0 per cent) higher than similar public offerings.

Private fund raising (bank loans, private placements) does not impose public disclosure requirements on borrowers. However, certain requirements of the lender as to the financial condition of the borrower are set out in (lengthy) loan covenants which form part of the loan agreement. If any of these requirements is not met as specified in the agreement, the loan goes into default – if the violation is minor, the situation is usually called 'technical default'. This can be important since many US debt agreements have cross default clauses: if the borrower goes into default on any of its loan agreements, it automatically triggers the others into default. Since having a loan in default allows a lender to renegotiate terms or move to claim any security, great care must be paid to understanding and complying with all loan covenant requirements. Typical examples include limitations on the payment of dividends, the sale (or pledging) of assets, incurring additional debt and requirements to maintain certain financial ratios. In essence, this merely requires the practical and prudent financial management normally practised in business operations.

Debt financing obtained from private placements or bank loans usually specifies its claim on assets, and indicates to which other debt it has senior claims and junior (subordinated) claims. Such rights may be indicated in the title – eg, $10\frac{1}{2}$ per cent subordinated debentures due 1992; 12 per cent sinking fund preferred shares, etc. (Sinking fund refers to the requirement to redeem, or place aside funds for future redemption of, a fixed principal amount in certain specified years over the life of the debt so that the principal is amortised over the term of the debt.)

Private placements can be used to raise debt or equity, or the hybrid preferred shares. This preference share capital usually has fixed percentage dividends, which can be cumulative or not, and may have mandatory redemption dates. Other variations include convertible preferred shares, or debt with warrants to purchase shares.

Private-activity financing – state or local governments

Previously named 'industrial revenue (or development) bonds', private-activity bonds are issued by state or local governments. These obligations are used to finance non-governmental activities and the interest payments received by lenders are often exempt from federal taxation. Tax exempt status is granted if payments from a non-government person total more than 10 per cent of the principal or interest to be paid, or if a non-government person uses more than 10 per cent of the bond proceeds in a trade or business. This form of financing is limited under federal law to $10 million per issue for one company in a specified location.

Since certain procedures exist which determine whether these types of bonds may be used for financing acquisitions and the requirements vary from state to state and sometimes county to county, it is advisable for investors to refer questions about this type of financing to professionals in the local area.

Financing through leasing

Long-term leasing is available in the US from various institutions including leasing companies, manufacturers, commercial banks and commercial finance companies. A form of secured lending, leasing requires little or no initial cash investment and may often be arranged for longer periods than many bank loans. Items typically leased include: equipment, office furniture and equipment and automobiles and aircraft.

Commercial financing

Commercial finance companies are a major source of secured financing in the United States. The financing is commonly secured by stock (inventory), debtors (accounts receivable), fixed assets, real estate or other assets. Commercial finance loans are another form of financing for those companies having difficulty obtaining commercial bank loans. Since there are often greater risks and higher costs involved, commercial finance companies tend to charge rates higher than commercial banks, sometimes up to 600 basis points above the bank prime rate.

Recently, many international acquisitions have been financed using leveraging techniques. In this case, the acquiror finances the purchase of another company by securing a loan with the collateral resting in the assets of the company being acquired. The borrower must have a predictable cash flow (for primary repayment of the debt) and secondary repayment abilities such as strong asset coverage and quality management.

Commercial paper

Some larger US companies issue commercial paper – a short-term promissory note with maturities ranging up to 270 days. It is an unsecured source of financing sold by investment banking firms and is generally a cheaper form of short-term financing than bank loans. Some of the larger commercial paper dealers may attach a commission of one-fourth to one-eighth of one per cent of the face value of the paper. However, issuing commercial paper is generally a route available only to quite large well-known entities with an established US presence.

Employee stock ownership plans (ESOP)

Plans which allow for the opportunity for employees and management to purchase equity in the company are called Employee Stock Ownership Plans ('ESOPs') Differing from profit-sharing plans or pensions, the ESOP is required to invest its cash in the shares of the employer company. Recently, the ESOP has developed into a method of financing acquisitions using employee pension funds to provide equity. It is popular as a way to expand equity buyout participation to a larger pool of employees. This might be a source of financing if the buyer wishes, or is willing, to share ownership with the employees. However, issues have developed such as who votes to ESOP shares held on trust etc. Since this is an extremely complex form of financing, it is best that acquirors seek professional assistance when contemplating an ESOP financing.

Part 4
Post-Acquisition Concerns

CHAPTER 13
Making the transaction work

Introduction

After the transaction has been closed, the work for the acquiror is far from complete. The immediate period following the acquisition is crucial for the ultimate success of the deal and acquiring management is wise not to neglect the post-acquisition stages. Companies should begin to consider this important phase of integration during the planning and negotiation processes, but unfortunately most acquirors disregard its importance. For example, during the planning and negotiating process, the foreign acquiror should consult with an executive compensation specialist to ensure that the levels of compensation at the acquired company are adequate, as well as to identify any improvements which may be needed to help the acquiror obtain the maximum effort from the executives and employees of the acquired company. John E. Robson, former CEO of G. D. Searle Pharmaceutical Company, expressed his view on the post-acquisition stages in *Joining Forces*. The authors quote Robson as saying: 'I am a real believer in gold-plated transitions, whether in the government or the private sector. The importance of a carefully planned, well-executed transition effort, one that is done with sensitivity and an eye for detail, cannot be over-emphasized'.[1] Acquirors, especially across foreign borders, need to give adequate attention to the post-acquisition concerns because they could make or break the long-term success of the deal.

It must be remembered that no acquisition is merely a purchase of assets or an assumption of liabilities – rather, the deal includes a complex array of relationships, arrangements and expectations. Customers, suppliers, employees and management all come along with the closing of the deal, and it is up to acquiring management to create an environment where integration will succeed. J. G. Williams, in his booklet, *Acquisitions and Mergers*, indicates that:

> there is a natural presumption that the purchaser can retain such relationships as wished.... But this is a dangerous presumption: there are bound to be some losses – of customers who dealt with the acquired firm from personal loyalty to the vendor ... of senior staff who are, or imagine themselves to be, adversely affected. The task after acquisition is to minimise those losses....[2]

It is the purpose of this section to set forth guidelines which assist in making the post-acquisition period successful.

Acquisitions which have been failures for reasons other than basic business problems or unrelated to any discord seem to be typified by four weaknesses:

- lack of a thorough understanding of the company that is sold and of its potential;

1 Joseph E. McCann and Roderick Gilkey *Joining Forces: Creating and Managing Successful Mergers and Acquisitions*, © 1988, p 147. Reprinted by permission of Prentice Hall Inc, Englewood Cliffs, New Jersey.
2 J. G. Williams *Acquisitions and Mergers* p 22.

- inadequate analysis of the seller, including what is necessary to manage and to finance the business;
- lack of understanding of how the seller will fit into the buyer's business; and
- institution of changes before the buyer has a real understanding of what has made the seller successful.

A study of leading industrial companies, all of which have engaged in extensive acquisition programmes, concluded that three major factors gave rise to problems with acquired companies:

- they did not assess the quality and nature of the talent necessary to integrate the seller into the buyer;
- they did not assess and plan for the kinds and levels of management skills required; and
- they did not plan management and organisation relations.

The common thread in both of these lists seems to be poor or inadequate planning and communication. In order to improve the odds for success during the transition period, the acquiring company should clearly define its future role: silent, passive, or active. Ideally, this should be done during the evaluation and negotiation period. In addition, probably the most important subject on which the two parties should reach agreement is the strategy for the acquired business. Acquirors should outline where and how the target is to fit within the parent company's organisation, and what objectives and goals are expected. They should be ready and able to communicate the targets formulated in their strategy for acquisitions, discussed in Chapter 5.

The buyer also must be aware that dealing with the seller's management or its employees requires willingness to listen and communicate. This is one of the most crucial elements for the post-acquisition period, because if acquiring management fails to communicate effectively with the purchased company, the entire acquisition may fall short of its goals.

It is also essential for acquiring management to deal with any anxieties which may be generated by the transaction. Many of the parties involved with the acquisition could have very genuine concerns for the aftermath. Customers, suppliers and employees of both entities and the local community all have a stake in the success of the acquisition and may have some anxieties about the future. Here are a number of suggestions which may help eliminate these concerns.

First, it is critical for the managing director of the acquired company to inform employees on the day of the closing that the acquisition has actually taken place. Employees' opportunities and benefits resulting from the transaction should be outlined, along with a reassurance from the director that the acquisition is in the best interests of both companies.

Second, acquiring management should announce its corporate plans for the acquisition and how the company will continue to operate.

Third, the acquiring company needs to present an overview of itself to the key constituents of the acquired company, including the employees. A general description of its business, operations, financial position, company personnel and other non-financial elements such as what attracted the buyer to the purchase in the first place should also be included.

Fourth, a detailed transition plan prepared by the acquiror is needed to shelter the value of the acquisition during this critical period. It should cover the following points with regard to the 'people question'.

- *Promptly address the maintenance of personnel morale in order to retain the services of the people.* One possible step is to send a letter from the managing director of the buyer to all employees welcoming them as a part of a stronger, more profitable entity. The employees should be assured that it is the desire of the purchaser to enhance the operation of the seller, allowing it to grow and prosper. The director needs to create an open atmosphere by welcoming suggestions and comments from the personnel of the acquired company. One means which may encourage employees to offer comments is a telephone answer-line or some designated (local) source for information and suggestions. Employees then have the opportunity to make suggestions, comments, or to ask questions about the intentions of the acquiror or the future of the company without the fear of being criticised.

- *Acquirors should provide the employees of the acquired company with some background on itself and its objectives.* This information can do much to relieve uncertainty among the ranks as well as offer employees the chance to evaluate its new owner. As Shakespeare stated in *Henry VI*, 'Ignorance is the curse of God, knowledge the wing wherewith we fly'. Employees desperately want to know that job positions are secure and that their authority is not threatened. To avoid ignorance or misunderstanding, buyers should make them feel part of the newly enlarged team.

- *It would also be wise to hold informal meetings with employees of both entities present.* Again, explanations of the background of the buyer and plans for the continued success and growth of the seller should be emphasised. Indications of which, if any, employee benefits will be affected will be welcomed and appreciated by the employees. Furthermore, it is a good practice to communicate the highlights of these meetings in writing to all employees. This report could be presented in the form of a regular company newsletter, including, in addition to the meeting notes, updates of company developments.

- *Acquirors should schedule regular meetings with acquired management.* Key managers need to be informed about their authority, responsibilities and reporting relationships. It is important to make certain that what was discussed or agreed upon during the negotiations has not changed without prior discussions with them. Acquirors should allow the management of the newly purchased company time to learn any new procedures and to prepare for any scheduled meetings. An acquired executive's morale can be devastated if unprepared for a meeting with the new boss.

- *In addition to writing letters, acquirors need to meet with key customers, key suppliers, and key officials of labour organisations.* Arrangements should be made for the appropriate managers of both companies to visit these people. Not only will this serve to enhance goodwill, but also the buyer and the executives of the acquired company may learn of problems which presently exist or opportunities that can be developed. Joint letters from management of each entity can also be a useful follow-up to clarify any points raised during the meetings.

- *Meetings with local community representatives should be organised as soon as possible.* The local community is always worried when a significant change occurs in the environs. Local officials should be given the necessary assurance that it is the desire of the acquiror to be an upstanding and contributing citizen of the community.

- *Develop immediately a clear understanding of company rules.* No one likes surprises, especially in business, so the sooner rules, procedures, systems and employee benefits are clarified, the quicker uncertainties can be resolved. Acquirors need to set these items forth as soon as possible in order to clear any misunderstandings.

- *Finally, the acquiring management should schedule at least one gathering for key personnel from both entities during the first week following the closing.* A social setting would provide the most comfortable atmosphere, but a small element of formality should also be present. The managing director from each of the companies should present his or her view of the transaction, including the objectives, expectations, value of existing personnel and immediate plans for the companies. This will undoubtedly help assuage any anxieties concerning employment security or other important issues.

Although most people consider an acquisition to be a financial or business transaction, the buyer should be aware that the human aspect of acquisitions often determines the overall success of the deal. The buyer should attempt to preserve essential people, values, positions, titles and authority to make decisions where possible. In order to acquire without damaging this vital component of the business, the acquiror should possess patience, tact and the ability to communicate effectively. In most cases, the more successful acquirors have a strong vision of what they desire from the acquired company, have taken the time to study the acquiree's strengths and weaknesses and have a plan to maintain a post-acquisition dialogue with acquired management.

The buyer should differentiate between problems requiring immediate decisions or solutions and those of a more general nature which can be solved after additional experience is gained. This will give the acquiror more time to understand the entire business and its more subtle characteristics. When a decision has to be made, it should be made speedily but only after thorough analysis. Nothing creates more apprehension than knowing a decision is coming and waiting for it to arrive.

The newly combined companies must establish clear reporting relationships. The managing director of the acquired company should report to someone that he or she can respect and rely on to make appropriate decisions. If this executive feels that his or her recommendations cannot be implemented or approved, some personal concern will arise. This lack of confidence will cause tremors to spread quickly throughout the organisation and could possibly damage the integration process. If possible, individual relationships which have been established by the acquiror with the acquired company should continue. Nothing is more demoralising than to report to one person one week and another person the next.

One technique for preventing damaging assumptions or reporting tactics involves a liaison arrangement. A team of senior personnel from the purchaser should be organised to meet with their respective counterparts of the acquired company. Members should represent areas such as finance and accounting, marketing, production, and personnel. By utilising a liaison group effectively, many uncertainties are addressed and apprehensions could be diminished.

The enlarged group should ensure that it is pursuing realistic goals. It should smooth the path for a transfer of ideas and let the acquired management share in the goal-setting process. The more the acquired company's management is involved with this process, the greater the chance for success.

Acquirors should not be afraid to compliment acquired company achievements. People want to be appreciated and may resent a distant attitude on the part of the acquiror. Meetings with employees should be held on a frequent and regular basis throughout the transition stages so that any incorrect or harmful assumptions can be dispelled.

Americans tend to be more direct in their discussions, asking for things immediately if needed, rather than saying 'when you get a moment' when as soon as possible is meant. Both criticism and praise are more frequently and directly communicated and silence is not assumed to be an indication of approval.

CHAPTER 14
Motivation

Another aspect which needs to be addressed by acquiring management is motivating the acquired personnel. After the excitement of the closing has passed, the buyer may find need for additional motivation of the management of the newly purchased company. The main target for the initial approach should be the managing director of the company, because the outlook and mood set by the director may very well spill over into the other ranks.

There are different methods of motivation which may be effective, some of which have nothing to do with monetary incentive packages. (Obviously, do not minimise the monetary incentive packages. It is advisable to speak to a compensation specialist prior to the closing of the deal to prevent problems from arising after the transaction is complete due to an inadequate compensation scheme.) It is wise, therefore, for acquiring management to explore various options available for motivating personnel and to choose those elements which best fit the combined company. After all, it is the natural 'spark' and energy of the people within the company which often means the difference between success and failure of a business. The following provides a few suggestions for some means of continuing motivation.

- *Maintain existing corporate culture as much as possible.* Companies which successfully keep alive their own culture after an acquisition are more likely to continue to operate smoothly. In this respect, acquired companies must remain somewhat independent and have a clear view of what they expect and desire from the purchaser.

- *Outline expectations for personnel.* The acquiror should outline any objectives or expectations for the acquired company in a manageable timetable. Employees can operate more productively and quickly if they understand what is expected from them and how they will be reviewed.

- *Include personnel from the acquired company in normal corporate events.* Bringing together members from both entities as much as possible in events such as divisional competitions, social functions and departmental sports will contribute to corporate motivation. Through these functions the acquired company will begin to feel more like part of the company team. If distances will not allow frequent participation, acquired management should encourage the events to take place locally.

- *Arrange for senior executives of the acquired company to visit the purchaser's headquarters.* Although this may initially appear to be an extravagant process, it could have outstanding results. Senior managers of the buyer have taken the opportunity to examine the seller's company, and now the opportunity should be reversed. This will help the executives understand the rationale and background of the acquisition as well as provide an opportunity to visit the foreign acquiror's homeland. In addition, it should be noted that the spouses of these executives need to be included in this activity, because in many cases, if the spouse is won over, he or she can persuade the executive.

- *Enquire and put to use input from acquired management.* It is all well and good to ask opinions and suggestions in an acquisition transition, but if the information is never considered for actual implementation, the efforts are useless. Furthermore, if acquired personnel see their comments or suggestions never included in planning, a feeling of resentment may emerge.

Four principles play a vital role in any acquisition process:

- a clear definition of responsibility;
- unity – working together for greater results;
- security – planning the integration with a set timetable; and
- creativity – maintaining an environment where a sense of accomplishment can flourish.

Managements should unite to work together, to understand the lines of authority, to avoid making changes without first notifying each other and to use their creative talents toward achieving results.

Like the union of two people through courtship and marriage, the chances for a successful business acquisition will be much stronger if time, effort and communication between the parties takes place before the ceremony and continues afterward. The joining of two parties must be entered into with good, sound reason, for both alliances are complicated and long-lasting commitments. Each should be undertaken with a sense of 'what you see is largely what you get' so both parties are advised to look carefully at exactly what they are getting. Afterwards, what is required resembles closely what author Jane Austen suggested for a good marriage – a foundation of mutual respect, fellow feeling and common purpose, some self-restraint, a good helping of conversation, and more than a grain of humour. This will set the combination in place for future success.

Part 5
A Summary

CHAPTER 15
The problem areas

For year acquirors have been the focal point for harsh criticism and numerous suggestions when it comes to a deal that has failed to meet management's expectations or when the deal has failed to actually come to a close. No investor should assume that the worst will happen, but it is important to outline any potential problems which may arise. If a foreign acquiror, or a domestic acquiror for that matter, takes the time and effort to identify what may potentially go wrong in an acquisition, he or she may be able to compensate for problems, lessen harmful impacts, or avoid trouble altogether. For many acquirors there are ten areas which may detrimentally affect the transaction. Referred to as the 'ten plagues' or 'what can go wrong', the list may help acquirors approach the acquisition more effectively.

1 Poor strategic planning

Foreign acquirors should understand why they want to go abroad for an acquisition and what they hope to achieve. Once they understand what is wanted out of the acquisition, the company can find the one good business niche in which to invest. From that existing business the acquiror can grow into a stronger competitor.

2 Paying too much

The second area is obvious, but sometimes forgotten: do not pay too much! Acquirors should not be afraid to admit that a company is overpriced and walk away from the deal, even after they have completed extensive work.

3 Going too far afield

The successful companies 'stick to their own knitting', that is to say, they stay in businesses that they understand. Foreign acquirors especially are advised not to go too far outside their standard business in search of a target. Investors bring more to a business transaction when they actually understand the industry, because these investors can bring more than just money to the table. When investors know the business, they bring in marketing and manufacturing understanding and both managements can feel comfortable with each other. For instance, when one company makes a request, the other easily understands it.

4 Not taking enough time

The fourth plague is straightforward but often lies victim to the heat of the deal. If the acquiror performs an inadequate investigation, the company may wind up with problems. There is a quote which relates to this issue extremely well: 'Analysis is cheaper than companies'. Acquirors should conduct their analysis thoroughly.

5 Management

Companies succeed not solely because of their products but principally through the people who make the entire operation work. Unfortunately, that fact is quite often forgotten. One of the mistakes that most people make in an acquisition is that they expect management to remain, no matter what the outcome of the deal. In a recent survey of major US companies that were acquired in the last two years, senior executives indicated that 75 per cent expected to leave within three years, and that 47 per cent sought to leave within one year. These can be fairly disturbing figures for the foreign acquiror. Investors must understand what management is being obtained and what additional people may need to be brought in. Considerations such as adding people or bringing over people from the 'home' country should be included.

6 Different cultures

This does not mean the UK versus US cultural differences; it means dealing with people in different working environments. Different ways of running businesses can affect the outcome of the acquisition. Once a major food company acquired a blouse manufacturer and asked the acquired company to make a five-year inventory projection. The executive from the acquired entity said, 'I don't know whether next month we'll need silk, nylon, or another synthetic material.' The whole acquisition was a disaster for the food company, because of different business cultures.

7 Making changes too quickly

The last thing in the world that needs to be done is for acquiring management to come in, promise no change, and then demand that personnel do it in a different way. Rather than make changes for the sake of doing something, only make the changes as they are needed. And inform management of your plans beforehand.

8 Inadequate communication

Foreign acquirors cannot purchase a business, go back to their home country and hope that the monthly report will always keep them informed. Acquirors must make sure that communication lines are firmly established and in place, whatever they may be, and that the lines remain intact.

9 & 10 Foreign currency exposure and financing and remittance relationships

The last two areas deal with foreign currency exposure and financing remittance relationships. An acquiror has to make sure that if money is borrowed in one currency and investments are made in another, all the risks involved are understood. These are easy to take care of by proper hedging. Fortunately, there is not a problem in the United States of repatriating dividends. In addition, management of the acquired company must know the remittance requirements of its new parent. It must also know the availability, or lack thereof, of finance.

Appendices

Contents

US states' offices located in Europe and economic trade and development offices

1 US STATES' OFFICES LOCATED IN EUROPE

Telephone country codes
Belgium   32; France   33; Sweden   46; Switzerland   41; W. Germany   49

Note: these must be used in addition to the telephone and fax numbers shown below, which begin with the city code.

Alabama
Waisenhausplatz 14, 3011 Berne, Switzerland; *tel* (31) 229 536, *tlx* 911865 aido CH, *fx* (31) 210 275; Col. William Y. Pennington – Exec. Director

Arkansas
Avenue Louise 437 Bte 4, 1050 Brussels, Belgium; *tel* (2) 649 6024, *tlx* 62062 *fx* (2) 649 4807; Peter C. Armstrong – Managing Director, Sybille Magee – Director Trade & Industrial Development

California
14 Curzon Street, London W1Y 7FH, England; *tel* (1) 629 8211, *fx* (1) 629 8223; James R. Phillips – Managing Director, Ms Isabella Kaliszczak – Associate Director

Connecticut
Schuetzenstrasse 4, 6000 Frankfurt, W. Germany; *tel* (69) 282 055/6, *tlx* 416067 ctdoc D, *fx* (69) 283 801; Ms Ute Volger – Director Industrial Development, Donald C. Burdon – Director of Trade

Florida
David Kuhlmeier, Director of Economic Development, 18–24 Westbourne Grove, London W2 5RH, England; *tel* (1) 727 8388, *tlx* 295096 floda G., *fx* (1) 792–8633

Rue Armand Campenhout 63, 1050 Brussels, Belgium; *tel* (2) 537 2900, *fx* (2) 537 5938; Gunnar Beeth – Director Europe

Georgia
Avenue Louise 380, 1050 Brussels, Belgium; *tel* (2) 647 7825, *tlx* 29520 gaeur B., *fx* (2) 640 6813; William Hulbert – Director

Illinois
Place du Champ de Mars 5 Box 14, 1050 Brussels, Belgium; *tel* (2) 512 0105, *tlx* 61534, *fx* (2) 512 5809; Bart A. Smit – Managing Director, Robert D. Miller – Director of Industrial Development, Susan M. Stiehl – Director of Trade Promotion

Indiana
11 Upper Brook Street, London W1Y 1PB, England; *tel* (1) 491 0593, *tlx* 23143 ubs G., *fx* (1) 408 1459; Calvin Berlin – Director

Iowa
An der Hauptwache 2, 6000 Frankfurt 1, West Germany; *tel* (69) 283 858, *tlx* 414623 iowa D., *fx* (69) 28 1493; Paul Wagner – Director

Kansas
Zettachring 10–A, 7000 Stuttgart 80, West Germany; *tel* (711) 728 7140, *tlx* 7255716 bpo D., *fx* (711) 728 7144; Rainer Mauser – Director

Kentucky
Hammond House, 117 Piccadilly, London W1V 9FJ, England; *tel* (1) 629 2484, *tlx* 291015 portag G., *fx* (1) 491 2367; Annemarie Topliss – Director

Maryland
Avenue Louise 222 Box 7, 1050 Brussels, Belgium; *tel* (2) 647 5367, *tlx* 64617, *fx* (2) 647 5700; Harry Geschwindt – European Director, Peter Uebe – Director of Industrial Development, Ronald E. Baker – Director International Trade

Michigan
Rue Ducale 41, 1000 Brussels, Belgium; *tel* (2) 511 0732, *tlx* 61573 miceur B., *fx* (2) 511 3617; Russell A. Leach – Director, Herbert Spaeth – Deputy Director

Missouri
Emanuel Leutze Strasse 1, 4000 Dusseldorf 11, W. Germany; *tel* (211) 592 025, *tlx* 8584645 dcmo D.; Wade K. Anderson – Director, Barbara Hillringhaus – Trade Specialist

New York
Panton House, 25 Haymarket, London SW1, England; *tel* (1) 839 5079, *tlx* 912721 nycom G, *fx* (1) 839 5401; Richard J. Kilner – Director Europe, Martin Lewis – Deputy Director (Trade) Europe

New Jersey
Leutschenbachstrasse 45, 8050 Zurich, Switzerland; *tel* (1) 302 1310, *tlx* 823678 pony, *fx* (1) 302 1368; John P. Cannizzo – General Manager Europe

North Carolina
Wasserstrasse 2, 4000 Dusseldorf 1, W. Germany; *tel* (211) 320 533, *tlx* 8581846; T. Davis Bunn – Director, Mariya A. Toohey – Manager Trade Coordination

Ohio
21 Avenue de la Toison D'Or, 1060 Brussels, Belgium; *tel* (2) 513 0752, *tlx* 26698 ohio B., *fx* (2) 513 2726; E. William Tatge – Director, Gabriele Alexander – Deputy Director

Pennsylvania
31 Rue Montoyer Box 4, 1040 Brussels, Belgium; *tel* (2) 513 7796/7/8, *tlx* 24757 pennst. B., *fx* (2) 514 2351; Jack L. Worms – Director

Puerto Rico (Commonwealth)
Pedro Teiceira 8, 28020 Madrid, Spain; *tel* (1) 250 3133, *tlx* 42339 slopr E., *fx* (1) 456 7286; Enrique Burgos Parez – Director for Europe, Jose Roberto Martinez – Director Spain

Rhode Island
Meir 24, 2000 Antwerp, Belgium; *tel* (3) 233 6021, *tlx* 33863 corgra B., *fx* (3) 232 9943; Frank J. Roovers – Director Europe

South Carolina
Post Box 750423, Frankfurt Airport Centre, Hudo Echever Ring, 6000 Frankfurt Main 75, W. Germany; *tel* (69) 697 90763, *tlx* 417775 wwbc D., *fx* (69) 697 90711; Steven A. Nodeau – Director

Virginia
Avenue Louise 479 Box 55, 1050 Brussels, Belgium; *tel* (2) 648 6179, *tlx* 29315 vded B., *fx* (2) 648 0698; Denis E. Rufin – Director Europe, Ingrid Westphal – Director Export Development

Wyoming
Rue du Brec, F-06360 Eze Village, France; *tel* (93) 410 272, *tlx* 469870; Xavier Cottier – Director

2 ECONOMIC TRADE AND DEVELOPMENT OFFICES

Telephone country code
The US telephone code is (1), which should be used in addition to any number shown below when calling from outside the US.

Alabama
Edgar Welden, Director, Development Office – Office of the Governor, Montgomery, AL 36130, USA; *tel* (205) 263 0048

Alaska
David Hoffman, Commissioner, Department of Commerce & Economic Development, State Office Building, 9th Floor, 333 Willoughby Avenue. Mail to: PO Box D, Juneau, AK 99811, USA; *tel* (907) 465 2500

Arizona
Jan Schaefer, Director, Business & Trade Division, Department of Commerce, Executive Tower, 5th Floor, 1700 W. Washington Street, Phoenix, AZ 85007, USA; *tel* (602) 255 5374

Arkansas
A. David Harrington, Director, Industrial Development Commission, One State Capital Mall, Little Rock, AR 72201, USA; *tel* (501) 371 1121

California
Christy Campbell-Walters, Director, Department of Commerce, 1121 L Street, Room 600, Sacramento, CA 95814, USA; *tel* (916) 322 5367

Colorado
Steve Schmitz, Director, Division of Commerce & Development, Department of Local Affairs, State Centennial Building, Room 523, 1313 Sherman Street, Denver, CO 80203, USA; *tel* (303) 866 2205

Connecticut
Mark Feinberg – Executive Director of Development, Department of Economic Development, 210 Washington Street, Hartford, CT 06106, USA; *tel* (203) 566 5546

Delaware
Louis Papineau, Jr, Director, Delaware Development Office, 99 Kings Highway. Mail to: PO Box 1401, Dover, DE 19903, USA; *tel* (301) 736 4271

District of Columbia
Kwasi Holman, Executive Director, Office of Business & Economic Development, Perpetual Bank Building, 7th Floor, 1111 E Street, NW, Washington, DC 20004, USA; *tel* (202) 727 6600

Florida
Steve Mayberry, Director, Division of Economic Development, Department of Commerce, Collins Building, Room 501B, 107 W. Gaines Street, Tallahassee, FL 32301, USA; *tel* (904) 488 6300

Georgia
George Berry, Commissioner, Department of Industry & Trade, 230 Peachtree Street, Suite 700. Mail to: PO Box 1776, Atlanta, GA 30301, USA; *tel* (404) 656 3556

Hawaii
Roger A. Ulveling, Director, Department of Planning & Economic Development, Kamamalu Building, 250 S. King Street. Mail to: PO Box 2359, Honolulu, HI 96804, USA; *tel* (808) 548 3033

Idaho
Jim Hawkins, Director, Department of Commerce, State Capital Building, Room 108, 700 W. Jefferson Street, Boise, ID 83720, USA; *tel* (208) 334 2470

Illinois
Jay R. Hedges, Director, Department of Commerce & Community Affairs, 620 E. Adams Street, Springfield, IL 62701, USA; *tel* (217) 782 7500

Indiana
Kurt G. Ellis, Director, Division of Business Expansion, Department of Commerce, Commerce Center, Room 700, One N Capital Street, Indianapolis, IN 46204-2243, USA; *tel* (317) 232 0160

Iowa
Allan Thomas, Director, Department of Economic Development, 200 E, Grand Avenue, Des Moines, IA 50309, USA; *tel* (515) 281 3251

Kansas
Harland E. Priddle, Secretary, Department of Commerce, Capitol Towers, 5th Floor, 400 SW 8th Street, Topeka, KS 66603-3957, USA; *tel* (913) 296 3481

Kentucky
David Lovelace, Commissioner, Department of Economic Development, Commerce Cabinet, Capital Plaza Tower, 24th Floor, Frankfort, KY 40601, USA; *tel* (502) 564 7670

Louisiana
Kay Jackson, Secretary, Department of Commerce, One Maritime Plaza, Room 236, 101 France Street. Mail to: PO Box 94185, Baton Rouge, LA 70804-9185, USA; *tel* (504) 342 5361

Maine
Mr. Leslie Stevens, Director, Development Office – Executive Department, 193 State Street. Mail to: State House, Station 59, Augusta, ME 04333, USA; *tel* (207) 289 2656

Maryland
J. Randall Evans, Secretary, Department of Economic & Community Development, 45 Calvert Street, Annapolis, MD 21401, USA; *tel* (301) 269 3176

Massachusetts
Joseph D. Aluani, Secretary, Executive Office of Economic Affairs, John W. McCormack State Office Building, Room 2101, One Ashburton Place, Boston, MA 02108, USA; *tel* (617) 727 8380

Michigan
William Lontz, Director, Community & Business Assistance Division, Department of Commerce, Law Building, 525 W. Ottawa Street. Mail to: PO Box 30225, Lansing, MI 48909, USA; *tel* (517) 373 0347

Minnesota
Mark Dayton, Commissioner, Department of Energy & Economic Development, American Center Building, Room 900, 150 E Kellogg Blvd, St Paul, MN 55101, USA; *tel* (612) 296 6424

Mississippi
Jerry McDonald, Executive Director, Department of Economic Development, Walter Sillers State Office Building, Room 1201, 550 High Street. Mail to: PO Box 849, Jackson, MS 39205, USA; *tel* (601) 359 3449

Missouri
Carl M. Kaupel, Director, Economic Development Programs, Department of Economic Development, Harry S. Truman State Office Building, Room 770, 301 W High Street. Mail to: PO Box 118, Jefferson City, MO 65101, USA; *tel* (314) 751 2133

Montana
Carol Daly, Administrator, Business Assistance Division, Department of Commerce, 1424 Ninth Avenue, Helena, MT 59620-0521, USA; *tel* (406) 444 3932

Nebraska
Rod Bates, Director, Department of Economic Development, State Office Building, 301 Centennial Mall, South. Mail to: PO Box 94666, Lincoln, NE 68509, USA; *tel* (402) 471 3747

Nevada
Andrew P. Grose, Director, Commission on Economic Development, 600 E William Street. Mail to: Capitol Complex, Carson City, NV 89710, USA; *tel* (702) 885 4325

New Hampshire
John E. Burns, Director, Division of Economic Development, Prescott Park, Building 2, 105 Loudon Road. Mail to: PO Box 856, Concord, NH 03301, USA; *tel* (603) 271 2341

New Jersey
Ben Ferrara, Director, Division of Economic Development, New Jersey National Bank Building, One W State Street. Mail to: CN 823, Trenton, NJ 08625, USA; *tel* (609) 292 7757

New Mexico
Gordon W. Thompson, Director, Economic Development Division, Bataan Memorial Building, Room 201, 1100 St Francis Drive, Santa Fe, NM 87503, USA; *tel* (505) 827 0270

New York
William Graper, Director, Department of Commerce, One Commerce Plaza, Room 930, 99 Washington Avenue, Albany, NY 12245, USA; *tel* (518) 474 2968

North Carolina
Alvah Ward, Director, Department of Commerce, Dobbs Building, Room 258, 430 N. Salisbury Street, Raleigh, NC 27611, USA; *tel* (919) 733 4151

North Dakota
William S. Patrie, Director, Economic Development Commission, Liberty Memorial Building, 2nd Floor, State Capitol Grounds, Bismark, ND 58505, USA; *tel* (701) 224 2810

Ohio
Clarence D. Tawlicki, Director, Department of Development, State Office Tower, 25th Floor, 30 E. Broad Street. Mail to: PO Box 1001, Columbus, OH 43266-0101, USA; *tel* (614) 466 7559

Oklahoma
Connie Irby, Deputy Executive Director, Department of Commerce, 6601 Broadway Extension, Oklahoma City, OK 73116, USA; *tel* (405) 521 2401

Oregon
Roger Smith, Acting Director, Department of Economic Development, 595 Cottage Street NE, Salem, OR 97310, USA; *tel* (503) 373 1205

Pennsylvania
Joy M. Pooler, Projects Director, Department of Commerce, Forum Building, Room 453, Walnut Street & Commonwealth Avenue, Harrisburg, PA 17120, USA; *tel* (717) 787 6500

Rhode Island
Louis A. Fazzano, Director, Department of Economic Development, Gilbane Building, 7 Jackson Walkway, Providence, RI 02903, USA; *tel* (401) 277 2601

South Carolina
Wayne Sterling, Director, State Development Board, AT&T Building, 1201 Main. Mail to: PO Box 927, Columbia, SC 29202, USA; *tel* (803) 734 1400

South Dakota
Ron Reed, Interim Director, Department of State Development, Capital Lake Plaza, 711 Wells Avenue, Pierre, SD 57501, USA; *tel* (605) 773 5032

Tennessee
Carl Johnson, Commissioner, Department of Economic & Community Development, Rachel Jackson Building, 8th Floor, 320 6th Avenue North, Nashville, TN 37219-5308, USA; *tel* (615) 714 1888

Texas
David V. Brandon, Executive Director, Economic Development Commission, Anson Jones State Office Building, 410 E 5th Street. Mail to: PO Box 12728, Capitol Station, Austin, TX 78711, USA; *tel* (512) 472 5059

Utah
David J. Grant, Director, Department of Community & Economic Development, State Office Building, Room 6150, Salt Lake City, UT 84114, USA; *tel* (801) 533 5325

Vermont
John Trethaway, Commissioner, Economic Development Department, Pavilion Office Building, 109 State Street, Montpelier, VT 05602, USA; *tel* (802) 828 3221

Virginia
P. Scott Eubanks, Director, Department of Economic Development, Washington Building – Capitol Square, Room 1000, 1100 Bank Street, Richmond, VA 23219, USA; *tel* (804) 786 3791

Washington
John C. Anderson, Director, Department of Trade & Economic Development, General Administration Building, Room 101, 11th Avenue & Columbia Street. Mail to: Mail Stop AX-13, Olympia, WA 98504-0613, USA; *tel* (206) 753 7426

West Virginia
Lysander L. Dudley, Sr, Acting Director, Governor's Office of Community & Industrial Development, State Capitol Complex, Room M-146, Charleston, WV 25305, USA; *tel* (304) 348 0400

Wisconsin
Richard J. Longabaugh, Executive Director, Housing & Economic Development Authority, First Wisconsin Plaza, Suite 500, One S. Pickney. Mail to: PO Box 1728, Madison, WI 53701-1728, USA; *tel* (608) 266 7884

Wyoming
Bill Budd, Executive Director, Economic Development & Stabilization Board, Herschler Building, 3rd Floor East, 122 W 25th Street, Cheyenne, WY 82002, USA; *tel* (307) 777 7287

Guam
David D. L. Flores, Administrator, Economic Development Authority. Mail to: PO Box 3280, Agana, GU 96910, USA; *tel* (671) 472 8821

Puerto Rico
Antonio J. Colorado, Administrator, Economic Development Administration, 355 Roosevelt Avenue, Hato Rey. Mail to: PO Box 2350, San Juan, PR 00936, USA; *tel* (809) 765 1303

Virgin Islands
Arnold M. Golden, Commissioner, Department of Commerce, Charlotte Amalie. Mail to: PO Box 6400, St Thomas, VI 00801, USA; *tel* (809) 774 8784

Standard US corporation information

The purpose of this chapter is to indicate the type of information which is usually contained in the Certificate of Incorporation of a US company, and the considerations which should be addressed if a US company is being formed. In the United States, a corporation must be incorporated under the laws of a specific state, and the guidelines vary between states, sometimes significantly. However, Delaware is often used, and therefore its requirements are presented in the following example.

Several US companies can handle the incorporation of a company for a fee. One of these is a Prentice Hall subsidiary, International Corporation Company Inc, which provided the following information.

Prentice Hall Corporate Service's materials are designed to provide accurate and authoritative information in regard to the subject matter covered. They are printed with the understanding that Prentice Hall Corporate Services is not engaged in rendering legal, accounting, or other professional service. If legal advice or other expert assistance is required, the services of a competent professional person should be sought.

Materials are reprinted with the permission of Prentice Hall Corporate Services. International Corporation Company Inc, a wholly owned subsidiary of Prentice Hall Corporate Services, which provides all international corporate services.

An example of the fees for incorporating a company are those of Delaware, where basic fees are about $50.00 and corporate services about $300.00 to prepare and file the proper documents. Further information concerning the range of available services can be obtained from:

International Corporation Company Inc, Simon & Schuster Professional Information Group, 1 Gulf + Western Plaza, New York, New York 10023; *tel* (212) 373 7588

The following are details describing the basic procedures and forms for incorporating in the US, and a specimen Certificate of Incorporation for the state of Delaware.

PRENTICE HALL CORPORATE SERVICES ('PHCS') ©

COMPRISING
The Prentice-Hall Corporation System Inc   United States Corporation Company

DELAWARE – DOMESTIC ORGANIZATION
Copyright 1988 by THE PRENTICE-HALL CORPORATION SYSTEM INC
1 Gulf-Western Plaza, New York, New York 10023-7773 – Telephone: 373-7500
(For distribution only to members of the Bar)

This information consists of three parts: I, an outline on organizational procedures; II, an outline setting forth certain related information; and III, a specimen Certificate of Incorporation. The information contained should be examined in conjunction with the outline on organizational procedures. Unless otherwise indicated, any section numbers refer to those under the 'General Corporation Law of the State of Delaware' (the 'Law').

Statutory representation
Statutory representation can be furnished by The Prentice-Hall Corporation System Inc.

I. ORGANIZATIONAL PROCEDURES

Estimated official disbursements

(a) *Payable to Secretary of State:*
1. Filing and indexing fee – $25.
2. Certification fee – $10.
3. Organization tax – At following rates on entire authorized share structure *with a minimum tax of $15* in any event:

Par value

Not exceeding $2,000,000	1¢ per $100.
Exceeding $2,000,000 but not exceeding $20,000,000	$200 plus $\frac{1}{2}$¢ ($0.005) per $100 in excess of $2,000,000.
Exceeding $20,000,000	$1100 plus $\frac{1}{5}$¢ ($0.002) per $100 in excess of $20,000,000.

Without par value

Not exceeding 20,000 shares	$\frac{1}{2}$¢ ($0.005) per share.
Exceeding 20,000 shares but not exceeding 2,000,000	$100 plus $\frac{1}{4}$¢ ($0.0025) per share in excess of 20,000 shares.
Exceeding 2,000,000 shares	$5050 plus $\frac{1}{5}$¢ ($0.002) per share in excess of 2,000,000 shares.

(b) *Payable to Recorder of Deeds:*
$5 per page (Kent County), plus flat surcharge of $3.

Note: If a corporation doesn't require numerous shares and/or shares without par value, Counsel may wish to consult caption ANNUAL FRANCHISE TAX at end of Part II of this information for possible alternative lower rates of annual Franchise Tax.

Expedited services – Expedited filing and other services by the Secretary of State are available at extra cost. Details as to the services available as well as the cost can be obtained from any corporate specialist on our staff.

Incorporator(s)
Only 1 incorporator is required. The statute provides that an incorporator may be any 'person, partnership, association or corporation, singly or jointly with others, and without regard to his or their residence, domicile or state of incorporation...'. There is no statutory requirement that an incorporator be a US citizen or a subscriber to shares. (101)

Execution, filing and recording of certificate of incorporation; corporate existence
One copy of the certificate of incorporation, as either signed only, or as both signed and acknowledged, by the incorporator(s), and one additional copy, which may be executed or conformed, are presented to Secretary of State, who files executed copy and endorses, certifies, and returns the other copy. The certified copy is presented to the Recorder of

Deeds of the county in Delaware in which the registered office is located. The Recorder ultimately releases this certified copy. Corporate existence commences upon filing by the Secretary of State unless certificate of incorporation specifies a subsequent effective time, which may be not later than, 'a time on the 90th day after the date of its filing.' (101, 103, 106)

The Law provides that, if the incorporator does not formally acknowledge the certificate before a Notary Public or other appropriate official, his signing alone 'shall constitute the ... acknowledgment ... under the penalties of perjury ... that the instrument is his act and deed ... and that the facts stated therein are true.' The specimen form which PHCS distributes to Counsel omits a formal acknowledgment. (103)

Certificate of incorporation – contents

Section 102 of the Law specifies the statements which must or may be set forth in the certificate of incorporation; and said statements will be quoted and discussed in the order specified in that section.

'The name'

'(1) The name of the corporation which shall contain 1 of the words "association," "company," "corporation," "club," "foundation," "fund," "incorporated," "institute," "society," "union," "syndicate," or "limited," or 1 of the abbreviations ["co.," "corp.," "inc.," "ltd."], or words or abbreviations of like import in other languages (provided they are written in roman characters or letters), and which shall be such as to distinguish it upon the records in the office of the Division of Corporations in the Department of State from the names of other corporations organized, reserved or registered as a foreign corporation under the laws of this State;'

For the extent to which, and the conditions under which a corporation may use the word 'trust' as part of its name, see section 395 of the Law.

There is no statutory authority for reserving a name; however, an available name may be reserved by administrative authority and without a reservation fee for a period of 30 days.

If a corporation is to obtain authority as a foreign corporation in any state, Counsel may wish to determine that a word or abbreviation which indicates corporate status in Delaware also indicates corporate status in the foreign jurisdiction involved.

The registered office and registered agent

'(2) The address (which shall include the street, number, city and county) of the corporation's registered office in this State, and the name of its registered agent at such address;'

Paragraph (a) of section 131 of the Law provides: 'Every corporation shall have and maintain in this State a registered office which may, but need not be, the same as its place of business.'

Paragraph (a) of section 132 of the Law provides: 'Every corporation shall have and maintain in this State a registered agent, which agent may be either an individual resident in this State whose business office is identical with the corporation's registered office, or a domestic corporation (which may be itself), or a foreign corporation authorized to transact business in this State, having a business office identical with such registered office.'

The business or purposes

'(3) The nature of the business or purposes to be conducted or promoted. It shall be sufficient to state, either alone or with other businesses or purposes, that the purpose of the corporation is to engage in any lawful act or activity for which corporations may be organized under the General Corporation Law of Delaware, and by such statement all lawful acts and activities shall be within the purposes of the corporation, except for express limitations, if any;'

Paragraphs (b) and (c) of section 101 of the Law provide: '(b) A corporation may be incorporated or organized under this chapter to conduct or promote any lawful business or purposes, except as may otherwise be provided by the Constitution or other law of this State. (c) Corporations for constructing, maintaining and operating public utilities within this State shall be subject to, in addition to this chapter, the special provisions and requirements of Title 26 applicable to such corporations.'

For a grant of general powers, see sections 121, 122, and 160 of the Law. Paragraph (c) of section 102 of the Law provides that it 'shall not be necessary to set forth in the certificate of incorporation any of the powers conferred on corporations by this chapter.'

Section 126 of the Law provides: '(a) No corporation organized under this chapter shall possess the power of issuing bills, notes, or other evidences of debt for circulation as money, or the power of carrying on the business of receiving deposits of money. (b) Corporations organized under this chapter to buy, sell and otherwise deal in notes, open accounts and other similar evidences of debt as collateral security therefor, shall not be deemed to be engaging in the business of banking.'

Authorized shares of stock

'(4) If the corporation is to be authorized to issue only 1 class of stock, the total number of shares of stock which the corporation shall have authority to issue and the par value of each of such shares, or a statement that all such shares are to be without par value. If the corporation is to be authorized to issue more than one class of stock, the certificate of incorporation shall set forth the total number of shares of all classes of stock which the corporation shall have authority to issue and the number of shares of each class, and shall specify with respect to each class those shares that are to be without par value and those shares that are to have a par value and the par value of each share of each such class. The certificate of incorporation shall also set forth a statement of the designations and the powers, preferences and rights, and the qualifications, limitations or restrictions thereof, which are permitted by §151 of this Title in respect of any class or classes of stock or any series of any class of stock of the corporation and the fixing of which by the certificate of incorporation is desired, and an express grant of such authority as it may then be desired to grant to the board of directors to fix by resolution or resolutions any thereof that may be desired but which shall not be fixed by the certificate of incorporation ...

Subsection (d) of section 141 provides that the 'certificate of incorporation may confer upon holders of any class or series of stock the right to elect 1 or more directors ... If the certificate of incorporation provides that directors elected by the holders of a class of series of stock shall have more or less than 1 vote per director on any matter, every reference in this chapter to a majority or other proportion of directors shall refer to a majority or other proportion of the votes of such directors.'

Section 151 of the Law relates to the designations, preferences, limitations, relative rights, etc. of shares or series when the corporation is authorized to issue 2 or more classes of shares or series. Where there are 2 or more classes of stock entitled to vote, and voting is *weighted*, the following language of section 212 of the Law should be noted: 'If the certificate of incorporation provides for more or less than 1 vote for any share, on any matter, every reference in this chapter to a majority or other proportion of stock shall refer to such majority or other proportion of the votes of such stock.' For related matters, including specific and general voting provisions, see caption STOCKHOLDERS in Part II of this information.

Subsection (c) of section 262 provides in part: 'Any corporation may provide in its certificate of incorporation that appraisal rights under this section shall be available for the shares of any class or series of its stock as a result of an amendment to its certificate of incorporation, any merger or consolidation in which the corporation is a constituent corporation or the sale of all or substantially all of the assets of the corporation . . . .'

The Incorporator(s)

'(5) The name and mailing address of the incorporator or incorporators;'

The qualifications and functions of the incorporator(s) have heretofore been discussed.

The directors (*optional provision*)

'(6) If the powers of the incorporator or incorporators are to terminate upon the filing of the certificate of incorporation, the names and mailing addresses of the persons who are to serve as directors until the first annual meeting of stockholders or until their successors are elected and qualify.'

The specimen form of certificate of incorporation which PHCS distributes to Counsel omits the naming of the initial director(s) of the corporation, since past experience indicates that the general preference of Counsel is to have the incorporator elect such directors, the incorporator's action not being a public record.

For number, qualifications, and related matters affecting directors, see caption DIRECTORS in Part II of this information.

Paragraph (b) of section 102 provides that in addition to any of the mandatory statements heretofore set forth, 'the certificate of incorporation may also contain any or all of the following matters . . .', which will be hereinafter quoted under appropriate captions. It is doubtful that Counsel will generally want to include the provisions under the captions *Limited duration* and *Stockholder personal liability*.

Regulatory matters

'(1) Any provision for the management of the business and for the conduct of the affairs of the corporation, and any provision creating, defining, limiting and regulating the powers of the corporation, the directors, and the stockholders, or any class of the stockholders, . . . if such provisions are not contrary to the laws of this State. Any provision which is required or permitted by any section of this chapter to be stated in the bylaws may instead be stated in the certificate of incorporation;'

Section 109 provides: 'The original or other bylaws of a corporation may be adopted, amended or repealed by the incorporators, by the initial directors if they were named in the certificate of incorporation, or, before a corporation has received any payment for any of its stock, by its board of directors. After a corporation has received any payment for any of its stock, the power to adopt, amend or repeal bylaws shall be in the stockholders entitled to vote, . . ., provided, however, any corporation may, in its certificate of incorporation, confer the power to adopt, amend or repeal bylaws upon the directors . . . The fact that such power has been so conferred upon the directors or governing body, as the case may be, shall not divest the stockholders . . . of the power, nor limit their power to adopt, amend or repeal bylaws.' The specimen form of certificate of incorporation which PHCS distributes to Counsel provides for conferring such additional powers upon the directors.

Subsection (e) of section 211 provides: 'All elections of directors shall be by written ballot, unless otherwise provided in the certificate of incorporation.'

The specimen form of certificate of incorporation which PHCS distributes to Counsel confers power upon the directors in connection with the Bylaws and provides that elections need not be by ballot.

Section 203 prescribes the conditions and procedures for tender offers for the purchase of a corporation's equity securities unless its certificate of incorporation provides 'that tender offers for the purchase of its equity securities shall not be subject to' section 203.

Compromise or arrangement clause

'(2) The following provisions, in haec verba, viz.—

"Whenever a compromise or arrangement is proposed between this corporation and its creditors or any class of them and/or between this corporation and its stockholders or any class of them, any court of equitable jurisdiction within the State of Delaware may, on the application in a summary way of this corporation or of any creditor or stockholder thereof or on the application of any receiver or receivers appointed for this corporation under §291 of Title 8 of the Delaware Code or on the application of trustees in dissolution or of any receiver or receivers appointed for this corporation under §279 of Title 8 of the Delaware Code order a meeting of the creditors or class of creditors, and/or of the stockholders or class of stockholders of this corporation, as the case may be, to be summoned in such manner as the said court directs. If a majority in number representing three fourths in value of the creditors or class of creditors, and/or of the stockholders or class of stockholders of this corporation, as the case may be, agree to any compromise or arrangement and to any reorganization of this corporation as consequence of such compromise or arrangement, the said compromise or arrangement and the said reorganization shall, if sanctioned by the court to which the said application has been made, be binding on all the creditors or class of creditors, and/or on all the stockholders or class of stockholders, of this corporation, as the case may be, and also on this corporation;"'

The specimen form which PHCS distributes to Counsel includes the foregoing clause.

Pre-emptive rights

'(3) Such provisions as may be desired granting to the holders of the stock of the corporation, or the holders of any class or series of a class thereof, the preemptive right to subscribe to any or all additional issues of stock of the corporation of any or all classes or series thereof, or to any securities of the corporation convertible into such stock. No stockholder shall have any preemptive right to subscribe to an additional issue of stock or to any security convertible into such stock, unless, and except to the extend [sic] that, such right is expressly granted to him in the certificate of incorporation ...'

The specimen form which PHCS distributes to Counsel contains provisions for granting preemptive rights for a limited period if the same are to be granted. Since the Law does not define *preemptive rights*, and since the Delaware *case* law on the subject is hardly replete, Counsel frequently includes provisions which enlarge upon the statutory denial.

Greater voting proportions

'(4) Provisions requiring for any corporate action, the vote of a larger portion of the stock or of any class or series thereof, or of any other securities having voting power, or a larger number of the directors, than is required by this chapter;'

Part II of this information sets forth the usual voting proportions.

Limited duration

'(5) A provision limiting the duration of the corporation's existence to a specified date; otherwise, the corporation shall have perpetual existence;'

Stockholder personal liability

'(6) A provision imposing personal liability for the debts of the corporation on its stockholders or members to a specified extent and upon specified conditions; otherwise, the stockholders or members of a corporation shall not be personally liable for the payment of the corporation's debts except as they may be liable by reason of their own conduct or acts;'

Director personal liability

'(7) A provision eliminating or limiting the personal liability of a director to the corporation or its stockholders for monetary damages for breach of fiduciary duty as a director, provided that such provision shall not eliminate or limit the liability of a director (i) for any breach of the director's duty of loyalty to the corporation or its stockholders, (ii) for acts or omissions not in good faith or which involve intentional misconduct or a knowing violation of law, (iii) under section 174 of this Title, or (iv) for any transaction from which the director derived an improper personal benefit. No such provision shall eliminate or limit the liability of a director for any act or omission occurring prior to the date when such provision becomes effective...'

Execution, filing and recording of certificate of incorporation; corporate existence
See same caption at the beginning of this outline.

Organization meeting or written action
Section 108 of the Law provides:

'(a) After the filing of the certificate of incorporation an organization meeting of the incorporator or incorporators, or of the board of directors if the initial directors were named in the certificate of incorporation, shall be held, either within or without this State, at the call of a majority of the incorporators or directors, as the case may be, for the purposes of adopting bylaws, electing directors (if the meeting is of the incorporators) to serve or hold office until the first annual meeting of stockholders or until their successors are elected and qualify, electing officers if the meeting is of the directors, doing any other or further acts to perfect the organization of the corporation, and transacting such other business as may come before the meeting. (b) The persons calling the meeting shall give to each other incorporator or director, as the case may be, at least 2 days' written notice thereof by any usual means of communication, which notice shall state the time, place and purposes of the meeting as fixed by the persons calling it. Notice of the meeting need not be given to anyone who attends the meeting or who signs a waiver of notice either before or after the meeting. (c) Any action permitted to be taken at the organization meeting of the incorporators or directors, as the case may be, may be taken without a meeting if each incorporator or director, where there is more than 1, or the sole incorporator or director where there is only 1, signs an instrument which states the action so taken.'

II. RELATED ORGANIZATIONAL INFORMATION

SHARES OF STOCK

Authorized minimum/maximum amount	None.
Par value stock	Permitted for any class and in any monetary amount, such as $\frac{1}{3}$ cent or 1 mill.
No par value stock	Permitted for any class. Directors evaluate unless certificate of incorporation vests authority in stockholders.
Minimum subscriptions before commencing business	None.

Minimum paid-in capital before commencing business	None.
Share consideration	Cash, services rendered, personal property, real property, leases of real property, or a combination thereof.

STOCKHOLDERS

Minimum number	1.
Maximum liability	Unpaid balance of subscription unless certificate of incorporation imposes personal liability for corporate debts.
Preemptive rights	Denied in absence of grant in certificate of incorporation.
Meetings and action	Meetings may be held anywhere provided in bylaws. Voting stockholders may act in writing in lieu of meeting unless otherwise provided in certificate of incorporation. Notice of meetings must generally be given to stockholders not less than 10 days nor more than 60 days before meeting (not less than 20 days for merger or consideration).
Quorum	Number of shares specified in certificate of incorporation or bylaws, but not less than $\frac{1}{3}$. If not so fixed, shares representing majority of all votes entitled to be cast.
Cumulative voting	Denied unless authorized by certificate of incorporation.
Voting restrictions	May be limited or denied any class except for adversely affected amendments.
Greater voting proportions	May provide for in certificate of incorporation.

Note: Special requirements may apply to certain 'business combinations', as defined.

General voting proportions

Amendments, dissolutions, mergers, consolidations and assets sales	Majority of all votes entitled to be cast.
Transactions for which statute prescribes no minimum	Proportion of votes fixed in certificate of incorporation or bylaws. If not so fixed, majority (plurality in election of directors) of all votes present or represented at meeting and entitled to be cast on the subject matter.
Stockholders' list	Must be prepared at least 10 days before each meeting and be open to inspection at place where meeting is held. Stockholders also have right to inspect stockholders' list upon demand during usual business hours.

DIRECTORS

Minimum number	1.
Qualifications	Need not be stockholders. There is no statutory requirement that directors be US citizens or Delaware residents. Certificate of incorporation or bylaws may prescribe qualifications.
Staggered terms	May be authorized by certificate of incor-

	poration, an initial bylaw, or a stockholders' bylaw.
Removal	Stockholders may remove directors with cause. They may also remove directors without cause with certain exceptions which otherwise require authority therefor in certificate of incorporation.
Vacancies and newly created directorships	Filled by a majority of directors in office unless otherwise provided in certificate of incorporation or bylaws.
Indemnification	Broad statutory coverage, including right to maintain insurance; but not exclusive of any bylaw, agreement, vote of stockholders or disinterested directors or otherwise.
Self-dealings	Broad statutory coverage.
Meetings and action	Meetings may be held anywhere provided in bylaws. Action in writing of all directors permitted, or directors may participate by conference telephone or similar communications equipment.

Quorum

Majority of total number unless certificate of incorporation or bylaws require a greater number. Bylaws may provide for lesser number which may be not less than $\frac{1}{3}$ of total number.

Act

The vote of a majority of directors present at the meeting at which the quorum is present is required, except that designating a committee or committees or initiating voluntary dissolution procedure requires majority of the whole Board. Section 102 permits provision in certificate of incorporation requiring greater number, while section 141 provides that either certificate of incorporation or bylaws may provide for greater number.

Personal liability

May be eliminated or limited in certificate of incorporation to extent provided in statute.

Control over bylaws

Original or other bylaws may be adopted, amended, or repealed by the incorporators, by the initial directors if they were named in the certificate of incorporation, or by the directors before payment for stock. Thereafter, stockholders entitled to vote have the power to adopt, amend, or repeal the bylaws, but such power may also be conferred upon the directors if the certificate of incorporation so provides. One exception is that the classification of directors for staggered terms requires provision therefor in certificate of incorporation, an initial bylaw, or a bylaw adopted by stockholders entitled to vote. Classifying directors for staggered terms may be authorized by the certificate of incorporation, an initial bylaw, or a stockholders' bylaw.

Annual franchise tax

The lesser of amounts determined under the following methods:

1. *Authorized share basis*

Authorized shares with or without par value (shares without par value are always taxed on this basis):

3,000 shares or less. $30
Over 3,000 shares but not more than 5,000. . . . . $35

Over 5,000 shares but not more than 10,000. . . . .$70
For each additional 10,000 shares (or part thereof). $35

2. *Gross asset basis*
Divide the total number of issued shares of all classes reported on the annual report into the total gross assets on annual report. If the quotient is more than par value per share, multiply the number of authorized par value shares by the quotient; if less than the par value per share, multiply the number of authorized shares by the par value per share. The result yields the assumed par value capital. The tax on this is computed at the rate of $140 per million dollars, or fraction thereof. When assumed capital is less than one million dollars, the tax is such part of $140 as the assumed par capital is to a million dollars. The tax is prorated for the number of days during which the corporation existed during the taxable year. If no par shares are combined with par shares, compute tax on no par shares on the share basis and add to the tax on par shares computed as above. Minimum tax is $30, maximum $130,000 (except for regulated investment companies, to which alternative rate may apply, maximum $65,000).

Corporations inactive during all or any part of a taxable year are taxed at one-half of the regular tax for the period of inactivity. A $30 minimum applies.

III. SPECIMEN FORM

CERTIFICATE OF INCORPORATION

OF

(Name of company)

The undersigned, a natural person, for the purpose of organizing a corporation for conducting the business and promoting the purposes hereinafter stated, under the provisions and subject to the requirements of the laws of the State of Delaware (particularly Chapter 1, Title 8 of the Delaware Code and the acts amendatory thereof and supplemental thereto, and known, identified and referred to as the 'General Corporation Law of the State of Delaware'), hereby certifies that:

FIRST: The name of the corporation (hereinafter called the 'corporation') is

(Name of company)

SECOND: The address, including street, number, city, and county, of the registered office of the corporation in the State of Delaware is 229 South State Street, City of Dover, County of Kent; and the name of the registered agent of the corporation in the State of Delaware at such address is The Prentice-Hall Corporation System Inc.

THIRD: The purpose of the corporation is to engage in any lawful act or activity for which corporations may be organized under the General Corporation Law of the State of Delaware.

(*Use either No Par or Par paragraph*)

FOURTH: The total number of shares of stock which the corporation shall have authority to issue is   , all of which are without par value. All such shares are of one class and are Common Stock. (*No par*)
FOURTH: The total number of shares of stock which the corporation shall have authority to issue is   . The par value of each of such shares is   . All such shares are of one class and are shares of Common Stock. (*Par value*)

(*Can grant or deny preemptive rights here*)

FIFTH: The name and the mailing address of the incorporator are as follows:

(Name of incorporator)

SIXTH: The corporation is to have perpetual existence.

SEVENTH: Whenever a compromise or arrangement is proposed between this corporation and its creditors or any class of them and/or between this corporation and its stockholders or any class of them, any court of equitable jurisdiction within the State of Delaware may, on the application in a summary way of this corporation or of any creditor or stockholder thereof or on the application of any receiver or receivers appointed for this corporation under the provisions of section 291 of Title 8 of the Delaware Code order a meeting of the creditors or class of creditors, and/or of the stockholders or class of stockholders of this corporation, as the case may be, to be summoned in such manner as the said court directs. If a majority in number representing three-fourths in value of the creditors or class of creditors, and/or of the stockholders or class of stockholders of this corporation, as the case may be, agree to any compromise or arrangement and to any reorganization of this corporation as consequence of such compromise or arrangement, the said compromise or arrangement and the said reorganization shall, if sanctioned by the court to which the said application has been made, be binding on all the creditors or class of creditors, and/or on all the stockholders or class of stockholders, of this corporation, as the case may be, and also on this corporation.

EIGHTH: For the management of the business and for the conduct of the affairs of the corporation, and in further definition, limitation and regulation of the powers of the corporation and of its directors and of its stockholders or any class thereof, as the case may be, it is further provided:

1. The management of the business and the conduct of the affairs of the corporation shall be vested in its Board of Directors. The number of directors which shall constitute the whole Board of Directors shall be fixed by, or in the manner provided in, the By-Laws. The phrase 'whole Board' and the phrase 'total number of directors' shall be deemed to have the same meaning, to wit, the total number of directors which the corporation would have if there were no vacancies. No election of directors need be by written ballot.
2. After the original or other By-Laws of the corporation have been adopted, amended, or repealed, as the case may be, in accordance with the provisions of section 109 of the General Corporation Law of the State of Delaware, and, after the corporation has received any payment for any of its stock, the power to adopt, amend, or repeal the By-Laws of the corporation may be exercised by the Board of Directors of the corporation; provided, however, that any provision for the classification of directors of the corporation for staggered terms pursuant to the provisions of subsection (d) of section 141 of the General Corporation Law of the State of Delaware shall be set forth in an initial By-Law or in a By-Law adopted by the stockholders entitled to vote of the corporation unless provisions for such classification shall be set forth in this certificate of incorporation.
3. Whenever the corporation shall be authorized to issue only one class of stock, each outstanding share shall entitle the holder thereof to notice of, and the right to vote at, any meeting of stockholders. Whenever the corporation shall be authorized to issue more than once class of stock, no outstanding share of any class of stock which is denied voting power under the provisions of the certificate of incorporation shall entitle the holder thereof to the right to vote at any meeting of stockholders except as the provisions of paragraph (2) of subsection (b) of section 242 of the General Corporation Law of the State of Delaware shall otherwise require; provided, that no share of any such class which is otherwise denied voting power shall entitle the holder thereof to vote upon the increase or decrease in the number of authorized shares of said class.

NINTH: The personal liability of the directors of the corporation is hereby eliminated to the fullest extent permitted by paragraph (7) of subsection (b) of section 102 of the General Corporation Law of the State of Delaware, as the same may be amended and supplemented.

TENTH: The corporation shall, to the fullest extent permitted by section 145 of the General Corporation Law of the State of Delaware, as the same may be amended and supplemented, indemnify any and all persons whom it shall have power to indemnify under said section from and against any and all of the expenses, liabilities or other matters referred to in or covered by said section, and the indemnification provided for herein shall not be deemed exclusive of any other rights to which those indemnified may be entitled under any By-Law, agreement, vote of stockholders or disinterested directors or otherwise, both as to action in his official capacity and as to action in another capacity while holding such office, and shall continue as to a person who has ceased to be a director, officer, employee or agent and shall inure to the benefit of the heirs, executors and administrators of such a person.

ELEVENTH: From time to time any of the provisions of this certificate of incorporation may be amended, altered or repealed, and other provisions authorized by the laws of the State of Delaware at the time in force may be added or inserted in the manner and at the time prescribed by said laws, and all rights at any time conferred upon the stockholders of the corporation by this certificate of incorporation are granted subject to the provisions of this Article ELEVENTH.

_____
(Name)
Incorporator

US visa requirements for UK nationals

This appendix, prepared by Austin T. Fragoman of the New York office of the law firm of Fragoman, Del Rey & Bernsen, PC, outlines those visas most utilised by UK nationals seeking employment in the United States; it is meant to provide background information only, and explain categories of options.

An investor planning to employ non-US residents in the US should be aware that obtaining a visa for anything more than a brief business trip is time consuming and uncertain. The US Embassy in London, and those located elsewhere, can discuss and advise on applications. It is likely to be useful to consult a law firm with immigration expertise prior to making an application to obtain advice on the preparation of an application and to expedite the process.

Introduction
Foreign nationals seeking entry into the United States are segregated into two principal categories for entering the country, according to the Immigration and Nationality Act. *Immigrants* are those who intend to reside permanently in the US, and *non-immigrants* are those who plan to remain for only a specific purpose and a fixed period of time. UK nationals may be admitted under either of these classifications.

Brief business trips
Commencing on 1 July 1988, the Immigration and Naturalization Service implemented special regulations designed to facilitate short-term travel to the United States by United Kingdom nationals for either business or pleasure. Pursuant to the visa waiver pilot programme, foreign nationals who (1) are classifiable as a tourist or a B-1 visitor for business, (2) seek admission for up to 90 days, and (3) hold a valid UK passport need not obtain a non-immigrant visa in order to obtain entry. To receive this benefit, the foreign national must purchase a round-trip, non-transferable airline ticket valid for a period of not less than one year and complete a visa waiver pilot programme information form that will be made available on the flight to the US. When entering the US without a visa pursuant to these special regulations no extensions of stay (beyond the 90 days) or changes in status will be granted. Not all airlines participate in this programme, so it is important when making a reservation to ensure that no visa is necessary. Alternatively, a UK passport holder wishing to travel to the US may obtain a multiple entry B-1 visa.

Non-immigrant classification
The immigration law presumes that all foreign nationals seeking entry into the US intend to remain permanently and the applicant for a non-immigrant visa must prove a desire to enter temporarily. Therefore, the burden is placed on the visa applicant to convince the consular officer that he or she will maintain ties abroad that will assure departure from the US at the end of the visit. Several categories of visas which are used most often by foreign nationals who seek temporary employment in the United States and are discussed below.

B-1 visa: temporary visitor for business
Business visitors who are UK citizens often use B-1 visas. Such visas are normally issued for an indefinite duration and for multiple entries. The visa does not authorise an unlimited stay but permits the bearer to travel to the US and present an application for

admission. This admission request must be made at the point of entry and it is generally for a period of less than six months. The maximum period for which a visitor for business may be admitted to the US under a B-1 visa is one year from the time of entry to the time of departure. While in the US, the visitor must maintain a foreign residence which he or she has no intention of abandoning. Adequate financial arrangements for the entire stay must also be demonstrated in order to gain entry. Most importantly, the business visitor must engage in legitimate B-1 business activities. (The major characteristic of B-1 activities is that the foreign national is employed abroad and is conducting activities beneficial to the foreign-based employer. In addition, in nearly all cases, the national must be paid from abroad. Also, the B-1 foreign national may not engage in local labour in the US.) There is no cost for UK applicants and it requires about ten working days to obtain through the post or 24 hours if an authorised courier service is used. Applications are available from US consulates and must be made by post or with authorised agencies with special visa processing facilities (the Embassy has additional details on both their services and available courier services).

E-1 and E-2 visas: treaty traders and treaty investors
Pursuant to treaties of commerce and navigation between the US and certain countries, including the UK, nationals of the UK normally resident there may receive visas temporarily to enter the US as part of an enterprise engaging in substantial international trade or having a substantial US investment. Both the enterprise and the foreign national must be 'nationals' of the same treaty country; for example, UK nationals who are permanent residents of Canada or the colony of Hong Kong do not qualify.

The nationality of the company engaging in trade or investment is the nationality of those persons who own at least 50 per cent of the shares of the corporation. The place of incorporation and principal place of business are not relevant. Foreign nationals who are also US permanent residents cannot be counted toward the minimum 50 per cent ownership.

E-1 treaty traders status is available for employees of companies engaging in trade – the exchange, purchase or sale of goods and/or services. *Goods* are tangible commodities or merchandise having intrinsic value, excluding money, securities and negotiable instruments. For E-1 purposes, the trade in *goods* conducted by the US office must be substantial and principally (at least 51 per cent) between the US and the treaty nation. *Services* are economic activities whose outputs are other than tangible *goods*. Such activities include, but are not limited to, banking, insurance, transportation, communications and data processing, advertising, accounting, design and engineering, management consulting and tourism. Firms involved in the trade of *services* will be judged on a case by case basis to determine whether the trade is 'substantial' and 'principally' between the US and the treaty nation. E-1 treaty trader foreign nationals must perform an executive or supervisory function or possess skills that are essential to the trading enterprise.

E-2 treaty investor status is granted either to foreign nationals who develop and direct a substantial personal investment in the US or employees of enterprises that have substantial US investments. The investment must be active, substantial (ie a minimum of $100,000 and normally in excess of $250,000) and not marginal – it must have true economic substance. It must represent a real operating enterprise productive of some service or commodity. There is no fixed rule with respect to substantiality, but passive or speculative investment held for appreciation does not apply. Some qualifying investments include loans secured by the foreign national's own assets and cash reserves placed in a business account. Non-qualifying investments include mortgage debt or other loans secured by the enterprise's assets and recurring business costs normally paid out of income generated by the operation (rent, inventory etc).

Since there is only a slight difference between the E-1 and E-2 status, it is important for the UK acquiror to seek assistance if either route is to be used. In general, however, the applicant must be prepared to present a company cover letter outlining the basic elements of E-1 or E-2 status and supporting detailed documentation. This documentation may include items such as articles of incorporation, sales reports, shipping records and quarterly reports. In addition to the letter and documentation, the Embassy in London requests that all foreign nationals complete a special questionnaire covering the nature of the enterprise, its nationality, and other matters relevant to E-1 and E-2 status.

E series visas for UK nationals can be valid for up to five years and can authorise an unlimited number of entries. At the point of entry, inspectors grant an E-visa holder an authorised admission for one year; once admitted to the US, the trader or investor can obtain extensions of stay for two years at a time. Alternatively, the person may leave the US, reenter on a currently valid visa and obtain a new one-year period of admission on each entry.

H-1 visa: temporary workers of distinguished merit and ability
This is a visa for professionals who desire to come temporarily to the US (normally for up to three years with extensions possible for up to five). However, the requirements are fairly rigid – the INS has a narrow definition of 'professional', virtually always requiring proof of a university degree, even where in the UK, non-degree apprenticeships exist as a route into a profession. The H-1 visa requires that the applicant be a professional, defined as having a baccalaureate or higher-level degree in a specialised course of study.

L-1 Visa: intracompany transferee
Employees of multinational organisations may enter the US as L-1 intracompany transferees. To qualify, the foreign national must have been employed abroad by a parent, subsidiary, branch, or affiliate of the US employer for a continuous period of one year prior to coming to the US. During the period the national was in overseas employment, he or she must have been employed as a manager, an executive, or in a capacity that required specialised, advance-level knowledge of information proprietary to the organisation. Furthermore, the foreign national must be going to the US to fill a position that is managerial or executive in nature or requires specialised knowledge. 'Executive' is defined as an assignment within an organisation in which the employee primarily directs the management of an organisation or a major component or function of the organisation. An 'executive' establishes goals and policies, exercises a wide latitude of discretionary decision making subject only to general supervision or direction from higher level executives and is not an employee who primarily performs the tasks necessary to produce the products or provides the services of the organisation. For start-up situations there may be slightly more flexibility about these requirements during the initial phase of operations.

In past years foreign nationals entered the US on H- or L-series visas and stayed for lengthy periods in valid non-immigrant classification. However, regulations published in 1987 now limit a foreign national's stay in either H-1 or L-1 status, and the combined stay in either category normally cannot exceed five years. A sixth year may be granted only when extraordinary circumstances exist.

J-1 visa: exchange visitors
The US government has approved a number of exchange visitor programmes through which certain foreign nationals are eligible to travel to the US in order to experience US culture, business procedures and educational opportunities. The purpose of these programmes is to provide cultural exchange, but also include development of business techniques which makes these programmes available to a foreign employer who conducts business through a US office or with US clients. These programmes are administered both by large multinational companies and by business groups such as a chamber of commerce. Much of the selection process is run by the sponsoring organisation which gives some measure of flexibility; the drawback to this point is that a visa is normally issued for a maximum of 18 months. Persons who are not UK nationals may be subject to a two year foreign residency requirement upon completion of their J-1 programme in the US.

Immigrant classification

Nearly all foreign nationals who seek permanent residence must apply for immigrant classification based on (a) a family relationship to a US citizen or permanent resident foreign national, or (b) an offer of full-time, permanent employment from a US employer. Two job-based immigration categories exist and the third preference category applies to professionals and foreign nationals of exceptional ability in the sciences or arts; a sixth preference category applies to skilled and unskilled workers in short supply. Job-based immigration generally requires interaction with more than one federal government agency. Immigration to the US is limited by country per year; there are very few applications granted outside the quota system. Therefore, the objective in applying for immigrant status is normally to identify the fastest route to an allocated slot usually either through a family reunification or job preference category.

If the foreign national properly entered the US in valid non-immigrant status and has never violated the terms for admission, he or she may be eligible for adjustment of status and is otherwise qualified, if an immigrant visa is currently available. (Availability of visa numbers is a key factor because a quota system exists which limits the number of third and sixth preference visas awarded annually in each category.)

Once the foreign national becomes a permanent resident, he or she must maintain his or her status by manifesting a subjective intent to reside permanently in the US. Absences from the US by a permanent resident for more than one year can lead to the forfeiting of a foreign national's permanent residence status unless advance permission is obtained from the US Immigration Service. Despite being a permanent resident, the foreign national is subject to exclusion each time he or she enters the US, unless he or she possesses a valid re-entry document, demonstrates intent to maintain permanent resident status and is not excludable under criminal or other enumerated grounds.

Conclusion

Although this section provides a basic overview of those visas most commonly affecting UK nationals entering the US market, it is not exhaustive. To obtain a complete overview of visas and foreign national requirements when entering the US, foreign acquirors should consult legal counsel and/or the American Embassy in London. The Embassy address is:

Embassy of the United States of America, 24 Grosvenor Square, London W1A 1EA; *tel* (1) 499–9000

US tax considerations and state corporate tax rates

1 US tax considerations

For certain items discussed briefly in the text of Chapter 3, additional detailed information is presented below. This section must be read in conjunction with Chapter 3 to understand both the context and significance of the items discussed within this appendix.

Depreciation
The classes and their assigned methods are:

Classes using 200 per cent declining balance method (with a switch to the straight-line method in order to maximise the deduction):

- 3 year property: this class includes certain short-lived tangible personal property (ie class life of four years or less);
- 5 year property: this class includes most types of machinery and equipment, automobiles, light-duty trucks, data handling equipment, computers, and other tangible personal property;
- 7 year property: this class includes office furniture, fixtures and equipment, and property without a class life that is not otherwise classified; and
- 10 year property: property with a class life of 16 or more years but less than 20 years (eg transportation property).

The following classes use 150 per cent declining balance method with a switch to the straight-line method in order to maximise the deduction:

- 15 year property – property with a class life of 20 or more years but less than 25 years;
- 20 year property – property with a class life of 25 or more years;

Property to which the straight-line method applies:

- residential real property – 27.5 years; and
- non residential real property – 31.5 years.

The cost of certain property eligible for ACRS deductions may instead be expensed currently. A taxpayer may elect to expense up to $10,000 of property. This ceiling is limited to an amount not in excess of taxable income, derived from the active conduct of a trade or business, computed without regard to the cost of the qualifying property being expensed and subject to a dollar-for-dollar reduction to the extent the cost of qualified property placed in service during the year exceeds $200,000. (Any amount disallowed can be carried forward indefinitely.) Amounts so expensed are then excluded from calculating the ACRS deduction.

In lieu of these accelerated cost recovery deductions, taxpayers may irrevocably elect to claim straight-line ACRS deductions over the regular recovery period. This election applies to all property in a class placed in service during the tax year. Certain other options are also available on both a class by class basis and asset by asset basis, including a limited ability to expense some property put in service during the year.

Other allowable expenses

Some additional allowable expenses include:

- Repair and maintenance – These expenses are deductible to the extent that they do not represent capital improvements.
- Research and development expenditures – These expenses, paid or incurred during the taxable year, are deductible currently. Alternatively, if such amounts are chargeable to a capital account during the year, and are not chargeable as depreciable or depletable property, an election may be made to amortise these expenditures over a period of not less than 60 months, beginning with the month in which the taxpayer first realises benefits from such expenditures.
- Advertising – Expenses spent on advertising are deductible.
- Bad debt – Bad debts are deductible, under the specific charge-off method, when they become worthless. The reserve method, whereby a deduction is allowed for a reasonable addition to a bad debt reserve, is allowable for commercial banks with total average assets of $500 million or less, and for thrift institutions.
- Start-up expenditures – generally, start-up costs, that is costs incurred in connection with investigating the creation or acquisition of an active trade or business or creating an active trade or business must be capitalised. However, a taxpayer may elect to amortise such costs over a period of 60 months, beginning with the month business begins.
- Employee benefit plans – Expenses of employee benefit plans, including contributions to employee pension, profit sharing, and other retirement plans, are deductible within limits.
- Charitable deduction – A domestic corporation may generally deduct up to 10 per cent of its taxable income, with adjustments, for charitable contributions to qualified US charities. Excess charitable deductions can be carried over for five years.

Non-business income

The following types of US source non-business income are generally not taxable to a foreign corporation.

- Gains from the sale of certain inventory, capital assets, and other property, except US real property interests.
- Interest received on deposits with banks and certain other financial institutions.
- Interest received on portfolio debt investments. Portfolio interest does not include interest received by a bank on a loan and interest received by a foreign creditor that also owns 10 per cent or more of the voting shares of the US debtor corporation.
- Interest on certain obligations issued by US state and local governments.
- Original issue discount on debt obligations that mature within 183 days or less after issuance or on certain debt obligations that pay tax-exempt interest.

Effectively connected income

For foreign entities not engaged in a US trade or business, no income is treated as effectively connected with a US trade or business except for gains from the disposition of US real property interests. For foreign entities engaged in a US trade or business, the determination of whether income is effectively connected is based in part on the type of income and in part on the source of that income.

Foreign source income is generally not treated as effectively connected. It will be so treated, however, if the foreign entity has an office in the US to which the income is attributable and the income consists of (1) rents or royalties for the use of certain intangible property outside the US or gains from the sale or exchange of such property or (2) dividends, interest or gains from the sale of shares and financial instruments derived from carrying on a banking, financing, or similar business in the US, or received by a corporation whose principal business is trading shares and securities for its own account.

Income from the disposition of a US real property interest is considered US source income; however, there are special treatments which may apply. In addition, income from the sale of personal property by a US resident generally is US source.

Other forms of taxes

- Environmental tax – An environmental tax is imposed on a corporation at 0.12 per cent on the excess of its modified AMTI (alternative minimum taxable income) over $2 million. The tax applies whether or not the corporation has AMT (alternative minimum tax) liability.
- Accumulated earnings tax – The accumulated earnings tax is a penalty tax imposed upon corporations that accumulate earnings with the purpose of avoiding taxes on shareholders. Accumulated taxable income is defined as taxable income of the corporation with special adjustments and reduced by the current earnings that are retained for the reasonable needs of the business.
- Personal holding company tax – An additional tax of 28 per cent (38.5 per cent in the case of taxable years beginning in 1987) is imposed on the undistributed personal holding company income of a personal holding company. This type of company is a domestic or foreign corporation of which more than 50 per cent of the value is owned directly or indirectly by five or fewer individuals and of which more than 60 per cent of the adjusted ordinary income is personal holding company income (certain passive income, etc).

Special tax entities

Foreign Sales Corporations (FSCs)
Domestic corporations with an active business of exporting their products to foreign countries may find it advantageous to form an FSC for their export activity. An FSC is a foreign corporation that generally derives substantially all of its income from exporting US goods. To benefit as a FSC, a corporation must:

- be organised under the laws of any foreign country or US possession (other than Puerto Rico) that has an exchange of information agreement or certified income tax treaty with the US;
- make a timely election to be treated as a FSC;
- maintain an office outside the US in either a US possession or in a country with an acceptable exchange of information agreement with the US;
- meet certain foreign management and economic process requirements; and
- meet other specified requirements.

The benefit of a FSC is that a portion of its income is exempt from US tax when earned. Also available is a small FSC status, which also holds certain benefits.

Domestic International Sales Corporations (DISCs)
The FSC provisions enacted into law under the Deficit Reduction Act 1984 eliminated to a large extent the use of DISCs. Small exporters may continue to use the DISC rules, as modified, which permit a deferral of tax on substantially all DISC income.

To qualify for DISC benefits, a DISC generally must be incorporated in the US, have outstanding capital shares with a par or stated value of $2,500, elect to be treated as a DISC, and satisfy the gross receipts test and the gross assets test. The gross receipts test requires that at least 95 per cent of the gross receipts be qualified export receipts; the gross assets test requires that 95 per cent of the corporation's assets be qualified export assets.

Foreign investment companies
US persons including resident aliens may be subject to special taxation on distributions from or on the disposition of the shares in a foreign investment company or a passive foreign investment company.

S corporations
An S corporation is a domestic corporation that elects to be taxed generally as if it were a partnership. The income, deductions, and credits flow through and are treated as such to the shareholders. An S corporation must have 35 or fewer shareholders, all of whom generally must be US citizens or resident aliens.

Additional reporting requirements
Domestic or foreign corporations that are engaged in a trade or business within the US and that are controlled by a foreign person (company) generally are required to file Form 5472, Information Return of a Foreign Owned Corporation, annually. This form requires the reporting of certain transactions between the corporation and its related parties.

Tax rates
Taxable income (gross income less deductions) of a corporation is taxed at the following rates, effective from 1 July 1987:

Taxable income	Rate (per cent)
$0 to $50,000	15
$50,001 to $75,000	25
Over $75,000	34

Additionally, a surtax at 5 per cent is imposed on taxable income between $100,000 and $335,000. This additional tax operates to phase out the benefits of graduated rates below 34 per cent for corporations with taxable income in excess of $100,000. The effect of this surtax is to tax every extra dollar of taxable income in the $100,000 to $335,000 range at a 39 per cent rate.

The top US corporate tax rate before 1 July 1987, is 46 per cent. Blended tax rates apply to taxable years that straddle 1 July 1987. The top blended 1987 tax rate for a calendar-year corporation is 40 per cent.

Capital gains generally are taxed at the same rates as other income. However, if the top statutory rate imposed for any taxable year exceeds 34 per cent (without regard to the 5 per cent surtax), the tax on net capital gains cannot exceed 34 per cent.

These rates are applied to taxable income. The tax is then reduced by allowable credits, such as the foreign tax credit and the research credit.

In addition, corporations are subject to the alternative minimum tax if amounts so calculated are higher than the tax computed at the regular rates; they are also subject to certain other taxes if applicable.

Dispositions of US real property interests
The Foreign Investment in the Real Property Tax Act of 1980 added provisions to the Internal Revenue Code that treat a foreign person's gain or loss from the disposition of US real property interest as if such gain or loss were effectively connected with a trade or business. Both non-recognition relief and treaty relief are limited, and significant withholding requirements are imposed to assist tax collection. Although currently no annual information reporting requirements exist, future regulations could require foreign persons to submit information returns to disclose such holdings.

US real property interest
A US real property interest (USRPI) generally includes any interest in real property located in the United States or in the US Virgin Islands and any interest (other than solely as a creditor) in a domestic corporation that is or was a US real property holding corporation (USRPHC). An interest in real property includes a direct interest in US real property, including land and improvements thereon, mines, wells, and other natural deposits, and personal property associated with real property (that is, moveable walls and furnishings). The term does not include a domestic corporation that was not a USRPHC during the testing period (the preceding five years or, if shorter, the period

during which the taxpayer held an ownership interest). Moreover, the term does not include an interest in a corporation that is no longer a USRPI because the corporation has disposed of all of its USRPIs held during the testing period in fully taxable transactions. A USRPI does not include an interest in a domestically controlled real estate investment trust, nor does it include an interest in a class of stock in a publicly traded corporation unless the person disposing of the stock held, during the testing period, more than 5 per cent of such class of stock. Furthermore, a foreign corporation is not a USRPI (unless it has elected to be taxed as a domestic corporation).

US real property holding corporation

A USRPHC is a corporation that holds USRPIs with a fair market value of at least 50 per cent of the sum of the fair market values of its USRPIs, plus its interests in real property located outside the United States and its other assets that are used or held for use in a trade or business. Although a foreign corporation may be a USRPHC, an interest in a foreign corporation is not a USRPI other than for purposes of determining whether another corporation is a USRPHC. Accordingly, a foreign person generally is not subject to US taxation on any gain from the disposition of an interest in a foreign corporation (unless it has elected to be taxed as a domestic corporation).

When assets of a USRPHC are held by a partnership, trust, or estate, they are considered to be held proportionately by the partners or beneficiaries. Moreover, use of the assets in a trade or business by the partnership, trust, or estate, will be treated as business use by the partners or beneficiaries. This constructive ownership rule applies to as many tiers as exist in the partnership or trust structure.

A corporation's controlling stock interest (50 per cent or more of the fair market value of all classes of stock) in another corporation is disregarded in determining whether the controlling corporation is a USRPHCC. Rather, the controlling corporation is deemed to hold a proportionate part of each of the assets of the controlled corporation, with each asset having the same status (for example, used in a trade or business) as in the hands of the controlled corporation.

Foreign corporate distributions

A foreign corporation must recognise gain on the distribution of a USRPI to the extent that its fair market value exceeds the corporation's adjusted basis in the interest. This recognition of gain will not occur, however, if the distributee would, at the time of receipt, be subject to US tax on a subsequent disposition of the USRPI, and if the property, in the hands of the distributee, has a basis that is no greater than the basis of the property before the distribution, increased by the amount of any gain recognised by the distributing corporation.

Any provision for the non-recognition of gain or loss generally applies only to the exchange of a USRPI for another interest, the sale of which would be subject to US taxation. Regulations may prescribe the extent that the non-recognition provisions will apply.

Domestic corporation distributions

If a domestic corporation makes a dividend distribution of a USRPI to a non-resident alien or foreign corporation, the basis of the USRPI in the hands of the distributee is limited to the adjusted basis of the property before the distribution, plus the amount of any gain recognised by the distributor and any tax paid by the distributee.

Sales or exchanges of interests in partnerships, trusts, or estates

Under regulations, these sales or exchanges are to be treated as sales or exchanges of USRPIs to the extent attributable to the USRPIs owned by a partnership, estate or trust.

Contributions to capital

A non-resident alien or foreign corporation must recognise gain upon the transfer of a

USRPI to a foreign corporation as a contribution to capital or as paid in surplus, despite the general non-recognition rules applicable to these types of transactions. The amount that must be recognised is the fair market value of the USRPI in excess of the sum of its adjusted basis and any other gain recognised by the transferor.

Domestic corporation treatment
A foreign corporation that holds USRPIs with respect to which it is entitled to non-discriminatory treatment under an applicable treaty (including the UK–US treaty), may elect to be treated as a domestic corporation, thereby treating the sale of its shares as effectively connected with a US trade or business. This election is the only remedy for a non-discrimination claim under a treaty with respect to the USRPI of a foreign corporation.

Withholding requirements
The transferee (eg, buyer) of any USRPI generally is required to deduct and withhold a tax equal to 10 per cent of the amount realised by the foreign transferor (eg, seller) upon disposition of the property. Exemptions from withholding are allowed when:

- the transferor furnishes the transferee with an affidavit stating that the transferor is not a foreign person;
- a non-publicly traded domestic corporation furnishes to the transferee an affidavit stating that the domestic corporation is not a USRPI;
- the property is acquired by the transferee for his or her use as a residence and the amount realised on the disposition does not exceed $300,000; and
- the disposition is of shares in a class of shares in a corporation that is regularly traded on an established securities market.

Special withholding rules apply in the following situations:

- a domestic partnership, trust, or estate is required to withhold a tax equal to 34 per cent of any gain it realises on the disposition of a USRPI to the extent that the gain is allowable to a foreign partner or beneficiary;
- a foreign corporation is required to withhold a tax equal to 34 per cent of the amount of gain recognised on certain distributions of USRPIs;
- a US corporation that is a USRPI is required to withhold a tax equal to 10 per cent of the amount realised by a foreign shareholder upon a distribution of property in connection with redemption of shares or in connection with a corporate liquidation;
- a domestic or foreign partnership, trust, or estate is required to withhold a tax equal to 10 per cent of the fair market value of any USRPI distributed to a foreign partner or beneficiary where the transaction would be taxable under the Foreign Investment in Real Property Act (FIRPTA); and
- the transferee of a partnership interest or of a beneficial interest in a trust or estate will be required to withhold a tax equal to 10 per cent of the amount realised on the disposition, to the extent required under future Treasury regulations.

The withholding otherwise required can be reduced or eliminated by obtaining a with-holding certificate from the IRS. Either the transferor or the transferee may apply for the withholding certificate. Withholding can be reduced or eliminated when the transferor's maximum tax liability on the disposition of a USRPI is less than the amount that would otherwise have to be withheld. Other reasons for reduced or eliminated withholding also exist. Moreover, the transferor can apply to the IRS for early refund of excess amounts withheld.

Taxation of foreign currency exchange rate gains and losses
The Tax Reform Act of 1986 provided a comprehensive set of rules for the US tax treatment of transactions involving foreign currency. The Act generally adopted the financial accounting concept of functional currency and requires all federal income tax determinations to be made in a taxpayer's functional currency. A taxpayer's functional

currency is the US dollar or, in the case of a qualified business unit, the currency in which a significant part of the unit's activities are conducted and that is used by the unit for accounting purposes. A qualified business unit is any separate and clearly identified unit of a business of a taxpayer for which separate books and records are maintained. US corporations and US branches operating in the United States generally have the US dollar as their functional currency. A taxpayer or a qualified business unit with a foreign functional currency must translate its income subject to US tax into US dollars at appropriate exchange rates.

Foreign currency exchange rate gains and losses attributable to certain transactions in a non-functional currency are calculated separately from any gains or losses on the underlying transactions and are taxable as ordinary income or losses which, to the extent provided in future Treasury regulations, may be characterised as interest income or expense, as the case may be. A foreign currency gain or loss is defined as a gain or loss from certain transactions realised by reasons of a change in the exchange rate between the date an asset or liability is taken into account and the date it is paid or otherwise disposed of. This gain or loss is generally recognised only when there is a closed or completed transaction. Moreover, the source of the exchange gain or loss is determined by reference to the residence of the taxpayer or the qualified business unit that realised the gain or loss.

The foreign currency transactions to which ordinary income and loss treatments apply are transactions where the amount that the taxpayer is entitled to receive or required to pay is denominated in a currency other than the functional currency of the taxpayer or is determined by reference to the value of one or more non-functional currencies, and where the taxpayer:

• acquires or becomes the obligator under a debt instrument;
• accrues or otherwise takes into account any item of expense or gross income or gross receipts that is to be paid or received at later date; and
• enters into or acquires any forward contract, futures contract, option, or similar financial instrument that is not 'marked to market' (treated as if sold at its fair market value) at the close of the taxable year under Internal Revenue Code section 1256.

Furthermore, the disposition of any non-functional currency, including demand or time deposits, is treated as a transaction to which these rules apply.

2 State corporate income tax rates

The following is a listing of the US states and their corresponding corporate income tax rate. The rate provided generally reflects the maximum income tax rate imposed by each state, however actual effective tax rates may vary. As these are subject to change, it is advisable for investors to consult their tax adviser for the most current rates. Note, however, that income tax is but one type of tax to which a corporation may be subject. States and/or local municipalities may impose additional taxes such as franchise taxes, excise taxes, sales and use taxes, property taxes, etc.

State	Tax rate %	State	Tax rate %
Alabama	5.0	Delaware	8.7
Alaska	9.4	Florida	5.5
Arizona	10.5	Georgia	6.0
Arkansas	6.0	Hawaii	6.4
California	9.3	Idaho	8.0
Colorado	5.5	Illinois	4.0
Connecticut	11.5	Indiana	3.4

State	Tax rate %	State	Tax rate %
Iowa	12	New Jersey	9.0
Kansas	4.5 + 2.25 surtax for income over $25,000	New Mexico	7.6
		New York	9.0
		North Carolina	7.0
Kentucky	7.25	North Dakota	10.5
Lousiania	8.0	Ohio	9.2
Maine	8.93	Oklahoma	5.0
Maryland	7.0	Oregon	6.6
Massachusetts	9.5	Pennsylvania	8.5
Michigan	2.35	Rhode Island	8.0
Minnesota	9.5	South Carolina	6.0
Mississippi	5.0	Tennessee	6.0
Missouri	5.0	Utah	5.0
Montana	6.75 + 4.0 surtax	Vermont	8.25
		Virginia	6.0
Nebraska	6.65	West Virginia	9.6
New Hampshire	8.0	Wisconsin	7.9

Note: Nevada, South Dakota, Texas, Washington, and Wyoming do not tax the income of corporations. However, other taxes may apply in these states.

Sources of information: US companies and industries

Sources of information: US companies and industries

1 Directories and yearbooks
Only the most generally useful directories and yearbooks are listed below; a number of more specialised directories are published and many are available in the UK through the British Library – Science Reference Library. In addition, for those more defined subjects or industries, it is useful to consult various trade publications. Generally, however, the British Library will be able to provide either the actual information or additional information for obtaining it. Details of additional sources may be obtained from the specialist publishers listed in section 13 of this appendix.

America's Corporate Families and International Affiliates
London: Dun & Bradstreet. Annual, published in April. Includes information on c22,000 companies, listed alphabetically by parent company. Details of business name, ultimate parent company, SIC codes, principal bank, accountants, legal counsel, and names and titles of officers are included.

The Billion Dollar Directory
London: Dun & Bradstreet. Annual, published in March. Details of corporate linkage and ownership of subsidiaries and divisions for some 8,000 US parents and 44,000 subsidiaries and divisions. Indexed by company, location, and SIC code.

Dun's Business Rankings
London: Dun & Bradstreet. Annual, published in April. A ranking of US public and private companies by sales volume and by number of employees. Details of name, address, telephone number, senior executives and SIC code are included.

MacRae's Blue Book
New York: MacRae's. Annual.   An industrial buying guide covering Original Equipment Market companies. Gives directory data and capital ratings. In five volumes.

Million Dollar Directory Series
London: Dun & Bradstreet. Annual, published in April. In six volumes, gives detailed information on US businesses with a net worth of over $500,000, with a separate volume for the top 50,000 companies with a net worth of over $1,850,000. The series gives details of parent company, subsidiaries, address, sales, number of employees, principal bank, division names, functions and titles of senior executives, legal counsel and accounting firm. Separate volumes list companies by location and by industry (SIC code).

Moody's Investment Guides
London: Dun & Bradstreet. The Moody's Investment Guides series consists of:

● *Moody's Handbook of Common Stocks*
   Published quarterly, lists business information, dividends, earnings, sales, address, principal directors and officers for some 950 of the most active US stocks.

● *Moody's Handbook of OTC Stocks*
   Published quarterly, gives financial and business information on the most active stocks traded on NASDAQ.

- *Moody's Industry Review*
  Comparative statistics and industry rankings for c3,600 companies with stocks traded on the NYSE, ASE, OTC and regional exchanges.

- *Moody's Dividend Record and Annual Dividend Record*
  The *Dividend Record*, published twice-weekly, includes data on c13,000 dividends. Eight cumulative issues are published each year and an Annual Cumulation is available for the calendar year.

- *Moody's Industrial*
  Twice-weekly news reports on all industrial companies listed on the NYSE and ASE, plus some 500 companies listed on regional stock exchanges.

- *Moody's Bank and Finance*
  Twice-weekly news reports on c11,000 banking and financial institutions.

Standard & Poor's Corporation Records
London: Standard & Poor's Corporation. Looseleaf with updating service. In six basic volumes. Detailed descriptions of general operations, plant locations, subsidiaries, financial structure and securities are given for c8,200 companies; abbreviated data is given for an additional 2,000 corporations. A *Daily News* supplement is issued five days a week and accumulated approximately every fifteen days. Indexed by topic, subsidiaries, affiliates and SIC code.

Standard & Poor's Register of Corporations, Directors and Executives
London: Standard & Poor's Corporation. Annual with cumulative supplements in April, July and October. In three volumes: *Corporate Listings*, which provides directory data for 45,000 nationally known companies; *Biographical Profiles*, with data on 70,000 top executives; and *Indexes*, by state and city, SIC code, subsidiaries and associates, ultimate parent company, new listings, and obituaries.

Standard & Poor's Stock Reports
London: Standard & Poor's Corporation. Two page reports on c3,700 companies. In three sets of four volumes each: NYSE Stock Reports, ASE Stock Reports, and OTC Stock Reports. Revised reports are issued weekly. Information given includes latest price and current year's range, a seven year chart of high/low prices, earnings and dividend rankings for common stocks, a summary of business operations, per share, income and balance sheet data.

Thomas Register of American Manufacturers and Thomas Register Catalog File
New York: Thomas Publishing Company Inc. Annual. In 26 volumes, it covers some 138,000 US companies. Gives details of name, address, telephone number, products and services. Some trade names are included with additional data (number of employees, names of parent and/or subsidiaries) for selected companies. Includes product catalogues from 1250 companies.

US Reference Book
London: Dun & Bradstreet. Published every two months. Gives company name, address, year of formation, activity, credit appraisal and credit rating, and estimated financial strength for c3 million businesses arranged by company location. In five volumes.

Ward's Business Directory
Belmont, California: Information Access Company. Annual. In three volumes, volume one lists the largest US companies, volume two the major US private companies. Volume three lists international companies. Each record gives details of name, address, chief executive, SIC, sales and employees. Indexed by SIC, location and company name.

Who owns Whom: North America
London: Dun & Bradstreet. Annual, published in June. In four sections, sections 1 and 2 list US and Canadian parent companies and give details of their subsidiaries and associates; section 3 lists non-US parent companies and their North American

subsidiaries and associates; section 4 consists of an alphabetical listing of some 60,000 subsidiaries and associates with the name of their parent company.

The titles and scope of other, suitable directories can be established using a directory of directories such as the *Directory of Directories*, published twice-yearly by Gale Research Co of Detroit.

2 Newspapers and periodicals
The major US business newspapers and journals are:

The New York Times
AO Sulzberger/ B Powers Ltd. Daily, Monday-Sunday.

The Wall Street Journal
Dow Jones & Co Inc/International Press Centre. Daily, Monday-Friday.

The Washington Post
Washington Post. Daily, Monday-Sunday

Barron's
Dow Jones & Co. Weekly. A tabloid newspaper concentrating on company reviews and stock market statistics.

Business Week
McGraw Hill Publications Co. Weekly. A leading US business magazine.

Forbes Magazine
Forbes Magazine. Fortnightly

Fortune
Time Inc. Fortnightly.

Institutional Investor
Institutional Investor Inc. Monthly.

Relevant UK/international publications include:

Economist
Economist Publications. Weekly.

Euromoney
Euromoney Publications Ltd. Monthly.

Financial Times
Financial Times Ltd. Daily, Monday-Saturday.

International Herald Tribune
International Herald Tribune, published jointly by the *New York Times* and *Washington Post*. Daily, Monday-Friday and a combined Saturday/Sunday edition.

Investors Chronicle
Financial Times Business Publishing Ltd. Weekly.

The two leading specialist publications on the subject of US and UK mergers and acquisitions are:

Acquisitions Monthly
Tudor House Publications. Monthly

Financial Times Mergers & Acquisitions
Financial Times Business Publishing. Monthly

For information about specific industries, trade journals (which frequently include trade directory type listings) should be used. Appropriate journals can be identified using sources such as *Willings Press Guide* (annual, British Media Publications), the *Standard*

Periodicals Directory (New York: Oxbridge Communications, 1987), the *Newsletters Directory* (Detroit: Gale Research Co), or *Trade Directory Information in Journals* published by the British Library Science Reference & Information Service.

3 Statistics
The major US statistical series are:

Business Conditions Digest (Monthly)
Business Statistics (Twice-yearly)
Survey of Current Business (Monthly)
The above titles are produced by the Bureau of Economic Analysis, Dept. of Commerce and are published by the US General Printing Office (USGPO).
Statistical Abstract of the United States (Annual)
Bureau of the Census. Published by the USGPO.
US Industrial Outlook (Annual)
Bureau of Industrial Economics, Dept. of Commerce. Published by the USGPO.

Many other statistical series are published; these can be traced in directories such as the *American Statistics Index* and *Statistical Reference Index*, compiled and published by the Congressional Information Service, Washington DC.

4 Online databases
Many of the published or 'hard copy' sources of information listed above are also available online. Online sources of information have the advantage of being more flexible for the purposes of searching and retrieving data and are usually more up-to-date than conventionally published sources. In many cases they may be accessed on a 'pay-as-you use' basis, thus removing the need to buy a range of expensive reference materials which may be used infrequently. The range and scope of available databases, and the costs of searching, vary enormously. It should be noted, however, that the following information was current at the time of writing, but developments and alterations are constantly taking place which may change specifics to some of the databases. An indication of databases available on a specific subject can be obtained using a specialist directory, eg *The Cuadra Directory of Databases*, published twice-yearly by Cuadra/Elsevier or *Books and Periodicals Online: A Guide to Publication Contents of Business and Legal Databases*, published twice yearly by Learned Information. The *Cuadra Directory* is also available online via the *Dialog* system. As a comprehensive listing of all relevant databases would be impossible to include, brief details of only the most general are given. These include:

ABI/Inform
A bibliographic database of abstracts of every article appearing in 500+ business and management journals with selective coverage of a further 300 journals. Updated weekly, available via *Dialog*, *Datastar* and others.

Businesswire
The full text of press releases of US companies. The press releases cover product news, mergers and acquisitions, financial results, share issues, personnel changes, etc. Updated daily and available via *Dialog*.

Cendata
Produced by the Bureau of the Census, US Dept. of Commerce, this database contains selected statistical data, press releases and product information from the Bureau of the Census. Available via *Dialog*.

Compustat
Produced by Standard & Poors, it is a database of financial statistics on c6,500 companies updated daily. The *Compustat* database is available via a variety of sources, including magnetic tapes, floppy diskettes, and commercial database host systems (see section 5).

Datastream
A databank of company, industry and economic information, with comprehensive US coverage. The database may be searched in a wide variety of ways and includes a graphics facility for charting the results of a search. Available only from Datastream International.

Disclosure
Produced by Disclosure Inc, it consists of financial and textual data taken from documents filed with the SEC. Updated weekly, it may be searched for financial, industrial, geographic, biographical and other data. It is available via at least 12 host sytems, including *Dialog, Mead Data Central* and *Dialcom*.

Donnelly Demographics
Produced by Donnelly Marketing Information Services, the Donnelly Demographics include selected demographic data from US censuses with current year estimates and five year projections in selected categories. Gives data for the US as a whole, and for individual states, counties, cities, and metropolitan areas.

Dow Jones News Service
Selected news items from leading US financial newspapers and journals (*Wall Street Journal, Barrons*, etc) and the Dow Jones News Wire Service. Available via the *Textline* service (updated daily) or the *Datastar* service (updated weekly).

Dun's Electronic Yellow Pages
Produced by Dun's Marketing Services, a division of Dun & Bradstreet. Online directory information for c8.5 million US businesses and professionals. A full directory listing is given for each entry, including address, telephone number, SIC codes and employee numbers. Updated quarterly and available via *Dialog*.

Dun's Financial Records
Produced by Dun & Bradstreet Credit Services & Dun's Marketing Services. Updated quarterly, it contains financial information, spreadsheet analysis, industry comparisons, company history and key ratios for some 1.5 million US business establishments. Available via *Dialog*.

Dun's Market Identifiers
Produced by Dun's Marketing Services and available via a number of host systems. Contains current address, financial and marketing data on almost 2 million US companies with 10 or more employees or $1 million or more in sales. Updated quarterly and available via *Dialog*.

Dun's Million Dollar Directory
This corresponds to the printed Directory; it is updated annually and available via a number of systems, including *Dialog*.

Dunsprint
Produced by *Dun & Bradstreet*. Includes comprehensive financial and credit rating information on some 10 million companies in the USA, UK and western Europe. Updated daily and available only from *Dun & Bradstreet*.

Exchange Service
Research reports on US and international companies and industries prepared by investment banks and stockbrokers, together with information taken from SEC filings and annual reports. Available from *Mead Data Central*.

Financial Times Company Information
Covers all articles in the *Financial Times* which refer to a company. Updated daily and available via *Datastar*.

Financial Times Full-Text
The full text of the *Financial Times*, available within two days of publication. Updated daily and available from *Profile Information, Dialog*, or *Mead Data Central*.

Findex
An index to market research and industry reports. Available via *Dialog*.

Frost & Sullivan Market Research Reports
Summaries of some 200 market reports prepared by Frost & Sullivan, covering industrial markets in the US and Europe, updated irregularly (as new reports are published) and available via *Datastar*.

Industry Data Sources
An index to marketing and financial data on 65 industries. Covers market research reports, industry newsletters, journals, etc. Available via *Datastar*, *Dialog*.

Investext
Produced by Technical Data International, it includes the full text of stockbrokers' reports issued by c50 stockbrokers (25 Wall Street, 10 US regional and 12 foreign) and is updated weekly. Available from some six host systems and direct from the producer.

M & A Filings
Detailed abstracts of every original and amended merger and acquisition document released by the SEC. Updated daily and produced by Charles E Simon & Company. Available via *Dialog*.

McCarthy Online
Press reports and company data sheets from some 60 leading business publications. Available via *Profile Information* and *BT Hotline*.

Moody's Corporate News
Financial and business information on some 13,000 US corporations; this is the online equivalent of *Moody's Bank & Finance*, *Moody's Industrial*, *Moody's OTC Industrial*, *Moody's Public Utility* and *Moody's Transportation*. Updated weekly.

Moody's Corporate Profiles
Financial and descriptive data on 4,000 of the most important publicly-held companies. Updated weekly and produced by Moody's Investors Service, a division of Dun & Bradstreet.

Newsnet
The full texts of c350 specialist business newsletters covering some 30 industries and sectors. Subscribers also have access to some ten major wire services, including AP, Reuters, UPI. Available from *Newsnet Inc*.

Nexis
A full-text news database covering more than 150 newspapers, journals, newsletters and wire services. Available from *Mead Data Central*.

Standard & Poor's Register
Corresponding to the printed Register, available via the *Dialog* system.

Textline
A database of company and industry news taken from over 1,500 international and national sources. The US service covers the *Dow Jones News Retrieval Service*, *Dow Jones Newswire* and the *Reuter* services. Updated daily and available from *Reuters*.

Thomas Register Online
Corresponds to listings in the first three volumes of the Thomas Register, updated annually and available via *Dialog*.

US M & A Database
Produced by IDD Information Services, a wholly-owned subsidiary of Extel Financial, it consists of details of US merger and acquisition deals, both public and private, over $1 million. Some 175 data items on both acquiring and target companies are included.

Washington Post
The full text of the *Washington Post*. Available via *Dialog*.

Who owns Whom
Produced by Dun & Bradstreet, it corresponds to the *Who owns Whom* directory series and is available via *Pergamon Financial Data Services*. Updated monthly.

5 Host systems

Host systems may provide access to only one database (eg Datastream) or to a vast number of systems. The following are the leading hosts in the UK; many other systems are also available and may be identified using directories such as the *Cuadra Directory* mentioned in section 4 or advisory services such as *Aslib*, detailed in section 11.

Datastar
Plaza Suite, 114 Jermyn Street, London SW1Y 6HJ; *tel* (01) 930 5503

Datastream International Ltd
58/64 City Road, London EC1Y 2AL; *tel* (01) 250 3000

Dialcom
Telecom Gold, PO Box 1351, London NW2 7HZ; *tel* (0800) 200 700

Dialog
Dialog Information Services (UK), PO Box 188, Abingdon, Oxford OX1 5AX; *tel* (0865) 730275
or
Dialog Information Services, 3460 Hillview Avenue, Palo Alto, CA 94304, USA; *tel* (1) (415) 858 3810

Dow News News/Retrieval
Dow Jones Information Service, PO Box 300, Princeton, New Jersey 08540, USA; *tel* (1) (609) 452 2000

Mead Data Central
International House, 1 St Katherine's Way, London E1 9UN
or
9393 Springboro Pike, PO Box 933, Dayton, Ohio 45401, USA; *tel* (1) 513 865 6800

Pergamon Financial Data Services
Achilles House, Western Avenue, London W3 0UA; *tel* (01) 992 3456

Profile Information
Sunbury House, 79 Staines Road West, Sunbury-on-Thames, Middlesex TW16 7AH; *tel* (0932) 761444; *tlx* 8811720; *fx* (0932) 761444 ext 2615

Reuters Holdings
UK Sales, Reuters Ltd, 85 Fleet Street, London EC4P 4AJ; *tel* (01) 250 1122

6 Stockbrokers' publications

Stockbrokers reports are an extremely valuable source of information on companies and industries/markets. They may, however, be very difficult to obtain. Many brokers' reports are now available via online databases (eg the *ICC Brokers Report* database on *Datastar* or *Dialog*, the *Investext* database on *Dialog*). Collections of stockbrokers' reports are also maintained by the British Library Science Reference and Information Service and by the University of Warwick Business Information Service.

7 Market research

A primary source of company and industry information. Market research reports are often extremely expensive, but are frequently held by major business libraries. The British Library holds an extensive collection of market research reports. The bulk of the collection is held by the Science Reference and Information Service at the Holborn reading room although the Document Supply Centre has an increasing collection of these reports which can be borrowed from the Document Supply Centre, in many cases via a local public library. A number of directories and indexes covering market research are available, both in paper format and online. Major sources include:

Findex
The Directory of Market Research Reports, Studies and Surveys. Published by Find/SVP. Annual with a mid-year supplement.

Marketing Surveys Index
A cumulative monthly directory of published market reseach. Coverage is world-wide. Published by Marketing Strategies for Industry (UK) Ltd.

8 Card services
The Extel and McCarthy card services are traditional sources of company information. These services will be found in most major business libraries, but Extel's North American service is limited to data on the top 550 US and Canadian companies. The information provided includes name, address, telephone number, directors, principal activities, subsidiaries, consolidated profit and loss accounts and balance sheets, and the Chairman's statement. The McCarthy North American Company Service contains records for all companies with common shares quoted on the New York, American, Toronto, or Montreal Exchanges. McCarthy cards consist of reprints of the full text of articles appearing in leading business periodicals and newspapers, including *Forbes*, *The New York Times*, *The Wall Street Journal* and *The Washington Post*, and company results. Card services are updated on a daily basis.

9 Microfiche

SEC Filings
Available from IPI, in either microfiche or paper format. SEC 10K, annual reports, 10Q and 8K documents, together with proxy and registration documents, acquisition documents and tender statements.

10 Libraries
The majority of the sources listed above will be available in major regional libraries such as:

Birmingham Public Libraries, Central Library, Chamberlain Square, Birmingham B3 3HQ; *tel* (0635) 34867
City Business Library (Until late 1988), Gillett House, 55 Basinghall Street, London EC2V 5BX; *tel* (01) 638 8215/6
then: Furness House, 105 Fenchurch Street, London EC3, (temporary accommodation for about 3 years)
City of Manchester Libraries, Commercial Library, St Peter's Square, Manchester M2 5PD; *tel* (061) 236 9422
Holborn Reference Library, 32 Theobald's Road, London WC1X 8PA; *tel* (01) 405 2706
Liverpool Public Library, Central Libraries, William Brown Street, Liverpool L3 8EW; *tel* (051) 207 2147
Newcastle upon Tyne City Libraries, Business & Technical Library, Central Library, PO Box IDX, Newcastle upon Tyne NE99 1DX; *tel* (0632) 617339
Sheffield City Libraries, Central Library, Surrey Street, Sheffield S1 1XZ; *tel* (0742) 734742/3
Westminster Central Reference Library, 35 St Martin's Street, London WC2H 7HP; *tel* (01) 798 2034/6

Other major business and specialist libraries include:

The British Library, Science Reference & Information Service, 25 Southampton Buildings, Chancery Lane, London WC2A 1AW; *tel* (01) 405 8721
United States Embassy, Commercial Library, Grosvenor Square, London W1A 1AE; *tel* (01) 499 7060

11 Information services
Several organisations with extensive collections of commercial reference materials will carry out research on a commercial basis. Services offered will include literature searches, the provision of documents such as annual reports, provision of copies of articles, reading lists and online searches. The principal UK commercial information services are:

BBC Data Enquiry Service, Room 7, 1 Portland Place, London W1A 1AA; *tel* (01) 927 5998

The British Library Business Information Service, 25 Southampton Buildings, Chancery Lane, London WC2A 1BR; *tel* (01) 323 7979

Financial Times Business Information Service, Bracken House, 10 Cannon Street, London EC4P 4BY; *tel* (01) 236 4000

London Business School Information Service, Sussex Place, Regents Park, London NW1 4SA; *tel* (01) 724 2300

Manchester Business School Information Service, Manchester Business School, Booth Street West, Manchester M15 6PB; *tel* (061) 275 6333

SVP United Kingdom, 12 Argyll Street, London W1V 1AB; *tel* (01) 734 9272

University of Warwick Business Information Service, University of Warwick Library, Gibbet Hill Road, Coventry CV4 7AL; *tel* (0203) 523251/523051

Major US business information services include:

Find/SVP, Information Clearing House, 625 6th Avenue, New York NY 10011; *tel* (1) 212 645 4500

Citicorp Information Center, Citicorp Center, New York NY 10043; *tel* (1) 212 559 9000

Center for Business Research, CW Post Campus, Long Island University, PO Box 121, Greenvale NY 11548; *tel* (1) 516 299 2832

Other US commercial information services can be identified using the *Directory of Fee-based Information Services*, published annually by Burwell Enterprises, Houston, Texas.

In addition to these commercial information services there are also a large number of information consultants who specialise in particular areas of business information and/or online searching. These consultants may be identified by specialist directories, eg Aslib's *Directory of Online Search Services*, or by contacting relevant organisations. Aslib, The Association for Information Management, is a particularly useful source of information.

Aslib
The Association for Information Management, Information House, 26/27 Boswell Street, London WC1N 3JZ; *tel* (01) 253 3030

A number of the most prominent UK information brokers are listed in the *Business Information Yearbook*, published by Headland Press. These include:

Business Information Associates, 34 Despard Road, Eastern Green, Coventry CV5 7DL; *tel* (0203) 470499

First Contact, Micrologic Suite, Adastra House, 401–405 Nether Street, London N3 1QG; *tel* (01) 346 9499

Personality Profiles, Kirkman House, 12–14 Whitfield Street, London W1P 5RD; *tel* (01) 436 4050

12 Bibliography
Business Information Yearbook 1988/89 Headland Press, 1988; 186p.
Business & Company Databases 1988 P Bater & H Parkinson; Aslib, 1988; 86p.
Market Research: A Guide to British Library Holdings S Ashpitel; British Library Science Reference & Information Service, 1988; 180p.

Directory of Online Databases Cuadra Associates, 1986.
Directory of Online Search Services Aslib, 1988.
How to find US Business Information Gerry Smith, in Business Information Review, vol 4, No 1, July 1987; Headland Press.
Paying for Business Information: A Survey of Fee-based Services Carmel McGrother, in Business Information Review, vol 4, No 4, April 1988; Headland Press.
Macmillan's Mergers & Acquisitions Yearbook K. D. George; Globe Book Services Ltd, 1988
Directory of International Sources of Business Information Sarah Ball; Pitman Publishing 1988

13 Publishers
Cuadra Associates Inc, 2001 Wilshire Boulevard, Suite 305, Santa Monica, California 90403, USA; *tel* (1) 213 829 9972; *tlx* 755814
or
1900 L Street N.W. Suite 614, Washington DC 20036, USA; *tel* (1) 202 463 2107
Dow Jones & Co Inc, 22 Cortlandt Street, New York NY 10007, USA; *tel* (1) 212 285 5000
Dun & Bradstreet International, 26/32 Clifton Street, London EC2B 2AQ; *tel* (01) 377 4295; *tlx* 886697; *fx* (01) 247 3836
The Economist Newspaper Ltd, 25 St James's Street, London SW1A 1HG; *tel* (01) 839 7000
Euromoney Publications, Nestor House, Playhouse Yard, London EC4V 5EX; *tel* (01) 236 3288
Financial Times Ltd, Bracken House, 10 Cannon Street, London EC4P 4BY; *tel* (01) 248 8000
Financial Times Business Publishing Ltd, Greystoke Place, Fetter Lane, London EC4A 1ND; *tel* (01) 405 6969
Forbes Magazine, 60 Fifth Avenue, New York NY 10011, USA
Frost & Sullivan Ltd, 4 Grosvenor Gardens, London SW1 0DH; *tel* (01) 730 3438
Globe Book Services Ltd, Stockton House, 1 Melbourne Place, London WC2B 4LF; *tel* (01) 379 4687
Headland Press, 1 Henry Smith's Terrace, Headland, Cleveland TS24 0PD; *tel* (0429) 231902
Institutional Investor Inc, 488 Madison Avenue, New York NY 10022, USA; *tel* (1) 212 303 3300
International Press Centre, 76 Shoe Lane, London EC4A 3IB; *tel* (01) 353 9503
McCarthy Information, Manor House, Ash Walk, Warminster, Wiltshire BA12 8PY; *tel* (0985) 215151
Standard & Poor's Corporation, 19 St Swithin's Lane, London EC4N 8AD; *tel* (01) 623 3226; *tlx* 8813444; *fx* (01) 626 3859
Marketing Strategies for Industry, 32 Mill Green Road, Mitcham, Surrey CR4 4HY; *tel* (01) 640 6621
McGraw Hill Publications, 1221 Avenue of the Americas, New York NY 10020, USA; *tel* (1) 212 512 2897
or
McGraw Hill House, Shoppenhangers Road, Maidenhead, Berkshire SL6 2QL; *tel* (044) 628 23431
Thomas Publishing Company Inc, One Penn Plaza, 250 W. 34th Street, New York, NY 10001, USA; *tel* (1) 212 290 7291
Time Inc, Time & Life Building, Rockefeller Center, New York NY 10020, USA; *tel* (1) 212 307 4821
Tudor House Publications Ltd, Lonsdale House, 7/9 Lonsdale Gardens, Tunbridge Wells, Kent TN1 1NU; *tel* (0892) 515454
US Bureau of the Census, Washington DC 20233, USA; *tel* (1) 301 763 2074
Washington Post, 1150 15th Street NW, Washington DC 20071, USA

Sample Dun & Bradstreet credit reports

Following are two sample Dun and Bradstreet credit reports. They are representative of the reports available through Dun & Bradstreet Credit Services for both quoted and privately held US companies. Charges are made for obtaining such reports; arrangements to obtain them can be made through Dun & Bradstreet in the UK, as discussed in Chapter 6.

The first, Exhibit A, is a 'Business Information Report' which includes full (summarised) financials. This type of report is prepared when the company releases financial information; the financial information summarised in the report is not prepared or independently verified by Dun & Bradstreet.

As discussed in the text of the book, there is no statutory audit requirement in the United States, and most unquoted companies do not file financial statements or disclose such information. Similarly, divisions of groups, whether the group is quoted or not, will not release, and sometimes not even prepare, separate financial information. In these circumstances, the second type of report, shown as Exhibit B, is prepared, and typically will not include financial information.

Exhibit A

FULL REVISION

```
          DUNS: 00-007-7743              DATE PRINTED              SUMMARY
GORMAN MANUFACTURING CO INC              AUG 23, 198-           RATING      3A3
GORMAN PRINTING
(Subsidiary of Gorman Holding Companies Inc)   COMMERCIAL PRINTING   STARTED     1965
492 KOLLER ST                            SIC NO.                PAYMENTS    SEE BELOW
(formerly 400 KOLLER ST)                 27 51                  SALES F     $18,931,956
(and Branches and Divisions)                                    WORTH F     $3,482,600
SAN FRANCISCO CA  94110-0012                                    EMPLOYS     500 (150 here)
   Tel: 415 555-9664                                            HISTORY     CLEAR
                                                                FINANCING   SECURED
CHIEF EXECUTIVE: LESLIE SMITH, PRES                             CONDITION   FAIR
                                                                TREND       DOWN
```

SPECIAL EVENTS 8/20/8-   On August 19, 198-, subject experienced a fire due to an electrical short in one of their printing machines. Damages amounted to $35,000, which was fully covered by their insurance company.

PAYMENTS (Amounts may be rounded to nearest figure in prescribed ranges)

REPORTED	PAYING RECORD	HIGH CREDIT	NOW OWES	PAST DUE	SELLING TERMS	LAST SALE WITHIN
07/8-	Ppt	1500	-0-	-0-	N30	1 Mo
07/8-	Ppt	500	-0-	-0-	N30	2-3 Mos
07/8-	Ppt	750	-0-	-0-	N30	2-3 Mos
07/8-	Slow-15	17000	6000	-0-	2 10 N30	1 Mo
07/8-	Slow-15	10000	500	-0-	2 10 N30	1 Mo
07/8-	Slow-30	3000	500	-0-	2 10 N30	1 Mo
07/8-	Slow-60	3000	3000	3000	N30	2-3 Mos
07/8-	Slow-60	2000	2000	2000	N30	2-3 Mos
06/8-	Ppt	7000	300	-0-	N30	2-3 Mos
06/8-	Ppt	5000	2500	-0-	N30	1 Mo
05/8-	Ppt	1000	-0-	-0-	EOM	2-3 Mos
05/8-	Slow-30	12000	2500	2500	N30	2-3 Mos
05/8-	Slow-30	2500	1000	1000	N30	2-3 Mos

Payment experiences reflect how bills are met in relation to the terms granted. In some instances payment beyond terms can be the result of disputes over merchandise, skipped invoices, etc.

CHANGES 03/17/8-   Subject moved from 400 KOLLER ST to 492 KOLLER ST on March 11, 198-.

UPDATE 08/17/8-   On August 17, 198- KEVIN J. HUNT Sec-treas stated for the six months ended June 30, 198- profits were up compared to same period last year.

FINANCE 03/17/8-

	Fiscal Dec 31, 198-	Fiscal Dec 31, 198-	Fiscal Dec 31, 198-
Curr Assets	7,151,675	7,055,442	6,770,968
Curr Liabs	3,379,403	4,015,903	4,192,046
Other Assets	1,354,469	1,336,009	1,309,375
Worth	4,056,901	3,893,231	3,482,600
Sales	26,577,608	20,432,522	18,931,956
Net Income	767,364	64,451	32,892

Fiscal statement dated Dec 31, 198-

Cash	$ 212,597	Accts Pay	$ 1,921,028
Acct Rec	1,733,380	Bank Loans	1,795,000
Inventory	4,439,597	Other Curr Liabs	476,018
Prepaid Exp	385,394		
	----------------		----------------
Curr Assets	6,770,968	Curr Liabs	4,192,046
Fixt & Equip	1,271,811	L.T. Liab-Other	405,697
Other Assets	37,564	CAPITAL STOCK	50,000
		RETAINED EARNINGS	3,432,600
	----------------		----------------
Total Assets	8,080,343	Total	8,080,343 (Continued)

Exhibit A, continued

This report has been prepared for:

Dun & Bradstreet, Inc.		
GORMAN MANUFACTURING CO INC SAN FRANCISCO CA	AUG 23 198-	PAGE 2 CONSOLIDATED REPORT

THIS REPORT MAY NOT BE REPRODUCED IN WHOLE OR IN PART IN ANY MANNER WHATEVER

	FULL REVISION

FINANCE   Annual sales $18,931,956; cost of goods sold $16,777,064. Gross profit $2,154,892;
(Cont'd) net income $32,892; dividends $29,640; monthly rent $2,500. Lease expires 1999.
Fire insurance on mdse & fixt $6,000,000.
        Submitted by Kevin J. Hunt, Sec-Treas. Prepared from statement(s) by Accountant:
Fred Mitchel, San Francisco, CA. Prepared from books without audit.
        Other assets are tangible, composed of miscellaneous deposits and deferred items. Other
current liabilities and long term liabilities are notes due on equipment.
        On Mar 15, 198- Kevin J. Hunt, Sec-Treas, referred to the above figures as still
representative.
        He stated that sales for the 12 months ended Dec 31, 198- were down compared to the same
period last year. Profit for the period was down but is expected to increase. Kevin J. Hunt
stated that the net worth decreased at 12/31/8-, attributed to the purchase and retirement
to treasury of a portion of the capital stock.
        Current debt is in excess of net worth. Inventory is large in relation to sales and working
capital is light compared to volume transacted.

PUBLIC   On Mar 25, 198-, a suit in the amount of $500 was filed against Gorman Manufacturing Co Inc. by
FILINGS   Z Henric Assoc.(Docket #27511) in San Francisco, CA. Cause of action was Goods sold and delivered.
03/17/8-   Financing statement #741170 filed 01-28-8 with the Secretary, State of CA. Debtor:
Gorman Manufacturing Co., Inc., San Francisco, CA. Secured party: Swinger Corp., Malibu, CA.
Collateral: Equipment.
        On March 17, 198- Kevin J. Hunt reported action filed by Z Henric Associates was due to damages
caused by faulty printer and has been settled. Count records reveal suit was withdrawn.

BANKING   Balances average moderate six figures. Account open over three years. Loans extended to low
03/8-   seven figures, now owes low seven figures, secured by accounts receivable and inventory,
and relation satisfactory.

HISTORY   LESLIE SMITH, PRES   KEVIN J. HUNT, SEC-TREAS
03/17/8- DIRECTOR(s): THE OFFICER(s)
        Incorporated California May 21, 1965. Authorized capital consists of 200 shares
common stock, no par value.
        Business started 1965 by principals. 100% of capital stock is owned by parent.
        LESLIE SMITH born 1926 married. Graduated from the University of California, Los Angeles,
June 1947. 1947-1965 was the general manager for Raymor Printing Co.San Francisco, CA.
1965 formed subject with Kevin J. Hunt.
        KEVIN J. HUNT born 1925 married. Graduated from Northwestern University, Evanston, IL,
in June 1946. 1946-1965 was the production manager for Raymor Printing Co., San Francisco, CA.
1965 formed subject with Leslie Smith.
        Related Companies: Through the financial interest of Gorman Holding Companies Inc.,
the Gorman Manufacturing Co Inc. is related to two other sister companies (Smith Lettershop Inc,
San Diego, CA and Gorman Suppliers Inc., Los Angeles, CA). These sister companies are
also engaged in commercial printing. There are no intercompany relations.

OPERATION   Subsidiary of Gorman Holding Companies Inc.,Los Angeles, CA, which operates as a holding
03/17/8- company for its underlying subsidiaries. Parent company has two other subsidiaries.
There are no intercompany relations between parent and subject. A consolidated financial
statement on the parent company, dated Dec 31, 198- showed a net worth of $7,842,226,
with a fair financial condition indicated.
        Commercial printing, engaged in letterpress and screen printing. Sells for cash
30% balance net 30 days. Has 1,000 accounts. Sells to commercial concerns. Territory:
Nationwide. Nonseasonal.
        EMPLOYEES: 500 including officers. 150 employed here.
        FACILITIES: Rents 40,000 sq. ft. in 1 story concrete block building in good condition.
Premises neat.
        LOCATION: Industrial section on side street.
        BRANCHES: Subject maintains a branch at 1073 Boyden Road, Los Angeles, CA.
        07-23)9D9 /5)0039/02 00000   052

Exhibit B

Dun & Bradstreet, Inc.

This report has been prepared for:

| BE SURE NAME, BUSINESS AND ADDRESS MATCH YOUR FILE | ANSWERING INQUIRY | |

THIS REPORT MAY NOT BE REPRODUCED IN WHOLE OR IN PART IN ANY MANNER WHATEVER

| | | FULL REVISION |

DUNS: 00-007-7743
GORMAN MANUFACTURING CO INC
GORMAN PRINTING
(Subsidiary of Gorman Holding Companies Inc)
492 KOLLER ST
(formerly 400 KOLLER ST)
(and Branches and Divisions)
SAN FRANCISCO CA 94110-0012
    Tel: 415-555-5555

DATE PRINTED
AUG 23 198-

COMMERCIAL PRINTING

SIC NO.
  27 51

SUMMARY
RATING   --

STARTED   1965
PAYMENTS   SEE BELOW
EMPLOYS   500 (150 HERE)
HISTORY   CLEAR
FINANCING SECURED
TREND   DOWN

CHIEF EXECUTIVE: LESLIE SMITH, PRES

SPECIAL   On August 19, 198-, subject experienced a fire due to an electrical short in one of their
EVENTS   printing machines. Damages amounted to $35,000, which was fully covered by their insurance company.
8/20/8-

PAYMENTS (Amounts may be rounded to the nearest figure in prescribed ranges)

REPORTED	PAYING RECORD	HIGH CREDIT	NOW OWES	PAST DUE	SELLING TERMS	LAST SALE WITHIN
07/8-	Ppt	1500	-0-	-0-	N30	1 Mo
07/8-	Ppt	500	-0-	-0-	N30	2-3 Mos
07/8-	Ppt	750	-0-	-0-	N30	2-3 Mos
07/8-	Slow-15	17000	6000	-0-	2 10 N30	1 Mo
07/8-	Slow-15	10000	500	-0-	2 10 N30	1 Mo
07/8-	Slow-30	3000	500	-0-	2 10 N30	1 Mo
07/8-	Slow-60	3000	3000	3000	N30	2-3 Mos
07/8-	Slow-60	2000	2000	2000	N30	2-3 Mos
06/8-	Ppt	7000	300	-0-	N30	2-3 Mos
06/8-	Ppt	5000	2500	-0-	N30	1 Mo
05/8-	Ppt	1000	-0-	-0-	EOM	2-3 Mos
05/8-	Slow-30	12000	2500	2500	N30	2-3 Mos
05/84-	Slow-30	2500	1000	1000	N30	2-3 Mos

        Payment experiences reflect how bills are met in relation to the terms granted. In some
    instances payment beyond terms can be the result of disputes over merchandise, skipped invoices, etc.

CHANGES   Subject moved from 400 KOLLER ST to 492 KOLLER ST on March 11, 198-.
03/17/8-

UPDATE   On August 17, 198- KEVIN J. HUNT Sec-Treas stated subject now has 500 employees, with
08/17/8- 150 here.

FINANCE   On Mar 15, 198- Kevin J. Hunt, Sec-Treas, declined financial information.
03/17/8-   He stated that sales for the 12 months ended Dec 31, 198- were down compared to the same
         period last year. Profit for the period was down but is expected to increase.

PUBLIC   On Mar 25, 198-, a suit in the amount of $500 was filed against Gorman Manufacturing Co Inc. by
FILINGS   Z Henric Assoc (Docket #27511) in San Francisco, CA. Cause of action was Goods sold and delivered.
03/17/8-   Financing statement #741170 filed 01-28-8- with the Secretary, State of CA. Debtor:
         Gorman Manufacturing Co Inc., San Francisco, CA. Secured party: Swinger Corp., Malibu, CA.
         Collateral: Equipment.
             On March 17, 198-Kevin J.Hunt reported action filed by Z Henric Associates was due to damages
         caused by faulty printer and has been settled. Court records reveal suit was withdrawn.
                                                                              (Continued)

Exhibit B, continued

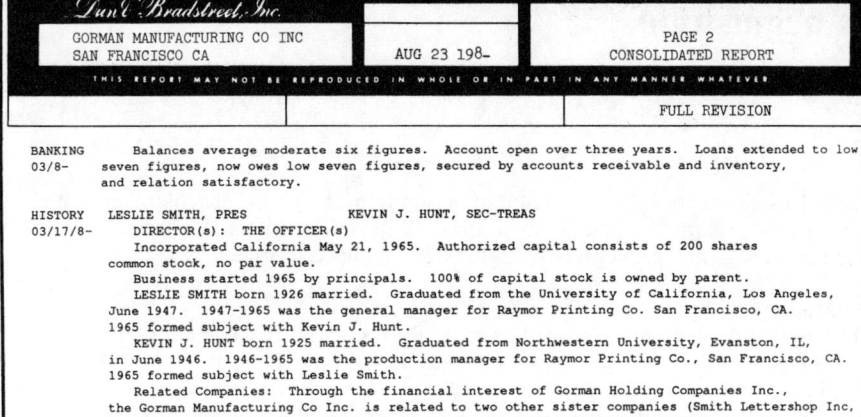

```
┌─────────────────────────────────────────────────────────────────────────────────┐
│  Dun & Bradstreet, Inc.                          This report has been prepared for:│
│  ┌──────────────────────────────┐ ┌──────────────┐ ┌──────────────────────────┐ │
│  │ GORMAN MANUFACTURING CO INC  │ │              │ │        PAGE 2            │ │
│  │ SAN FRANCISCO CA             │ │ AUG 23 198-  │ │  CONSOLIDATED REPORT     │ │
│  └──────────────────────────────┘ └──────────────┘ └──────────────────────────┘ │
│       THIS REPORT MAY NOT BE REPRODUCED IN WHOLE OR IN PART IN ANY MANNER WHATEVER │
│  ┌────────────────────────────────────────────┐ ┌──────────────────────────────┐ │
│  │                                            │ │      FULL REVISION           │ │
│  └────────────────────────────────────────────┘ └──────────────────────────────┘ │
└─────────────────────────────────────────────────────────────────────────────────┘
```

BANKING   Balances average moderate six figures. Account open over three years. Loans extended to low
03/8-   seven figures, now owes low seven figures, secured by accounts receivable and inventory,
          and relation satisfactory.

HISTORY   LESLIE SMITH, PRES   KEVIN J. HUNT, SEC-TREAS
03/17/8-   DIRECTOR(s): THE OFFICER(s)
          Incorporated California May 21, 1965. Authorized capital consists of 200 shares
          common stock, no par value.
               Business started 1965 by principals. 100% of capital stock is owned by parent.
               LESLIE SMITH born 1926 married. Graduated from the University of California, Los Angeles,
          June 1947. 1947-1965 was the general manager for Raymor Printing Co. San Francisco, CA.
          1965 formed subject with Kevin J. Hunt.
               KEVIN J. HUNT born 1925 married. Graduated from Northwestern University, Evanston, IL,
          in June 1946. 1946-1965 was the production manager for Raymor Printing Co., San Francisco, CA.
          1965 formed subject with Leslie Smith.
               Related Companies: Through the financial interest of Gorman Holding Companies Inc.,
          the Gorman Manufacturing Co Inc. is related to two other sister companies (Smith Lettershop Inc,
          San Diego, CA and Gorman Suppliers Inc., Los Angeles, CA). These sister companies are
          also engaged in commercial printing. There are no intercompany relations.

OPERATION   Subsidiary of Gorman Holding Companies Inc., Los Angeles, CA, which operates as a holding
03/17/8- company for its underlying subsidiaries. Parent company has two other subsidiaries.
          There are no intercompany relations between parent and subject. A consolidated financial
          statement on the parent company, dated Dec 31, 198- showed a net worth of $7,842,226,
          with a fair financial condition indicated.
               Commercial printing, engaged in letterpress and screen printing. Sells for cash
          30% balance net 30 days. Has 1,000 accounts. Sells to commercial concerns,. Territory:
          Nationwide. Nonseasonal.
               EMPLOYEES: 500 including officers. 150 employed here.
               FACILITIES: Rents 40,000 sq. ft. in 1 story concrete block building in good condition.
          Premises neat.
               LOCATION: Industrial section on side street.
               BRANCHES: Subject maintains a branch at 1073 Boyden Road, Los Angeles, CA.
               07-23)9D9 /5)0039/02 00000   052

Thermal Scientific plc: a case study in development by acquisition

Note: This case is based on a presentation made by Hugh Sykes, chairman and chief executive of Thermal Scientific, at a 1988 'Acquisitions in the US' seminar and on discussions with him concerning the company's acquisition strategies.

1 Introduction
This case study concentrated on the personal experience of a company building up a technology based group and gives a practical view of development by acquisition with specific reference to the USA. No one experience is either original or definitive; the experience reflected here is based on acquisitions in both the UK and US of moderately sized private companies which were bought generally from their founders or owners. Thermal Scientific was not involved in US public company acquisitions, tender offers, contested bids or similar situations.

The case study which follows is presented under four headings.

(1) What has Thermal Scientific done?
(2) Why did they do it?
(3) How did they do it?
(4) What has the company achieved and what do they expect for the future?

2 What has Thermal Scientific done?
Thermal Scientific had its origins in the Sheffield based Carbolite company – a small, long established manufacturer of electric furnaces which was purchased by a group of individuals in 1972. Carbolite faced bankruptcy but the change of ownership, coupled with the appointment of a new managing director, brought solid progress in home and overseas markets. By 1983, the company had sales of £2 million, profits of £300,000, 100 employees and had won the Queen's Award for Export Achievement.

The opportunity then came to purchase a scientific instrument company from GEC. This was merged with Carbolite to form Thermal Scientific which was simultaneously floated on the USM in August 1983. A period of rapid expansion followed and prior to transferring to the main market in December 1987, Thermal Scientific was one of the largest industrial concerns on the USM.

The group now has an international reputation in its specialist markets, annual sales of £60 million, latest reported profits of over £5 million, more than 1,200 employees and 19 operations including seven in the United States. The product range has expanded from basic laboratory equipment to include:

- specialised furnaces and ovens
- electron beam equipment
- electronic test systems
- sub-contract thermal and laser processing
- plastic extrusion machinery
- scientific instruments
- materials testing machines

This rapid, orderly expansion has been achieved by a combination of steady organic growth – the original companies have more than doubled their profits – and an intensive acquisition programme. In the last three years, 18 acquisitions including seven in the

USA have been completed. Some 50 per cent of the total business is now in North America.

Appendix A shows various charts of growth 1983–1987.

3 Why did Thermal Scientific do it?

Hugh Sykes, the chairman and chief executive, emphasised that a well conceived long term strategy was essential to the success of the company's acquisition programme:

> 'First, it is important to realise that the mainspring of our growth has been the vision of creating an international technology group with individual companies becoming world leaders in their respective activities. I believe vision is an essential pre-requisite of any business venture and our acquisition programme would not have succeeded without it.'

Pursuit of this vision required a coherent campaign of acquisition, which has been pursued in both the US and UK since adopting the above goals.

Shortly after forming the Group this vision was committed to writing as a company philosophy. It is reproduced as Appendix B.

Second, Thermal Scientific's growth by acquisition has been driven by logical operational and financial needs, many of which are not unique to the company. It is, therefore, interesting to consider those reasons identified by the company which led to the choice of the US as the primary venue for foreign acquisitions. Having clear cut reasons for going to the US helps shape specific criteria for evaluating candidates, and streamlines the entire search process. Sykes believes that the US is a sound basis for growing globally: 'If you're going to be an international company, you cannot ignore the States.'

To understand further Thermal Scientific's rationale for entering the US market, it is useful to look at a few contributing factors identified by Mr Sykes:

* at least 50 per cent of world sales for many of the Group's products are within the US home market;
* the UK companies had successful though modest reciprocal trading links with several US manufacturers and distributors;
* whilst recognising that acquisitions in mainland Europe or the Far East were inevitable for longer term growth, the absence of language or significant cultural barriers made the US more attractive initially;
* by linking known US companies with certain of the existing UK operations, the Group could move into world leadership in specific sectors of its activities whilst exploiting joint technical and market co-operation; and
* operating in the US is the only way to gain access to certain 'leading edge' technologies, both in terms of products and markets.

Thermal Scientific pursued opportunities in the United States market because its directors believed that more opportunities for the company's growth existed within that area than in many other places in world. The access to current technology because of substantial product development and strong marketing capabilities also attracted the company towards American acquisitions.

4 How did Thermal Scientific do it?

Before looking at the US acquisitions made by Thermal Scientific in detail, it is worth highlighting three broad but important features of the company's acquisition strategy – planning, human resources and technique.

i Planning

This is the means by which vision becomes reality. The group began by looking at its commercial and economic environment. It looked at its strengths and weaknesses, the impact of new technology, likely changes in customer and market requirements, new product development and a host of other items which would help or hinder the Group in achieving its objectives. It directed its energies at looking for activity sectors which held the best potential for good long-term growth. Electronics, advanced materials, test instruments and systems and emerging technologies were examples of areas analysed.

The company set very basic criteria as a general guideline for potential acquisitions. This framework actually did not change dramatically from one deal to another; however, in some instances the criteria were 'customised' to suit the specifics of the transaction. Sykes believes that such guidelines are vital for clearly directed acquisition growth, and indicates that the basics are revised in almost every acquisition. Keeping to a rigid timetable, however, is quite difficult as fast growth emerges; therefore he suggests the importance of re-evaluating the criteria periodically to check their validity.

There is of course the problem that competitors are often formulating exactly the same plan with very similar criteria and guidelines. The plan should reflect this assumption and should try to answer the question 'Why and how are we going to succeed against competitors who have similar plans?' The answer to that problem is the secret of success!

Mr Sykes, however, emphasised that the need for planning and analysis must never be allowed to dampen that elusive quality – the ability to grasp an opportunity. Many 'experts' will say that the best acquisitions have come not from detailed planning but from the ability to see and grasp an opportunity.

In pricing acquisition candidates, Thermal Scientific tends to place greater emphasis on what a business is rather than on what it might become. Forecasting the way in which a company may develop is important and is always part of the investigation exercise. Paying for performance to date, however, rather than potential for improvement, avoids the pitfall of paying for indefinite future benefits which will in any event be the responsibility of the buyer rather than the vendor.

ii Human resource concerns
There is no point in having an ambitious plan without the human resources to achieve it. Thermal Scientific established several key principles to address this problem:

- have plenty of people available before they are actually needed;
- always try to recruit the best; and
- maintain organisational flexibility.

No acquisition programme can be successful unless there is a management team in place who have personal confidence and commitment to the task. Building such a team has been, in Mr Sykes' opinion, a key ingredient for Thermal Scientific's success.

Subsequent to acquisition, all of the operations have been controlled by local management teams who enjoy a high level of decentralised independence to achieve their goals. A US subsidiary, Thermal Scientific Inc., was established, staffed by a US Chief Executive and two accountants (all from the UK) to co-ordinate the US operations. The basic role of Group Head Office is to encourage and assist subsidiary company management teams to set and reach challenging targets.

Sykes recognises the difficulty in achieving the unique combination between independence and cross-fertilisation, yet he feels that his company has made some progress in this area. He feels that the way to obtain cross-fertilisation in the long-term is to organise along product lines rather than geographic regions or historical structure. This encourages interchanges of ideas and makes one director the focal point for all information about an area or technology.

iii Technique
Thermal Scientific's method for planning and managing the various stages of the acquisition process are basic, straightforward and proven:

- identification;
- negotiation;
- drafting heads of agreement;
- investigation;
- further negotiation; and
- completion.

With few exceptions, Thermal Scientific followed this pattern in each of its acquisitions.

Hugh Sykes made the following observations about the identification, negotiation and investigation stages:

Identification – *Though we maintain contact with perhaps 50 UK and US intermediaries and have used formal search techniques in the USA, we have in fact identified all our acquisitions using our own internal resources. Some have resulted from detailed search, others have been more obvious as competitors, trading partners, or distributors. In practice, the Company places little or no restrictions on members of the group from pursuing opportunities. It is from this practice that many candidates have emerged from contacts within the group itself.*

The company also maintained and updated an acquisition criteria document (Appendix C). This was then used as a screening tool, because as the company became known as a company growing by acquisition, many opportunities were sent our way. We could then quickly review and evaluate these by comparison against a written standard. We found that nearly all of them were rejected as being unsuitable primarily on grounds of lack of an activity 'fit', poor financial performance or inadequate management.

Negotiation – *This is when the adrenalin flows – every negotiation is different. All our acquisitions have been of private companies with a sole vendor or occasionally a small group of controlling shareholders which makes negotiation a particularly personal affair.*

For the private deals, the emotionl attachment is an extremely important factor. With these deals the personal concerns must be handled more carefully than in public acquisitions. Also, when there are various family members involved, it is vital to the negotiation stage to remember that personal rapport is much more important than the final price.

There are no set rules. We have burnt the midnight oil, walked away and returned (sometimes after several months) and very occasionally come to terms immediately. I think I can say we have never failed to negotiate terms except when we have seen a competitor offer what we believe was an unjustified price or when our investigation has revealed previously hidden problems. This highlights how vital a thorough investigation and analysis are.

Investigation – *This is an area where I believe we have refined our skills through experience. In company investigations work there is no substitute for experience and several of our executives had a 'baptism of fire' in profit improvement and recovery consultancy. It's surprising how quickly you can form a judgement on a potential acquisition. For us, an important first step is to hold monthly reviews of potential candidates and keep abreast of any possibilities. Therefore, when the time is right, we are able to approach a deal with our 'homework' already done – that's what makes the difference in the deal.*

Regardless of first impressions, however, we always investigate thoroughly. We aim, even in a relatively small company, to have a multi-disciplinary team of three or four people spend, say, two weeks in detailed due diligence. Our rules are:

- *have a checklist and use it;*
- *do as much of an investigation as you can using your own staff;*
- *never rely solely on figures or accountants' reports; and*
- *give high priority to product technology, market competitiveness and management competence.*

Very early we learned the truth of the statement – 'You can sell a second-rate product with first-rate management, but never the other way round!'

Typically, when looking at a US company, we ask seven basic questions:

1. *Can we understand the business?*
2. *Can we manage the business?*
3. *Can we market the products?*
4. *Is the technology in demand?*
5. *Can we retain key personnel?*

6. Can we apply financial controls?
7. Can we investigate thoroughly and pay a fair price?

In addition to these, we understand the need to think through the downside of each deal. This has been one key factor in making successful acquisitions.

iv Thermal's US acquisition programme
Over the past three years the Group's searches in the UK and USA produced listings of approximately 200–300 companies which broadly met its criteria. From this listing, the company looked at the size, products, and market position of the candidates to assist in narrowing the list. Of these candidates, it looked in detail at perhaps 30 companies in the US, positively listed or investigated 15 and completed seven acquisitions.

The move from 20 to 30 possibilities down to the few seriously considered for an acquisition is an interesting one. Sykes believes that it is important to make the initial contact to these 20 or 30 by either writing or phoning the chairman of the target. He also suggests that under certain circumstances, it may be more appropriate to use a banker rather than someone internally for this contact. The purpose of this stage is to actually 'feel out' the potential candidate for responsiveness and willingness to consider a sale. In Mr Sykes' opinion, the best approach is a 'soft lead-in' on non-threatening grounds; in that way the acquiror can listen to the potential seller's objectives and concerns.

The following is a history of the Group's acquisitions:

Centorr, a New Hampshire based manufacturer of high temperature vacuum furnaces, was the Group's introduction to US acquisitions in 1985. It had known the company some time from its international furnace connections. Despite the fact that Gerry Lavoie, its founder/owner, had spoken to several US suitors, he sold to Thermal Scientific after long, hard negotiations for a fair commercial price. Interestingly enough, the deal almost fell through; but realising the importance of this acquisition, Thermal decided to play its final and most significant trump card – its chairman. Hugh Sykes understood the concerns of the vendor and because of his personal attention, the acquisition became a reality. Centorr has since been considered a success story. In less than three years, sales and profits more than doubled. In addition, the company gave the Group access to the research and development markets in large technically based US corporations and was the first overseas link in building its world presence in the high temperature vacuum furnace market, which has since become one of the main legs of the Group.

Later in 1985, Thermal Scientific bought Killion, a company operating in New Jersey and Florida. As the leading US supplier of precision plastic extruders for research and development, it was highly complementary to the Group's UK based company, Betol – a point also taken by the Killion vendors.

Killion and Betol together are world leaders in small extrusion technology. Currently, sales and profits are running at 50 per cent above the levels at acquisition.

The Group's most active year for US acquisitions was 1986. Ebtec and E.B. Engineering, companies in Massachusetts and California respectively, gave entry to the important US specialist subcontract welding industry on both the East and West coasts. These were tough acquisitions, because the businesses needed a combination of restructuring and relocating and there were difficult decisions to make in setting up separate profit centres. These companies are now seeing positive results and profits are growing – in one business segment dramatically so. This reorganisation would not have been possibly without having corporate executives located in the USA.

Uniplex (New Jersey) and Omnitherm (Illinois), the other 1986 acquisitions, were quite different. Uniplex produces plastic profiles by extrusion and the Group was able to capitalise on its extrusion machine experience. These two companies had difficulties which included customer dependence, margin pressure and poor management organisation. Omnitherm has been a major success both in its own right and as a US distributor for scientific instruments produced by Stanton Redcroft, one of Thermal's UK subsidiaries. Omnitherm's profits for 1988 are 300 per cent up on the prior year and the forecasts are that the investment of approximately $1m will be recovered in less than three years.

Thermal Scientific's last and largest acquisition, Vacuum Industries, was completed in December 1986. It was a positive response to the company's view that vacuum furnace techniques, which are vital to the production of new and advanced materials such as engineering ceramics, were set for sustained long-term growth. These assumptions are being borne out by the company's subsequent performance. The negotiations for this business were unusual in that the vendor was a US entrepreneur well used to the acquisition process; despite the size of the consideration ($15 million) the negotiations and investigation were carried out in record time.

v Thermal's acquisition experience
Certain features of Thermal Scientific's acquisition experience are summarised below:

MARKETS AND PRODUCTS

- Good market survey work in advance is essential. At times this work was performed by US consultants, but not always with success. Market and product intelligence in the US is generally much more comprehensive and more widely available than in the UK.
- It is essential to identify the rate of change of the technology involved, to avoid being caught out by sudden leaps ahead by the competition.
- The US home market is huge, which depresses their need to export. Internally, the characteristics of the East and West coasts are quite different. A high tech company in Los Angeles loosely managed by 'work any time' Californians is totally different from an apparently identical company in conservative New England.
- The US isn't all 'high gloss', 'high tech'. While the marketing expertise has always been impressive, manufacturing facilities in smaller companies have often appeared outdated in UK terms.

FINANCIAL AND LEGAL

- Thermal Scientific found it useful to list in detail the assumptions made in the analysis and compare that to the acquisition consideration. This allowed management to analyse what it was buying in terms of products, profit performance and assets.
- US legal, accountancy, and banking activities are more cautious, less flexible and inevitably more expensive. Strict control of work and fees is essential.
- The Group learned to be aware of legal problems such as anti-trust legislation or the New Jersey Environmental Clearance certification.
- Smaller US companies are unused to budgeting and forecasting. Very often, it was Thermal Scientific who drafted the first budgets in the course of the investigation.
- Audited accounts for small companies are rare. This leads to problems in UK stock exchange requirements.
- Many US companies, particularly larger ones, are sold 'by auction'. It is possible to waste time and money on abortive investigation and professional costs if this is the manner of the sale. Also, Thermal found it best to avoid companies being 'touted around' for sale.
- Typically, financial staff in smaller US companies sometimes lack the status and calibre of their UK equivalents.
- The vendors and sometimes their professional advisers often do not understand the complications of vendor placings and UK stock exchange requirements generally.

MANAGEMENT

- In general, US managers are more optimistic, more independent and more decisive that their UK counterparts. In short, they're different! While they are easy to meet, they are hard to evaluate. An excellent presentation socially and professionally can

sometimes mask the facts from UK observers. Also, it was generally difficult to recruit management and financial staff of the required standard.
- Americans respect forthrightness and expect changes and performance evaluation.
- They speak a different language! If you 'table' something, it means you forget it.
- Fringe benefits have different values. Company cars are rare, but medical benefits are widespread. The company found it complicated to implement a US stock option scheme.

vi Funding
While this is a subject in its own right it is useful to review the funding of Thermal Scientific's US acquisitions to demonstrate the range of options used:

		£m
Centorr	cash placing	3.6
	share issue	0.4
		4.0
Killion	rights issue	1.9
Ebtec	open offer-placing	5.8
E.B. Engineering	with clawback	
Omnitherm	share issue	0.1
	cash resources	0.6
		0.7
Uniplex	cash placing	2.3
Vacuum Industries	cash placing	7.6
	cash resources	1.7
		9.3

5 What has Thermal achieved and what are the prospects for the future?
Hugh Sykes believes strongly in the value and success of the group's acquisition programme. He offered the following summary of this, and the company's experience.

I believe we have built a soundly based group with strong core business, leading market positions and the capacity for steady long-term growth. We have followed our vision and objectives. Perhaps more importantly we have developed motivated experienced management teams able to face the future with confidence.

Inevitably, the recent events in the stock markets mean that in the short term our acquisition programme is unlikely to be as aggressive as in the past. Currently, we are concentrating on the organic growth of our existing businesses but our strong balance sheet will allow us to take advantage of particularly appropriate acquisition opportunities as they arise.

In September 1988, Thermal Scientific agreed to be acquired by TI Group. TI and Thermal Scientific described the acquisition as a unique opportunity for TI, given the complementary fit of the thermal interests of the two. This combination will create the world's largest thermal technology business.

APPENDIX A
Thermal Scientific plc 1983–1987

Thermal Scientific plc 1983–1987

	1984	1985	1986	**1987**
Turnover	3,805	4,718	7,655	20,045	**36,720**
Profit before taxation	369	507	1,031	3,183	**5,515**
Profit after taxation	212	291	571	2,004	**3,511**
Earnings per share	2.6p	3.4p	5.7p	11.1p	**14.4p**

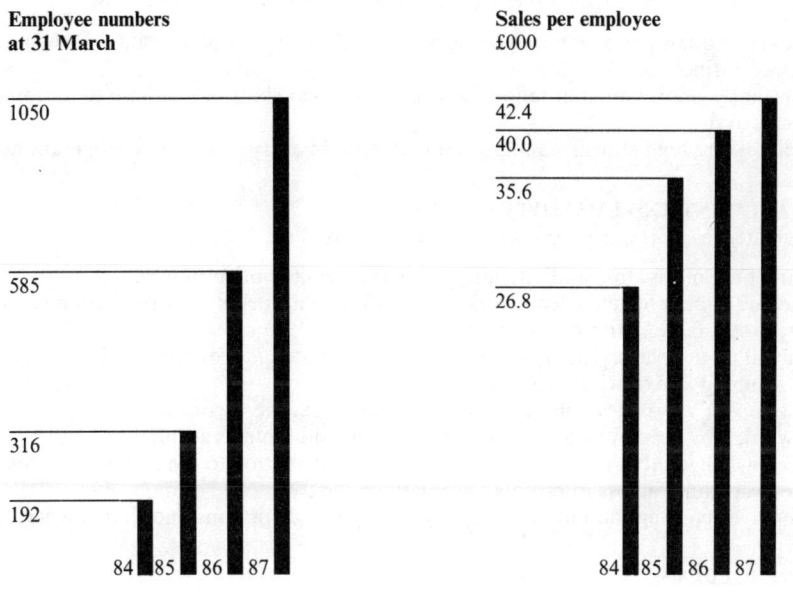

**Employee numbers
at 31 March**

1050
585
316
192
84 85 86 87

Sales per employee
£000

42.4
40.0
35.6
26.8
84 85 86 87

APPENDIX B
Thermal Scientific philosophy

OBJECTIVE
Our group corporate objective is consistent long-term growth based on an expanding international group of professionally managed companies and a comprehensive range of products in thermal and related technologies. We aim to be world leaders in the main activities and markets in which we operate.

CUSTOMERS
We are committed to earning the respect and goodwill of our customers by:

- providing quality products and services which allow a reasonable profit and encourage repeat business;
- constantly improving and refining our products and skills in response to customers' needs; and
- maintaining high ethical standards and integrity in every aspect of our operations.

MANAGEMENT AND EMPLOYEES
Our greatest asset is our people and we are committed to:

- attracting, motivating and retaining the highest calibre of employee;
- encouragement of active teamwork and creation of a working environment conducive to job satisfaction and productivity;
- pursuit of an open style of management, enquiring attitudes of mind and participation in planning and decision making;
- developing ways in which personal achievement can be encouraged, recognised and rewarded by development, training, promotion and remuneration;
- acknowledging that loyalty, performance and contribution to the company's progress are overriding factors in personal evaluation; and
- employee participation in the company through stock options and share ownership.

SHAREHOLDERS
We are committed to maintaining the trust and support of our shareholders by:

- managing the group with a clear definition of long-term objectives, strategy and responsibilities;
- planning and generating funds for successful development of the business;
- making strategic acquisitions which complement our activities and enhance earnings for shareholders; and
- achieving an above-average growth in earnings per share and consequently in the value of shareholders' investment.

APPENDIX C
Thermal Scientific plc: acquisition criteria

Thermal Scientific has defined a policy of further development by acquisition in 1987/88. The criteria for acquisition candidates are:

FINANCIAL
A private business or a subsidiary/division of a public company.
Pre-tax profits in the range £2–7m ($3–10m).

MARKETS
Preference given to product or market leaders.
Candidates should ideally have a range of products serving several market sectors.

MANAGEMENT
The preference will be for existing management to remain with profit responsibility.

LOCATION
UK, USA and Europe.

ACTIVITIES
Related to existing thermal scientific group activities:

laboratory electric furnaces and ovens
vacuum, high temperature and other specialised industrial electric furnaces and ovens
sub-contract metallurgical services operations
energy beam (laser and electron beam) equipment and services
machinery for plastics processing
production of specialised plastic products
analytical instruments particularly related to materials testing
environmental test equipment and systems including 'burn-in'

Areas of additional interest:

temperature controlled laboratory equipment
electronic components in niche markets (manufacture or distribution)
infra red equipment
instrumentation relating to sensing, measurement, testing and process control
instruments and systems for materials testing
specialised optical equipment
independent testing laboratories

NOTE: A more detailed listing of the preferred activities follows.

Acquisition criteria – detailed activity listing

Related to existing group activities

FURNACES
(1) Laboratory electric furnaces and ovens
(2) Vacuum, high temperature and other electric furnaces and ovens for industrial use

(3) Sub-contract metallurgical processing operations including heat treatment, vacuum brazing, plasma coating and surface engineering
(4) Electron beam and laser welding/machinery equipment and services
(5) Environmental chambers and systems
(6) 'Burn in' equipment and systems.

PLASTICS
(1) Extrusion machinery (preferably less than 60mm barrel diameter)
(2) Downstream equipment for extrusion systems
(3) Secondary and ancillary equipment for plastics processing, eg for laminating, coating, cutting, chilling and mixing
(4) Production of specialised plastics products eg extrusions and profiles.

INSTRUMENTS
(1) Analytical instruments for thermal and gas analysis
(2) Materials testing equipment for physical and chemical testing
(3) Environmental/safety testing equipment, eg for flammability, smoke testing and similar safety standards
(4) Instrument distribution in niche markets, eg thermal analysis.

Areas of additional interest

(1) Manufacture or distribution of electronic instruments/components in niche markets
(2) Infra red equipment for sensing, heating and measurement
(3) Instruments and components for sensing, measurements, test and process control eg transducers, temperature control systems
(4) Instruments and systems for materials testing including physical and chemical testing and equipment for specific materials (eg polymers)
(5) Optical instruments and equipment in niche sectors but excluding microscopes, photographic equipment
(6) Temperature controlled laboratory equipment including incubators, water baths, block baths and thermal calibration devices
(7) Independent electronic/electrical/mechanical test laboratories and consultancies.

(Other activities may also be considered if the required criteria are fulfilled.)

APPENDIX 7
Significant differences in US and UK accounting

A discussion of the differences between US and UK accounting principles can go on for pages and pages, and even hundreds of pages. For the most part, these differences exist because there is much more specific guidance in the US for virtually every type of situation; in the UK, accounting principles take the form of statements of principles and objectives rather than detailed accounting guidance. The US principles take very much the latter approach; quite often, the more specific US accounting requirements are allowable for UK accounting purposes, although they might be more restrictive or conservative than ones which might be chosen by a UK company given a free hand. Therefore, on an ongoing basis, it might not be necessary to make a great number of adjustments; however, it might be preferable to do so to bring the accounts of the US subsidiary onto a comparable basis with those of the UK parent.

In addition to those differences relating to goodwill, fixed assets, pensions, taxes, and foreign exchange discussed in the text of Chapter 8, there are a number of additional items covered below. Please note that this is not a comprehensive listing, which is appropriate for an entire book rather than a brief discussion. The purpose of this listing is, rather than being an exhaustive detailing of variances, to identify those differences most likely to affect comparability of US and UK financial statements. The citation shown after the title is the principal, but normally not the sole, reference on the topic.

Imputation of interest (APB 21)
This is required in connection with long term transactions at non market interest rates. At the date a transaction originates, eg a note payable is given or received as consideration, the nominal interest rate must be evaluated in light of the risk, terms, credit worthiness of the borrower, securities given, etc. If the stated rate is not a realistic one, US accounting principles require that the face amount be discounted so that the stated rate plus amortisation of the discount yield a market rate of interest. This discounting is not revisited subsequently or adjusted for interest rate fluctuation; of course, ongoing assessments of collectibility should be made.

Capitalisation of interest (SFAS 34)
Capitalisation of interest is required in connection with certain qualifying assets. Interest capitalised is based on the cost of average expenditures during the acquisition period, up to the total actual interest expended by the group in the period. Qualifying assets are those which are discrete projects which require a period of time to get them ready for use. They do not include items which are routinely manufactured or produced for inventory.

Non-monetary transactions (APB 29)
In the US, the use of fair values is required in most cases. Historical cost is to be used for exchanges which are not essentially the culmination of the earnings process, ie an exchange of similar productive assets or interests therein. Book values are also to be used for exchanges between certain related entities (eg two subsidiaries of a parent).

Marketable securities (SFAS 12)
Marketable equity securities are classified into current and non-current portfolios. Each portfolio is then valued to be carried at the lower of aggregate cost or market value.

Any writeoff required for the current portfolio is an income statement adjustment in the current period; any adjustment on the long-term portfolio, other than one representing permanent impairment, is a valuation adjustment carried in the shareholders' equity section, and not written off to profit and loss. The use of such an aggregate portfolio method is prohibited for UK purposes by the Companies Act. Also, certain specialised industries in the US (eg brokers and dealers in securities, and insurance companies), use other (eg 'marked to market') methods.

Shares repurchased by companies (ARB 43)
A company may repurchase its own shares in the US with much less difficulty than in the UK. Such shares, if not immediately retired, are commonly referred to as 'treasury stock'. They are shown as a deduction from shareholders' equity based upon the cost of the treasury shares reacquired. This treatment is also applied to shares held for contribution to an ESOP (Employees' Stock Ownership Plan) until they are contributed to that plan.

Compensated absences (SFAS 43)
US accounting principles require that a liability for compensated absences (eg holiday, illness and public holidays) must be accrued if the obligation is attributable to services already rendered and it is expected that payment will be made.

'In-Substance' defeasance (SFAS 76)
In certain situations in the US, debt can be treated as extinguished for financial reporting purposes (even though it has not yet been legally repaid) where the borrower irrevocably places cash or certain assets in a trust to be used solely for satisfying scheduled payment of both interest and principal. Any gain or loss on such a retirement, as on any early extinguishment of debt, is to be treated as an extraordinary item.

Research and development costs (SFAS 2)
Generally, no deferral of research and development costs is allowed in the US other than certain qualifying development costs for computer software. However, as investments in computer software have become more significant especially in service industries, other types of entities are beginning to capitalise substantial software costs.

Stocks and work in progress (ARB 43)
The use of the LIFO ('Last In, First Out') method of accounting for stocks (inventory) is permitted in the US. In periods of inflation, this increases the cost of sales and decreases the carrying amounts of stock by flowing out the most expensive stock first. While this decreases reported earnings because of the higher cost of goods sold, it can provide substantial tax savings by reducing taxable income. Companies adopt it for book purposes as well as for tax purposes since the Internal Revenue Service in the US requires that it be used for both to be used for tax purposes. Use of LIFO is prohibited in the UK by SSAP 9.

Earnings per share (APB 15)
Earnings per share ('EPS') are shown before and after extraordinary items, based on average shares and common share equivalents outstanding. Rather complex rules exist to cover situations where significant amounts of options, warrants or convertible debt are outstanding. Primary EPS are often lower in a US calculation than a UK one because a greater number of common shares are deemed to be outstanding, therefore increasing the denominator of the equation.

Shares issued to employees (ARB 25 and 43)
In the US it is required that any discount on shares issued to employees be treated as remuneration and charged as an expense in the period in which the related services are performed. The amount of the discount is the difference between the employee's cost (or

the exercise price of an option granted) and the market price of the shares at the date the grant becomes unconditional. There is no standard for accounting for share option schemes in the UK.

Dividends payable
Dividends are not required to be associated with a particular period's earnings for US purposes and are shown as a deduction from retained earnings rather than on the face of the profit and loss account. They are recorded in the period in which they are approved by the Board of Directors.

Revenue recognition when right of return exists (SFAS 48)
A general rule of revenue recognition is that recognition of income is delayed until substantially all the economic risks and rewards related to the sale have been transferred to the purchaser. This requires therefore that the seller is able to make a reasonable estimate of the amount of future returns where the right of return exists. The provision for these returns is calculated in a fashion similar to that used for reserves for bad debtors.

Sales of receivables with recourse (SFAS 77)
If an entity sells receivables but the purchaser retains recourse to the seller, then the gain or loss on the sale is based on the balance of the net receivable. Proceeds from the sale are adjusted for 'probable adjustments'. 'Net receivables' as used here is a term defined in SFAS 77 to reflect unearned income including service and other charges.

Leases (SFAS 13 and others)
With the adoption of revised SSAP 21, accounting guidance for leases is broadly the same in the US and the UK. However, there are more specific requirements for designating a lease as a capital lease in the US. For a lessee to record a capital lease, one of four specific criteria must be satisfied; if none are, it would be classified as an operating lease. From the perspective of a lessor, one of the four tests must be met, and additionally, both of two additional criteria designed to ensure that the lessor's ongoing economic involvement is not significant, and there are no major uncertainties regarding collectibility. Therefore, it is possible that a lease classified as a finance lease for UK purposes would not be treated similarly for US purposes.

POINTS REGARDING PRESENTATION OF FINANCIAL STATEMENTS

Consolidation (ARB 43)
In the US it has been possible to exclude certain majority owned subsidiaries from consolidation into group accounts on the basis that they are involved in dissimilar activities to those of the main group. Non-consolidated subsidiaries are generally accounted for under the equity method. Large conglomerates have used this as a basis for excluding certain of their operations, typically those such as real estate, leasing and finance subsidiaries, from the consolidated accounts, despite the growing significance of such activities to the group as a whole.

However, a new pronouncement, SFAS 94, has eliminated the dissimilar activities exemption. It requires consolidation of all majority owned subsidiaries for all fiscal years ending after 15 December 1988, with restatement of prior periods required. The only remaining exemptions from consolidation of majority owned subsidiaries relate to lack of control (eg bankruptcy, restrictions on earnings remittance for foreign subsidiaries, etc).

Business combinations (APB 16)
This is another area where the accounting is broadly the same in the US and UK, once the categorisation of the transaction has been determined. In the US, to qualify for

'pooling of interest' accounting (UK merger accounting), twelve strict tests must all be met, including a requirement for an all share deal (cash is allowed for fractional shares only). If any one of the twelve tests is failed, purchase accounting (UK acquisition accounting) is usually applied, though in certain circumstances, the historical cost of assets will continue to be used in something referred to as 'as if pooling'. This last, somewhat unusual method is used where there has not been a demonstrated change in control, for example, in certain leveraged buyout situations.

Once the classification of the transaction as a purchase or pooling has been determined, the accounting treatments are broadly the same, apart from the previously discussed difference in treatment of goodwill.

Discontinued operations (APB 30)

The US format requires that the results of discontinued operations be presented separately on an income statement below the results from continuing operations but above extraordinary items. Once it is appropriate to classify operations as discontinued, all comparative periods presented must be restated. In all those statements, *all* the trading revenues and expenses are netted down into the income or loss from discontinued operations, even those from the period preceding the decision to discontinue the segment.

Section I13 of the *Current Text* describes in detail the qualifications for classification as discontinued operations. Under that guidance, if an entire segment of business is being abandoned or sold, any anticipated losses shall be provided at the *measurement date*, which is the date a formal plan to dispose of a business, through sale or abandonment, is adopted by management with the authority to take such a decision. If losses from future trading, or from sale, are anticipated, these must be provided for at the measurement date. If gains are anticipated from operations or dispositions, they can be netted off against losses anticipated to a maximum of those losses (in which case no provision for losses would be necessary at the measurement date), although no anticipation of a net gain can be recognised.

To qualify for treatment as a discontinued operation, the entire segment, worldwide, must be exited, and the segment must not be defined in an overly narrow sense. For example, a furniture manufacturer who decides to cease making standing case clocks, but will continue to produce wall clocks, would not be eligible to apply discontinued operations accounting for its standing case clock operations. Similarly, a decision to get out of all clock manufacturing in the UK, shifting some production to Asia, would not qualify for discontinued operation. Note, however, that the definition of what does and does not constitute a segment of a business does not have to parallel that used by SFAS 14, Segment reporting.

Acquisition evaluation checklist

General information
- Exact corporate name
- Address
- Date and state of incorporation
- States in which the company is qualified to do business
- Location of minute books, by-laws and certificate of incorporation
- History
- Description of products
- Fiscal year
- Capitalisation
- Rights of each class of stock and other securities
- Stockholders' agreements and terms thereof
- Names of stockholders and holdings
- Bank depositaries and average bank balances
- Bank references
- Credit rating
- Location of company records
- Accountants: Name, address, and reputation
- Attorneys: Name and address

Personnel
- Directors and their affiliations
- Officers. For each – position, duties, age, health, salary, service, experience, personal plans for the future, other interests (including time devoted thereto), and stockholdings
- Organization chart
- Employee contracts: Terms, expiration date(s)
- Number of employees in production, sales, administration etc
- Union contracts: Terms, expiration dates
- Strike record, labor morale, handling of labor relations
- Labor market
- Pension, profit sharing, insurance, stock

bonus, deferred compensation and severance plans
- Comparison with industry as to number of employees, hours per week and wage rates for the past five years and for the past twelve months

Operations
- Description, including significant changes in the past few years
  (1) Capacity and per cent of utilisation
  (2) Production controls (scheduling and inventories)
  (3) Shipping and receiving controls
  (4) Accounting controls
- Principal suppliers and terms
- Distribution methods and terms (also, brokers or agents and compensation arrangements)
- Branch offices and their operations
- Subsidiaries, their operations and intercompany dealings
- Government contracts and subcontracts
- Seasonal factors
- Public and stockholder relations

Sales
- Description of market
- Number of customers and names of principal customers
- Gross and net sales for the past five years and for the past twelve months
  (1) Penetration of market by product
  (2) Possibilities of increase through existing lines and by diversification
- Sales comparison with the industry for the past five years and for the past twelve months
- Sales backlog, accounts receivable activity, customer continuity
- Sales correspondence
- Sales policies and method of compensation of sales personnel

- Pricing policies and fluctuations in the past five years
- Principal competitors
- Relative size in the industry
- Comparative advantages and disadvantages
- Revenues produced by new products introduced in the past few years
- Any nonrelated activities
- Missing product lines
- Advertising and other sales promotion programs: Cost and effectiveness in the past five years
- Research program: Costs, history, scope, potential, results, work by outsiders
- New developments
- Industry trends
- Current and future prospects

Earnings and dividends
- Earnings record and budget for the past five years and the last twelve months, break-even point, gross profit margins and reasons for variations, non-recurring income and expenses, changes in overabsorbed and underabsorbed burden
- Earnings comparison with the industry for the past five years
- Dividend and earnings record for the past five years in total and per share
- Potential economies
- Current and future prospects
- Analysis of selling and general and administrative expenses
- Contribution of company's effort to profit

Plant facilities
- Location
- Shipping facilities
- Real estate taxes
- Land
  (1) Acreage
  (2) Cost
  (3) Assessed value
  (4) Fair market value
- Buildings
  (1) Description, including pictures, if available
  (2) Age and condition
  (3) Area
  (4) Depreciation: Reserves, methods, rates, policies
  (5) Assessed value

(6) Fair market value (recent appraisals)
(7) Fire insurance
- Title to realty and title policy
- Machinery and equipment
  (1) Description
  (2) Age, condition, efficiency, insurance coverage
  (3) Depreciation: Reserves, methods, rates, policies
  (4) Total acquisitions during the past five years
  (5) Analysis of most recent additions
- Future plant, machinery and equipment requirements
- Capitalisation versus repair policies
- Capital expenditures and repairs for the past five years
- Percentage relationship of production costs and comparison with the industry
- Efficiency of operations
- Subcontracting done by others
- Certificates of necessity
- Facility contracts or leases
- Surplus or idle buildings or equipment

Assets
- Relationship of cash to current liabilities
- Age and number of accounts receivable (debtors) (latest accounts receivable ageing)
- Provision for bad debts
- Inventories (stocks) for the past five years
  (1) Relationship of inventories to current assets
  (2) Location
  (3) Finished goods by product
  (4) Work in process by product
  (5) Raw materials by product
  (6) Pricing methods
  (7) Accounting procedures and practices
  (8) Provision for obsolete or slow-moving stock (latest inventory aging)
- Analysis of notes receivable
- Analysis of investments
- Subsidiaries
  (1) Treatment on parent company's balance sheet
  (2) Analysis (per check list) of significant items
- Analysis of other assets
- Patents held

Liabilities
- Renegotiable business
- Renegotiation status
- Current federal and state tax status and tax payments for the past three years
- Commitments for new buildings, machinery, inventories
- Long-term loans outstanding and terms
- Debentures outstanding and terms
- Dividend and interest arrearages
- Leases: Locations, areas, terms
- Insurance coverage, fidelity bonds and amounts
- Pensions, etc
- Contingent liabilities: Warranties; patent, etc, infringements; loss contracts; compensation for services
- Litigation record and present status

Financial data
- Annual statements and audit reports for the past five years
- Tax returns for the past five years
- Surplus statements
- Disposition of funds statements
- Reports to Securities and Exchange Commission
- Explanation of how consolidations, if any, were effected and separate statement for each company involved
- Chart of accounts
- Book, net quick, liquidating, and market values for the past five years
- Working capital for the past five years and normal requirements based on trade practices, credit terms to customers, consignments, finished inventory, and raw inventory

- Net working capital ratios for the past five years
- Net quick position for the past five years
- Annual depreciation compared with capital additions for the past five years
- Inventory turnover for the past five years
- Cash, inventory and working capital requirements for the past two years
- Interest charges for the past five years
- Exchange, if any, on which the company's stock is traded
- Recent stock sales and prices paid

Comparison with comparable companies
The following ratios for the subject company should be compared with those of comparable companies for the past five years and, if data are available, by quarters for the current year
- Price to earnings
- Price to book value
- Sales to accounts receivable
- Sales to inventories
- Sales to fixed assets
- Earnings to book value

Terms of acquisition
- Reasons for sale
- Price to be paid
- Terms of payment
- Financing
- Brokerage fees
- Tax considerations

Projected financial data
- Pro forma balance sheet
- Earnings forecast

Frequently asked questions (with answers)

How are US businesses organised?
Usually as corporations, since the corporate form offers shareholders the advantage of limited liability. There are two types of companies in the US:

(1) public companies, the shares of which are traded on the major exchanges; and
(2) private (closely held) companies which are usually owned by a small number of shareholders; for sole proprietorships, partnerships and unincorporated joint ventures there is normally unlimited liability.

How can suitable acquisition targets be located?
Once an acquiror's investment criteria have been defined, it is possible to identify public companies that meet the specific criteria. Information pertaining to public companies is available from a number of databases, research reports, bond-rating companies, industry trade associations and governmental filings. Information on private companies is primarily limited to reports prepared by various credit agencies, trade association memberships, and sales oriented product information.

Is it easier to find a company if the acquisition criteria are specific? Or does it make more sense to keep the criteria broad so as not to miss out on any good opportunities?
In most cases it is useful first to determine what exactly the acquisition is to achieve and to state that clearly. From this statement, the acquiror is able to outline objectives and goals of the transaction. The specific acquisition criteria should be broad enough to cover the basics of the company and its acquisition purposes, such as core business and potential size, yet be suitable to state in more specific terms if a particular company appears to be 'borderline'. The acquisition criteria should be determined by acquiring management depending on its goals and capabilities, and should be specific to the extent that its major objectives are represented. See the example at the end of the Thermal Scientific case, Appendix 6.

How long will it take to complete a search? To complete a transaction?
The search process time will depend greatly on the amount of experience of the acquiring team. A wide-ranging thorough search is likely to be a six month project for executives working on it part time; however, the time may range from a few weeks to a few months. The search time should take no longer than is absolutely necessary, so as to not extend management's time and costs. Many acquirors hire a professional firm to conduct the search in order to free up management time at the beginning of the acquisition process. The time to negotiate and complete a transaction is often six to eight months, with time required afterwards for the transition stages with the newly acquired company. The most important thing to remember is to take the time necessary and to put adequate emphasis on the investment's importance; in other words, do not rush through any of the search and analysis stages as these tend to lay the groundwork for the entire transaction.

What are the criteria used to screen for the ideal target company? (ie in terms of strategic fit, size, growth potential, location, etc)
Some of the basic criteria used in preliminary screening of candidates include, but are not limited to, the following: lines of business; set guidelines on turnover or employment,

or both; compatibility with the company's long-term objectives; geographic location; position in an industry and/or specific market and price range. The criteria and screening are covered in detail in Chapter 7.

What is the SIC code system and how does it work?
The Standard Industrial Classification (SIC) Codes is a system of coding organised by the Office of Management and Budget of the US government. The SIC codes numerically classify all US economic activity into coded groups, with the system ranging from a two digit major group code down to an industry segment four digit code. The hierarchical system classifies the activities and defines the industries in accordance with the composition and structure of the economy. The Standard Industrial Classification Manual is the reference source for the SIC codes.

Where can industry information on similar companies be obtained?
General industry information on similar companies can be obtained through various sources but most focus on public companies. The most common of these sources include Dun & Bradstreet publications and Standard and Poor's information. Moody's also puts out some industrial and financial information in their Dividend Record and Industry Review. Databases in the UK also provide information on similar companies; these sources include *Compustat*, *Datastream* and *Investext*. Appendix 5 provides a detailed review of available sources of information.

What information is available publicly on companies identified as suitable?
The Securities Act of 1934 requires most issuers of securities registered with the Securities and Exchange Commission (SEC), that is publicly traded companies, to file annual and other periodic reports designed to provide a public file of current, material information. Contained in these filings are the company's audited financial statements, and other information about:

- the company's business, including products and services, principal markets, and methods of distribution;
- properties;
- legal proceedings pending against the company;
- securities holdings of management and significant shareholders;
- selected financial data for the most recent five-year period;
- management's discussion and analysis of financial condition and results of operations; and
- remuneration of directors and officers.

Annual reports are distributed to all shareholders and are available to any other interested party at no charge. In addition, securities analysts' reports on the company, its industry, and forecasted short and long-term prospects are also available.

If a division of a public company seems interesting for an acquisition and there is no segment information in the 10–K, where can information be found?
As with privately held companies, financial and operational information for subsidiaries and divisions is difficult to obtain. In the case of a division of a publicly held company, limited information may be gathered in the annual reports or other SEC filings.

What information is available on privately held companies?
For privately held companies information is generally difficult to obtain. Much of the required information can only be obtained from the company itself. However, the *Thomas Register* provides product information and Dun & Bradstreet has credit reports. Other information which may prove useful are product and marketing publications from the target company.

Where does one obtain adequate data on recent mergers and acquisition activity? (ie recent transactions, prices paid, buyers and sellers by industry)
Current and relevant information on recent merger and acquisition activity may be obtained from a variety of sources which are outlined in detail in the 'Sources of information' appendix. Some specialist journals which provide valuable information include *Acquisitions Monthly* from Tudor House Publications and *Mergers & Acquisitions* from *The Financial Times*.

What are the procedures for acquiring a US company?
The foreign investor's acquisition of a US corporation usually may be accomplished by one of the following:

- purchase of the US corporation's assets;
- purchase of all of the shares or the controlling share interest in the corporation from existing shareholders;
- subscription to a capital increase in the corporation itself; or
- merger of the US corporation into the acquiring corporation or a subsidiary corporation formed for the acquisition.

When acquiring a US private company, the principal shareholders/directors may be freely approached by a prospective buyer, which is often done through an intermediary. The intermediary may be an investment banker, a commercial banker, an accounting firm, or a business broker. It may be necessary to sign a confidentiality letter to obtain information.

What is a letter of intent?
If the target company is willing to sell, a 'letter of intent' (heads of agreement) may be drawn up between the parties. This letter, while not legally binding, creates the basis for further negotiations and eventually a detailed acquisition agreement. The proposed acquiror generally undertakes to maintain confidentiality of information obtained during the negotiations regarding the target corporation; the target corporation does the same for the acquiror.

Are there any tax or governmental impediments for overseas companies acquiring US operations?
There are no tax impediments for overseas companies acquiring US operations; however, in structuring the purchase, it is best to consult a tax adviser before detailed negotiations for guidance in this area.
A few industries are subject to restrictions on foreign ownership, including those involving the exportation of natural resources, communications, shipping, nuclear and other power-generating facilities, and aviation. These are the exceptions to the general rule of free flow of capital in and out of the US.

Is there monopoly or antitrust legislation affecting acquisitions?
The antitrust laws of the US, as administered by the Federal Trade Commission (FTC) and the Justice Department, encourage market forces to freely influence supply and demand. The most common regulation is a preacquisition filing requirement known as Hart-Scott-Rodino. It requires advance notification of a proposed merger in situations in which one party has annual net sales or total assets of at least $100 million and the other party has net sales or total assets of $10 million or more. The filing requirements are broadly the same for foreign and domestic acquirors.

Is there foreign investment review?
Although there are no substantial restrictions on foreign investment in the US, the federal government imposes reporting requirements through the Commerce and Agriculture Departments. Most foreign investments in US business enterprises in which foreign persons own a 10 per cent or more voting interest must be reported to the Commerce Department. If the acquisition involves the purchase of 200 or more acres of US land,

it must be reported, regardless of the total cost of the acquisition. The Agriculture Department requires reporting by foreign persons who acquire or transfer interests in agricultural land. (See Chapter 2 on the legal concerns.)

Are there exchange control regulations?
No.

Are there any restrictions on repatriation of dividends or an investment?
No.

What professional advisers are required? When in the process should they be consulted?
Accountants, lawyers, and investment bankers are invaluable additions to the team involved in the acquisition process.

- The accountant is involved in investigations and due diligence reviews of the entity to be acquired, examining its operations and financial and fiscal condition. Tax advisers should assist by making recommendations about the structure of the acquisition, seeking the most advantageous position from a tax standpoint. The accountant may also assist in selecting the overall structuring of the package and in the pricing negotiations.
- The attorneys do far more than prepare the appropriate legal documentation. They assume responsibility for clearing regulatory hurdles, for example state regulatory agencies, Hart-Scott-Rodino and other information filing requirements, as well as SEC regulations if a quoted company is involved. The status of all material outstanding contracts of the target, all product liability and insurance policies, and all patents, trademarks, and copyrights, is also reviewed.
- The investment banker can act as the chief architect of the structure particularly with regards to the financial support of the acquisition and also oversee matters pertaining to the strategy and timing of negotiations. His or her role is critical in public takeovers.

Any one adviser can also act as a negotiator at times, particularly if it helps deflect antagonism between principals. All of the above parties can assist in the search process.

Must an investment banker be used to represent the interest of the acquiror? And at what point during the process should he or she be involved?
An investment banker is essential in the purchase of a publicly traded company. These advisers are involved in the larger transactions and often charge a monthly retainer as well as a success fee. The investment banker should be brought into the process at the point where the acquiror has narrowed the possible candidates to only a few and the contact phase is about to proceed. If, however, the acquiror elects to have the investment banker assist in the candidate search process, then this adviser will undoubtedly become involved at an earlier stage. The investment banker is not required in private transactions and is not usually involved in transactions of less than $25 million.

What fees should be expected for the use of professional advisers?
Fees for investment bankers can be negotiated! In general, however, the proposal for smaller transactions follows the 'Lehman Formula' as the basis for establishing the fees. This sets the fees in the following manner: five per cent of the first $1 million of the purchase price; four per cent of the second million; three per cent of the third million; two per cent of the fourth million; and one per cent of any amount thereafter. In some cases there may also be a monthly retainer fee which will be offset against the success fee charged. These again should be determined prior to securing the services of the professionals so that the acquiror may utilise the prerogative to 'shop around' for the most suitable fees. Accountants and attorneys normally charge on a time basis.

How can financing be raised in the US?
Institutional lenders, private or public debt placements in the US, and to a limited extent,

industrial development bonds are among the primary financing sources in the US. The timing and/or amount of the purchase price may be made contingent upon the subsequent success of the target corporations.

There are no legal restrictions on the borrowing of funds in the US by a foreign investor, whether the purpose is to finance a US acquisition or another investment.

What are earn-out deals?

An earn out gives the seller the right to receive additional monies if certain profit goals are reached in the post-acquisition period. Earn outs can act as an incentive for the seller to continue as part of the management team after the transaction is complete. An earn out may bridge the gap between what the buyer has offered and the seller is asking. One example of an earn out is the opportunity for management to buy back some of the shares of the company.

How can acquired management, employees, customers and creditors be retained after the sale?

As mentioned in Section IV, the acquiror should keep in mind the past relationship and positions of these interested parties. More specifically, acquiring management should inform these parties as soon as possible of its intentions and potential changes which may occur due to the acquisition. Furthermore, management should be kept abreast of objectives and goals for the integration as well as their position within the newly enlarged group. Some of these concerns may be eased if acquiring management attempts to understand the concerns of the acquired company and realises that changes will always cause unrest. To aid in retaining management, the acquiror should consult compensation experts before the deal is closed.

What are the unique legal, accounting, tax and financing encumbrances associated with an international investment in the US? Where does one find professionals equipped to address these issues?

From the UK perspective, it is advisable to consult both UK legal and accounting advisers. This will initiate the information flow between the acquiror and professional advisers, so that the acquiror may be made aware of any restrictions or effects of an acquisition in the US. In addition to the UK advisers, the investor is advised to consult US counterparts in order to fully understand what restrictions, etc, may apply on such an investment. Many of the larger legal, financial and accounting firms have offices located in the larger European cities, including London.

How can the appropriate due diligence programme and team be structured?

'Due diligence' is a legal defence against charges of negligence; documentation of due diligence by the advisers is used to demonstrate that adequate professional care was taken. The term is often used loosely to describe much of the pre-closing work undertaken, including investigations by the company, its accountants, and attorneys; reviews of documents; any regulatory filings, etc.

To ensure that all necessary work is going forward on schedule, all professional advisers should be involved and a detailed schedule agreed.

Should a contact letter be used? Should a letter of intent be used?

A contact letter should be employed by the acquiror when the analysis and investigation has progressed to the degree where an actual meeting of the two parties would be beneficial. In some cases, the managing director may decide to meet a few candidates merely to 'get a feel' for them and their operations. In others, however, the acquiror may decide that only one or two are to be contacted and may wish to use a contact letter to initiate negotiation. Typically, the contact letter helps to outline the acquiror's intentions and position and makes for a less abrupt start to the process.

A letter of intent is normally used in transactions involving unquoted companies. The acquiror can use this letter to reassure the potential candidate of the sincerity and confidentiality of the deal and of any information shared. A letter of this type often assists in the transfer of key financial and operational information from the candidate to the acquiror as well as indicating the acquiror's sincere and genuine intentions. Such a letter is no longer used in most transactions involving large quoted companies.

At what point in the process should key management contracts be negotiated?
In some cases, the contracts for acquired management are discussed in the earlier stages of the transaction. This would help indicate to the acquired management that the acquiror is concerned and interested in their ongoing involvement. Furthermore, the acquiror should set out clearly their objectives for management, eg place within the organisation, responsibilties and how their performance will be measured. If management of the acquired company has concerns or considerations they would like the acquiror to deal with, it is useful to indicate these early in the process so that the acquiring management will be able to respond to them adequately.

What are some of the key reporting differences between the US and the UK?
For a look at the key accounting differences, acquirors should examine Chapter 8 and Appendix 7. Most notable are reporting and disclosure requirements, including reporting for goodwill, fixed asset valuation and pensions. The US does not have a blanket requirement to prepare or file audited or unaudited accounts other than for quoted companies.

Glossary

The following provides a listing of some of the more frequently used terms and phrases employed in merger and acquisition activity, as well as some general business terms. Note that some of the terms have not appeared in the text of this book.

Acceptance – the agreement by a shareholder to take up an offer made for his or her interest in a company.

Acid test ratio (quick ratio) – a measure of a company's financial strength which relates quick assets to current liabilities. Considered a rigorous measure of a company's ability to pay off short-term obligations.

American Bar Association – professional organisation for US attorneys.

American Institute of Certified Public Accountants – professional accounting body which issues technical auditing guidance.

Articles of Incorporation – document prepared by persons establishing a corporation and filed with state authorities.

Bank credit – amount of borrowing with interest from commercial banks.

Basis point – one one-hundredth of one per cent; used to express differences in yields on bonds or interest rates.

Bid – offer to buy an interest in a company.

Bid price – price at which prospective owner offers to buy a security, commodity, or other property.

Blue sky – term for US state laws (differing from federal laws) regulating the issue and sale of securities.

Board – Board of Directors.

Broker – person who arranges transactions between other parties and receives commission for doing so.

Buy-out – to purchase the entire interest in a business; may be deemed a leveraged buyout where the transaction is initiated by a financial group, or a management buyout where the business is purchased by existing management.

Cap – upper limit on the interest rate of a floating note.

Capital – (1) amount invested in an enterprise; (2) owners' equity.

Cash flow – net cash generated by a company's operations for a given period.

Cashier's cheque (American spelling: check) – American term for a banker's draft.

Completion – the final stage of the acquisition process, after which the company has legally changed owners.

Consideration – the amount paid for an interest in a company.

Consolidation – combination of the financial statements and accounts of two or more enterprises for presentation as if they were a single unit.

Contested bid – offer to purchase a company which is opposed by the Board of Directors.

Date of acquisition – (1) the effective purchase date of an asset; from this date the asset must appear in the accounts and financial statements of the owner; (2) the date on which control of a subsidiary was obtained as the result of a share purchase or other actions by a parent.

Debt/equity ratio – ratio used to measure a company's capital structure. Total liabilities divided by total shareholders' equity or long term debt divided by shareholders' equity.

Depreciation – a decrease in the value of an asset to indicate lost usefulness or expired utilisation.

Discount – (1) difference between an estimate of future worth and its present value; (2) allowance given against the face amount of debt to be repaid.

Discount rate – a rate used to calculate the present value of future cash flows.

DTC (Depository Trust Company) – a co-operative share registry and depository company run by the large brokers and dealers in the US. Trades are settled by entries on DTC's books rather than by physical delivery. Shares held at DTC often show up on shareholder lists as 'Cee Dee'.

Due diligence – thorough analysis and appraisal of a target's background and financial reliability. Sometimes used to describe a process undertaken by underwriters and other experts associated with an SEC filing; proof of performance of a due diligence examination can be a valid defence against suits charging negligence.

Earn out – a price setting method where the consideration is dependent on the subsequent performance of the company and/or executive(s) concerned.

Earnings per share – net income of a stated period (less preferred share dividends) divided by the average number of common shares outstanding during that period or shares outstanding at end of period.

Effective – declaration by the SEC of final permission to commence distribution of a prospectus for a new issue of securities.

Equity – ordinary share capital of a company, distinct from preference shares (preferred stock).

ERISA (Employee Retirement Income Security Act) – law governing the operation of most private pension and benefit plans.

FASB (Financial Accounting Standards Board) – independent board responsible for establishing and interpreting generally accepted accounting principles in the US.

Fair market value – the price a willing buyer would be willing to pay a seller under no compulsion to sell. This may be determined by a bona fide transaction, or estimated by experts.

Fed – abbreviation for the Federal Reserve System which is the central banking system in the US.

Foreign corporation – in state corporation laws, a foreign corporation is one created under the laws of another state or country.

Fundamental analysis – investment analysis to determine whether to buy or sell shares of a company and what their worth should be.

GAAP (Generally Accepted Accounting Principles) – accounting principles and conventions used in the preparation of accounts.

Gearing – British term for financial leverage. It is not normally equal to a US debt/equity ratio.

Golden parachute (defence tactic) – a provision in senior managements' contracts of service that a large payment or an extentsion of the contract must be made to the manager if the contract is brought to an end as a result of a change in control.

Greenfields operation – form of investment usually referring to a start-up operation.

Greenmail – the purchase by a company, at a price representing a premium to market value, of a block of shares held by an unfriendly investor.

Hands-on – an investor who approaches an investment 'hands-on' aims to add value to the business by actively participating in the management of the company.

Heads of agreement – the essential business terms of the acquisition deal – may or may not be legally binding. This is the UK equivalent of a US letter of intent.

Holding company – company whose function is to hold shares of other companies and subsidiaries.

Horizontal merger – combination of companies engaged in similar business activities (eg production or sale of similar products).

Indemnities – undertaking by a seller to hold the purchaser harmless from any losses resulting from the seller's breach of representation or warranty.

IRS (Internal Revenue Service) – US Treasury Department agency responsible for administering the tax laws.

Investment – expenditure to acquire property yielding some income or services.

Investment banker – an adviser retained to provide financial, strategic and other advice in connection with acquisitions or dispositions. These advisers often act also as underwriters, and buy stock or bond issues in their entirety for an issuing corporation and who may distribute the issues either to dealers or directly to investors.

Joint venture – commercial undertaking by two or more persons with a limited duration and for a defined purpose.

Junior debt – another term for subordinated debt.

Letter of credit – letter from bank stating that a line of credit has been established in a company's name which can be drawn upon by the seller receiving the letter.

Letter of intent – letter by acquiring company to a target signifying sincere interest and intent of the possible transaction; it may also outline confidentiality concerns. (See 'Heads of Agreement'.)

Leverage – American term for gearing; generally the proportion of debt to equity in a company's capital structure.

Line of credit – agreement by a bank to extend loan(s) not to exceed a certain limit.

Merger – (1) acquisition in which all assets and liabilities are absorbed by the buyer; (2) legal expression meaning putting two or more companies into solvent liquidation and transferring their assets to a newly formed company, whose shareholders are those of all the other companies.

Mezzanine finance – unsecured loans which rank after senior debt but before equity.

Net present value (NPV) – a project's net contribution to wealth; total present value minus initial investment.

Net worth (owners' equity) – book value of a company's common shares, surplus, and retained earnings. (Total assets less liabilities.)

Offer document – official document prepared by a bidder in a takeover which is sent to shareholders of the target company.

P/E ratio (price/earnings ratio) – quoted share price divided by earnings per share; often used as a measure of how much an investor is paying for the company's earning power.

Poison pill – action taken by a target to make it unattractive to a buyer, eg the issue of a stock purchase right entitling the holder to purchase common stock at a price that would drastically dilute a buyer's interest.

Preacquisition profits – retained earnings of a corporation prior to the assumption of control by another company.

Preferred stock – US term for preference shares.

Prospectus – document published by a company making an issue of shares to the public.

Pyramiding – (1) use of multiple layers of holding companies to control a relatively large amount in corporate assets; (2) an increase on the holding of a stock financed out of the margin created by a rise in the price of stock already owned.

Quoted – usually refers to a company whose shares are traded on a public market.

Real interest rate – interest rate expressed in real terms, ie adjusting for effects of inflation.

Rescission – legal right to extricate oneself from a legally binding deal (very difficult to do).

Reverse takeover – (1) in the UK the buying of a public company by a private company (instead of visa versa); (2) the purchase of a larger company by a smaller one. Also used in the US is the term 'Pac-man' defence where the target, as a defensive strategy, attempts to acquire its predator.

Rights issue – an invitation to shareholders to subscribe for new shares in their company in proportion to their shareholdings.

Rollover – renewal of short term debt at the option of the borrower.

SEC (Securities and Exchange Commission) – US agency responsible for overseeing the securities industry and all stock markets and reporting by, and trading in the shares of, quoted companies.

Seed capital – investment which enables a project or idea to begin development.

Senior – US term for debt which ranks ahead of other debts.

Shark repellants – term for the defence tactics implemented to protect the company from takeovers.

Systematic risk (market risk) – risk inherent to the market which can not be diversified away.

Takeover – acquisition of an ongoing business by another through outright purchase or exchange of shares.

Tender offer – typically used only to refer to acquisitions of public companies; refers in the US to an offer made to the public for a specific aggregate amount of securities (normally cash but could be a share or security exchange).

Tombstone – advertisement announcing an issue of securities or completed acquisition.

Treasury bill – a non-interest bearing obligation of the US government, payable to the bearer, and maturing in less than a year from date of issue; it is issued at a discount to face value.

Underwriter (investment banker) – firm which buys an issue of securities for a company and resells it to investors.

Vertical merger – combination between companies in a customer/supplier relationship – may be a direct or indirect relationship.

Voting rights – most common shares carry voting rights with regards to matters pertaining to the company, however all do not.

Warranties – contractual term expressed by the seller that the target is as it was held out to be.

White knight – defence tactic whereby the target searches for a friendly acquiror when threatened by a hostile bidder.

Yankee bond – a dollar bond issued in the US by a non-US borrower.

APPENDIX 11
Reference list

Books

Allen, Mike and Robert Hodgkinson *Buying A Business: A Guide to the Decisions* (Graham & Trotman, London, 1986).

Cooke, Terence E. *Mergers & Acquisitions* (Basil Blackwell Inc, New York, 1986).

Davidson, Kenneth M. *Mega Mergers: Corporate America's Billion Dollar Takeovers* (Ballinger Publishing Co, Cambridge, MA, 1985).

French, Derek *Dictionary of Accounting Terms* (Financial Training Publications, London, 1985).

A Guide for the Foreign Investor: Doing Business in the USA, edited by Robert F. Cushman and Herbert A. Morey (Dow Jones-Irwin, Homewood, Illinois, 1984).

Handbook of Mergers, Acquisitions, & Buyouts, edited by Steven James Lee and Robert Douglas Colman (Prentice-Hall Inc, Englewood Cliffs, New Jersey, 1981).

Kohlers Dictionary for Accountants, 6th edition, edited by W. W. Cooper and Yuji Ijiri (Prentice-Hall, Englewood Cliffs, New Jersey, 1983).

McCann, Joseph E. and Roderick Gilkey *Joining Forces: Creating and Managing Successful Mergers and Acquisitions* (Prentice Hall, Englewood Cliffs, NJ, 1988).

Moore, Brian and Kit Stenning *The Takeover Guide* (Longman Group UK Limited, London, 1988).

OECD Economic Surveys – United States: 1987/1988 (OECD Publications, Paris, France, 1984).

Tolchin, Martin and Susan Tolchin *Buying Into America: How Corporate Money is Changing the Face of Our Nation* (Times Books, NY, 1988).

Forry, John I. *A Practical Guide to Foreign Investment in the United States*, 1st edition (Tax Management International, London, 1979).

Starr, Robert and Robert B. Donin *Doing Business in the United States – An Executive's Guide* (Oyez Publishing Ltd, London, 1979).

Williams, J. G. *Acquisitions and Mergers* (The Institute of Chartered Accountants in England and Wales, 1980).

Articles (by journal)

Academy of Management Review
'Mergers and the Performance of the Acquiring Firm' Michael Lubatin (1983) vol 8, no 2, 218–225.
'Corporate Acquisitions: A Process Perspective', David B. Jemison and Sim B. Sitkin (1986) vol 11, no 1, 145–163.

Accountancy Age
'Achieving Post-Acquisition Success' Keith Harrison and Bill Neale (1988) 24 March, 24–25.

Acquisitions Monthly
'Hitting the Acquisition Trail' Peter Osborne (1988) March, 32–34.
'How to Make the International Acquisition Work' Peter A. Firmin and Alain Ged (1985) December, 19–23.
'Identifying and Contacting a US Acquisition Opportunity' Herbert S. Adler and Christopher G. Sneath (1986) May, 30–35.

230

'Managing the US Acquisition Process' Michael Stallibrass (1987) March, 36–37.
'Strategy – The Key to Acquisition Success' Ronald A. Sandler and J. Alex Rentoul (1987) September, 25–28.
'Post Acquisition Problems and Opportunities in the USA' Tom Angear (1985) March, 11–12.

Economist
'America's Friendly Invaders' (1988) 30 April, 16–17.

Euromoney
'Foreigners Rush To Buy Into the US' Lori Ioannou (1988) May, 41–42.

Financial Weekly
'Watch Out ... The Brits are Coming' Jonathan Gregson (1987) 24 September, 12–13.

Fortune
'Acquiring Without Smothering' Myron Magnet (1984) 12 November, 54–59.

Harvard Business Review
'Compatibility in Corporate Marriages' Richard E. Davis (1968) July/August, 86–93.
'After the Acquisition: Continuing Challenge' Charles M. Leighton and G. Robert Tod (1969) March/April, 90–102.
'Plan to Integrate your Acquisitions' Robert A. Howell (1970) November/December, 66–76.
'Takeovers: Folklore and Science' Michael C. Jensen (1984) November/December, 109–121.
'Acquisitions: The Process Can Be A Problem' David B. Jemison and Sim B. Sitkin (1986) March/April,107–116.
'From Competitive Advantage to Corporate Strategy' Michael E. Porter (1987) May/June, 43–59.

Journal of Financial Economics
'Assessing Competition in the Market for Corporate Acquisitions' Richard S. Ruback (1983) April, 141–153.

Long Range Planning
'Acquiring Companies in the USA' Herbert S. Adler and Christopher G. Sneath (1987) April, 42–50.
'Alternatives to Merger – Joint Ventures and Other Strategies' Jeffery S. Harrison (1987) December, 78–83.

Management Review
'Planning: The Key to Successful Mergers and Acquisitions' John J. Fox (1987) September, 12–18.

Mergers and Acquisitions
'Roundtable: Putting the Deal Together' (1982) Winter, 22–28.

The Texas Business Executive
'An Approach Toward Successful Acquisition' James B. Farley and Edward H. Schwallie (1981) Fall/Winter, 32–39.

Time
'For Sale: America' Stephen Koepp (1987) 14 September, 30–37.

Other

Berkshire-Hathaway 1982 Annual Report, Letter from Chairman – Warren Buffet.
'Doing Business in the United States of America – A Guide for the Foreign Investor' (Deloitte Haskins & Sells, New York, 1985).
'Doing Business in the United States' (Price Waterhouse, US, 1988).

'Executive Summary – On US/Great Britian Investment' Daniel McRae – Hurt, Richardson, Todd, Garner and Cadenhead Attorneys at Law (Atlanta, Georgia, 1988).

'Mergers and Acquisitions in the United States – Legal and Practical Considerations' (Willkie Farr & Gallagher, London, July 1988).

'Investment in the United States' KPMG Peat Marwick (New York, 1987).

Index

(*Note*: Entries refer to the United States, unless the sense or the text indicate otherwise, eg 'Acquiror' refers to the UK firm making a purchase, 'Department of Commerce' is the United States Department of Commerce, 'Tax Reform Act, 1986' is the US Act but 'Financial Services Act, 1986 (UK)' is the British Act.)